SYSTEMATIC THEOLOGY AND CLIMATE CHANGE

This book offers the first comprehensive systematic theological reflection on arguably the most serious issue facing humanity and other creatures today. Responding to climate change is often left to scientists, policy makers and activists, but what understanding does theology have to offer? In this collection, the authors demonstrate that there is vital cultural and intellectual work for theologians to perform in responding to climate science and in commending a habitable way forward. Written from a range of denominations and traditions yet with ecumenical intent, the authors explore key Christian doctrines and engage with some of the profound issues raised by climate change. Key questions considered include: What may be said about the goodness of creation in the face of anthropogenic climate change? And how does theology handle a projected future without the human? The volume provides students and scholars with fascinating theological insight into the complexity of climate change.

Michael S. Northcott is Professor of Ethics in the School of Divinity at the University of Edinburgh, UK.

Peter M. Scott is Samuel Ferguson Professor of Applied Theology and Director of the Lincoln Theological Institute at the University of Manchester, UK.

SYSTEMATIC THEOLOGY AND CLIMATE CHANGE

Ecumenical Perspectives

Edited by
Michael S. Northcott and Peter M. Scott

Routledge
Taylor & Francis Group

LONDON AND NEW YORK

First published in 2014
by Routledge
2 Park Square, Milton Park, Abingdon, Oxon OX14 4RN

And published by Routledge
711 Third Avenue, New York, NY 10017

Routledge is an imprint of the Taylor & Francis Group, an informa business

British Library Cataloguing in Publication Data
A catalogue record for this book is available from the British Library

Library of Congress Cataloging in Publication Data
Systematic theology and climate change : ecumenical perspectives / edited by Michael S. Northcott and Peter M. Scott.
pages cm
1. Theology, Doctrinal. 2. Ecotheology. 3. Climatic changes. I. Northcott, Michael S., editor of compilation.
BT78.S97 2014
261.8'8--dc23
2013050742

ISBN: 978-0-415-74278-8 (hbk)
ISBN: 978-0-415-74279-5 (pbk)
ISBN: 978-1-315-76887-8 (ebk)

Typeset in Bembo
by Taylor & Francis Books

Printed and bound in the United States of America
by Edwards Brothers Malloy on sustainably sourced paper.

CONTENTS

CONTRIBUTORS

Celia Deane-Drummond is full Professor in Theology at the University of Notre Dame, USA. Her research interests are in the engagement of theology and natural science, including specifically ecology, evolution, animal behaviour and anthropology. Her most recent books include *Wonder and Wisdom: Conversations in Science, Spirituality and Theology* (UK: DLT, 2006), *Genetics and Christian Ethics* (Cambridge: CUP, 2006), *Ecotheology* (UK: DLT, 2008), *Christ and Evolution* (Minneapolis: Fortress Press, 2009), *The Wisdom of the Liminal: Human Nature, Evolution and Other Animals* (Grand Rapids: Eerdmans, 2014).

Timothy Gorringe has worked in India, Oxford, St Andrews and Exeter. He is the author, most recently, of *The Common Good and the Global Emergency* (Cambridge: CUP, 2011) and *Earthly Visions: Theology and the Challenges of Art* (New Haven, CT: Yale, 2011). He is currently working on a book on values.

Niels Henrik Gregersen is Professor of Systematic Theology at Copenhagen University, Co-Director of the Centre for Naturalism and Christian Semantics 2008–13 and Co-PI of the Centre for Changing Disasters 2013–17, Copenhagen University.

Tamara Grdzelidze (Orthodox Church of Georgia), is a Programme Executive within the Faith and Order Secretariat of the World Council of Churches in Geneva, Switzerland. She holds a DPhil from the University of Oxford, a doctorate in Medieval Georgian Literature from the Tbilisi State University and a doctorate *honoris causa* from the Faculty of Theology of the University of Bern, Switzerland.

Neil Messer is Professor of Theology and Head of the Department of Theology and Religious Studies, University of Winchester, and an ordained minister of the

United Reformed Church. His publications include *Flourishing: Health, Disease and Bioethics in Theological Perspective* (Grand Rapids: Eerdmans, 2013), *Respecting Life: Theology and Bioethics* (London: SCM Press, 2011) and *Selfish Genes and Christian Ethics: Theological and Ethical Reflections on Evolutionary Biology* (London: SCM Press, 2007).

Rachel Muers is Senior Lecturer in Christian Studies at the University of Leeds. She was previously Lecturer in Theology at the University of Exeter, and before that Margaret Smith Research Fellow at Girton College, University of Cambridge. Her publications include *Living for the Future: Theological Ethics for Coming Generations* (London: T&T Clark, 2008); *Keeping God's Silence: Towards a Theological Ethics of Communication* (Oxford: Blackwell, 2004); (with David Grumett) *Theology on the Menu: Asceticism, Meat and Christian Diet* (London: Routledge, 2010); and (with Mike Higton) *The Text in Play: Experiments in Reading Scripture* (Eugene, OR: Wipf and Stock, 2012).

Michael S. Northcott is Professor of Ethics in the School of Divinity of the University of Edinburgh, a priest in the Scottish Episcopal Church, and keeps a large vegetable garden in the Scottish Borders. He is the author of *The Environment and Christian Ethics* (Cambridge: Cambridge University Press, 1996); *A Moral Climate: The Ethics of Global Warming* (London: Darton Longman and Todd, 2007); (with R. J. Berry) *Theology After Darwin* (Milton Keynes: Paternoster, 2009); (with Kyle S. Van Houtan) *Diversity and Dominion* (Eugene, OR: Wipf and Stock, 2010); and *A Political Theology of Climate Change* (London: SPCK, 2014).

Peter M. Scott is Samuel Ferguson Professor of Applied Theology and Director of the Lincoln Theological Institute at the University of Manchester, UK. He is the author of *Theology, Ideology and Liberation* (Cambridge: CUP, 1994), *A Political Theology of Nature* (Cambridge: CUP, 2003) and *Anti-human Theology: Nature, Technology and the Postnatural* (London: SCM Press, 2010).

Stefan Skrimshire is a lecturer in Theology and Religious Studies at the University of Leeds, UK. Previous to this appointment he was a post-doctoral researcher at the Lincoln Theological Institute at The University of Manchester, where he led a research project on Religion and Climate Change. He is the author of *Politics of Fear, Practices of Hope* (London: Continuum, 2008) and editor of *Future Ethics: Climate Change and Apocalyptic Imagination* (London: Continuum, 2010).

PREFACE

This project began in a breakfast discussion at the 2010 conference of the Society of Christian Ethics at Westcott House in Cambridge. The theme of the conference was 'Climate Change and Christian Ethics', and we were both there to give papers. Noting that the ethical discussion of climate change was well advanced, we agreed on the need for a comparable systematic theological engagement with climate change and lamented that it would be a difficult book to write. Then we happened on the idea that perhaps a group of theologians could write such a systematic theology together, with each theologian taking a doctrine apiece. And so this book was born.

We would like to thank the contributors for their work. We met as a group at the University of Manchester in 2011 and 2012 for intensive discussion of draft chapters and we are grateful for the spirit in which contributors engaged with process and the generosity and warm-heartedness that pervaded the conversation. There was no consensus but there was a readiness to work hard on an issue that all agreed was highly important.

Routledge has done a fantastic job in guiding the volume through the production process, and we would like especially to thank Jonathan Merrett, Katherine Ong and Andrew Watts for their work.

Finally, we would like to thank the trustees of the Lincoln Theological Institute at the University of Manchester whose financial support has made this project a reality. Through their commitment to theological research, the trustees are now providing occasions for important theological conversations to take place in the UK and beyond, and we are grateful to them for their willingness to fund such conversations.

MSN/PMS
Advent 2013

1

INTRODUCTION

Michael S. Northcott and Peter M. Scott

In this innovative book, Anglican, Catholic, Lutheran, Orthodox and Reformed theologians come together for the first time to consider the implications for Christian doctrine of the scientific reporting of anthropogenic climate change, and its effects on humanity and the earth. Christian theology is defined, first by Anselm of Canterbury and then by many theologians since, as '*fides quaerens intellectum*' or 'faith seeking understanding'.[1] It is an activity that has occurred continuously within, and flows from, the Church's proclamation and worship of Jesus as the Christ since the birth of the Church at Pentecost.[2] Theologians since Thomas Aquinas have adopted a classic order in their systematic reflection on faith and worship whose shape arises from the Trinitarian understanding of the nature of God, Creation, Church and Eschaton. We do not significantly depart from this traditional shape here. But this volume reflects the fact that in the history of the Church, Christians have responded to civilizational crises through a combination of fidelity to scripture and tradition, and theological and ethical innovation. That new contexts call forth new teachings is for Christian theologians underwritten by the Trinitarian belief that the Holy Spirit, who was gifted to the Church at Pentecost, continues to reveal new truth as Christians reflect on scripture and tradition in new contexts. We therefore offer in this volume a number of new insights, and a new systematic theological topic – *creatures* – in response to the emergent civilizational challenge of climate change.

The phrase 'climate change' is shorthand for the scientific realization that human industrial activities, especially burning fossil fuels, clearing or burning forests and making cement, are taking place on such a scale that they are changing the earth's climate. This is manifest in more extreme weather, drought, flood, melting ice, rising oceans and strengthening storms. But the *experience* of climate change is not directly empirical. The scientific prediction of momentous change in future atmospheres, without radical transformation in industrial practices, is not perceptible to the senses, although this is of course true of many other scientific claims that are less widely disputed. Nonetheless, vociferous voices and organisations – not least those which represent fossil fuel and forestry interests – contest with climate scientists, and developing world farmers, about the claim that the weather is becoming more extreme – and moving beyond historic norms – and that these extremes are anthropogenic. In the midst of the global contest of opinion on climate science, for Christians the witness that has most import is that of farmers, fishers and the urban and rural poor in the developing world for whom increasing weather extremes are already a threat to their ability to feed their families, or even to continue to dwell in their ancestral homes.

The threat from extreme weather is not, however, confined to the developing world or to future generations. Increasingly, farmers and residents of low-lying areas are also experiencing the effects of extreme weather in the developed world. Australia's rural farmers and rural poor are among the most severely affected by growing weather extremes, but Australian politics is also deeply shaped by climate change denialism and the intention of the Australian government and corporations to continue to mine, burn and export its large coal reserves. The former Prime Minister, Kevin Rudd, won and lost elections over his efforts to fashion an economic and political response to climate change science in Australian government policy. For Rudd, an Anglican evangelical, the moral and political challenge of climate change arises from Christ's parable of the Last Judgment, in which the judgment rests on how people responded in their lives to the hungry, the poor, prisoners and the sick. Climate change is already having grave effects on the poor and giving rise to forced migration, and this makes response to climate change part of the 'prophetic mission of Christians'.[3] And the planet, like the working people of the developing world, 'cannot speak for itself' and hence the planet is also among the weak that Christians are called to serve.[4]

The refusal of fossil fuel corporations, investment banks and governments to reduce climate impacts by reducing investment in fossil fuel extraction and infrastructure, and by restraining deforestation and cement making, is fundamentally about *political economy* and not science. Few in government challenge climate science, but given the very great wealth derived from fossil fuels no government whose terrain includes them has yet shown a willingness to legally restrain licensing of their extraction and use. Some governments have adopted *emissions* targets in the Kyoto Protocol but these targets do not affect fossil fuel extraction. They are therefore easily avoided by importing carbon-intense goods and services from other domains and emissions targets do not include fossil fuel production.[5] The Fifth Assessment Report of the Intergovernmental Panel on Climate Change estimates for the first time a 'global carbon budget' of anthropogenic greenhouse gas emissions which can be emitted without provoking more than 2 degrees Celsius of warming. The IPCC estimate this budget at 1000 billion tons and estimate that humanity has emitted just over half this budget since the beginning of the Industrial Revolution.[6]

In the last fifteen years there has been a 'great acceleration' in both CO_2 emissions and deforestation which shows no sign of letting up.[7] Some argue this is because corporations and governments are anxious to extract and burn what they can before any global treaty restrains them. The refusal to act is despite the widespread availability of substitutes for fossil fuels, including electricity sourced from renewable energy, building insulation and other energy conservation technologies including heat pumps, low energy lighting, electric bicycles and so on. But investment decisions on energy use in the built environment, and for mobility, are still, in the main, driven by short-term cost considerations instead of future climate instability.

One of us argues elsewhere that the unfolding civilizational crisis that climate change will provoke in the twenty-first century is analogous to the crisis of German nationalism and Nazism in the twentieth, and that it calls for an equivalent confessional response from Christians.[8] This is because the climate crisis threatens to reduce the habitability of the planet – of what Christians know and experience as the divine Creation – for billions of people including not only present farmers, fishers and coastal dwellers but all future humans.

The response to German nationalism and Nazism came to be known as the theology of crisis. The theologians of crisis, who included not only Barth, but also Brunner and Bonhoeffer in Europe and Reinhold Niebuhr in North America, called for the bold reassertion of the intellectual distinctiveness of Christian confessional doctrines, and the cultural distinctiveness of Christian moral and worshipping practices in the face of the crises of the twentieth century. For the theologians of crisis, modern Western culture represented an existential challenge to authentic Christian faith and witness that arises from the secular scientific and technological subversion of Christian doctrine and ethics, especially as represented in German nationalism and scientific racism, and their radically evil outcomes in world war and the Holocaust.

We suggest that climate change provides a different and yet parallel crisis, and thereby an opportunity for theological development and the necessity for confession. Climate crisis confronts the tendency of modern historians since the Enlightenment to separate natural history and human history and narrate them independently of one another.[9] Climate change challenges this separation by remixing human and natural history, and this remixing also finds resonances in the New Testament. For the Evangelists, and the writer of the Book of Acts, the God who is revealed in Jesus Christ is still revealed in observable events in the created order. Hence Christ's birth, Christ's baptism in the Jordan, the revelation of Jesus as the Christ at the Transfiguration and his death and resurrection are all clearly marked with earthly and heavenly phenomena which include a star, a dove, clouds, a partial solar eclipse and mild earth tremors. Similarly, at Pentecost the Spirit is heralded by strange atmospheric effects: these included a 'rushing mighty wind' and 'the appearance of tongues of fire' on the heads of the apostles (Acts 2.3–4) as well as more obviously 'religious' phenomena such as ecstatic utterance and boldness and clarity in preaching the gospel. These resonances also challenge the broader post-scientific distinction between nature and culture which, as one of us argues elsewhere, is an obstacle to proper theological response to human industrial influence on the climate in the present century.[10]

Responding to and intervening in this remixing of human and natural histories, climate science involves a combination of new theory and new kinds of observation. In the mid-nineteenth century, the English scientist John Tyndall first theorized that carbon in the atmosphere is the reason for the modest diurnal change of temperatures between day and night on earth: the night time temperatures that were theorized are higher than they would be in the absence of direct radiated heat from the sun because a quotient of that heat is conserved inside the atmospheric envelope. In 1896, the Swedish physicist Svante Arhenius first estimated the likely warming effects of atmospheric CO_2 from coal burning on the earth's temperature. But it was not until the mid-twentieth century that physicists began to model a 'biogeochemical' network of relationships between mammals, plants, rocks, soils, oceans and the atmosphere which could begin to explain their complex interactions, and, more precisely, how anthropogenic movement of carbon from underground into the atmosphere would change these interactions. It is from an account of these interactions that the contributors to this volume work, because we recognize that climate science raises vital issues for the future of human, and more than human, life to which Christians must respond.

Science and technology were crucially implicated in the twentieth century theology of crisis, as they are in the climate crisis.[11] The use by Germany and the Allies of technologies of war − including chemical weapons and aerial bombing − took the violence and ecological destructiveness of war to unprecedented heights, so much so that the Vatican significantly revised Roman Catholic just war doctrine subsequent to World War II to respond to these new military technologies. In his systematic theological reflections on Genesis 1–3, which originated as lectures in 1932 in the context of the rise of the Third Reich, Bonhoeffer argues that a scientific and technologically advanced form of civilization carries particular threats to human beings, and to life on earth more broadly, precisely because its inhabitants refuse to know the earth as divine creation. Consequently, 'the earth is no longer our earth, and then we become strangers on earth', and from strangers we finally become earth's subjects: through the power of technology 'the earth grips man and subdues him'.[12]

Some argue that the Christian tradition is unable to adapt to modern scientific cosmology without denying revealed truths in scripture and tradition, and that Christians should therefore resist scientific theories about the origins of life and the nature of the universe as conceived by modern physicists and biologists.[13] Others argue that modern scientific cosmology, as classically framed by Isaac Newton's account of a universe governed by immutable laws which are independent of human or divine willing, is challenged by the new era that some scientists are now calling the 'Anthropocene'.[14] This is because in the climate changing era of the Anthropocene the human is *in* the observed: the carbon atoms now studied in recent ice cores, the hurricanes and typhoons bearing more strongly down on American and Asian cities, also now carry a human element. In this new context, religion, and especially religions like Christianity which are open to creative doctrinal reformulations in new contexts, offer cultural resources for enduring, and finding meaning in, the new world of the Anthropocene. We find a parallel here in Sallie McFague's reflection on the implications for theodicy of the nuclear age. In earlier eras, Christians and Jews understood that human beings lived their lives on earth under the influence of a spiritual contest between principalities and powers in heavenly places where evil powers contested with God for influence over human and creaturely life.[15] Something like this is envisaged in the Book of Job. In this worldview,

> the metaphor of Christ as the victorious king and lord, crushing the evil spirits and thereby freeing the world from their control, is indeed a powerful one. In our situation, however, to envision evil as separate from human beings rather than as the outcome of human decisions and actions, and to see the solution of evil as totally a divine responsibility, would be not only irrelevant to our time and its needs but harmful to them, for that would run counter to one of the central insights of the new sensibility: the need for human responsibility in a nuclear age. In other words to do theology, one must in each epoch do it differently.[16]

Analoously, in the new era of the Anthropocene, the Church and humanity face a genuinely novel occasion which 'teaches new duties'. Perhaps the central theological question for this new occasion is, in Bonhoeffer's terms, who is Jesus Christ in the Anthropocene? In the chapters that follow we develop our answers to this question across the full range of Christian doctrines.

Ours is not the first attempt to think ecumenically about climate change. From the 1970s, the World Council of Churches began to articulate the emerging faith and moral challenges raised by the impacts of science and technology on the habitability of the earth and her ecosystems. It was at a consultation of the WCC in Bucharest in 1974 that Charles Birch, working with the scientists who had authored the Club of Rome report *Limits to Growth,* coined the phrase 'ecological sustainable society' for the first time.[17] This was followed by Birch's speech on the 'sustainable society' to the fifth WCC Assembly in Nairobi in 1975, which was widely acknowledged as a key moment in the awakening of ecological consciousness in the ecumenical churches. As the WCC continued to reflect on the ecological, social and technological challenges of an increasingly rampant takeover by science-informed humans of the natural systems of the planet, the WCC developed a theological agenda for the response of the churches. Under the banner of a quest for Justice, Peace and the Integrity of Creation (JPIC) the WCC sought to lead its member churches in challenging a pattern and scale of industrial development which was increasingly pushing at planetary and social limits to growth.[18] In the 1990s, the WCC sponsored a number of ecumenical meetings on climate change, at the conclusion of which the delegates noted that 'the concept of "sustainable development" was in danger of being eviscerated of its transformative potency by being expanded to include "sustainable economic growth"'.[19]

In the present work we argue, with the WCC, that climate change represents a radical challenge to the contemporary belief in the intrinsic relationship between progress, defined as economic growth, and the welfare of humanity and the human habitat. In Chapter 2, 'The Trinity', Tim Gorringe argues that a particular account of the rights of private property owners is core to the modern grand narrative of progress. He argues that the adulation of private wealth is a modern form of idolatry and that the Temples of this modern form of idolatry are the world's Stock Exchanges. The 'god concept' of monetary value is therefore the theistic ground of modern society. This idolatrous value is the reason for the failure of the nations to honour and care for Creation by mitigating climate change, and it competes with the Christian knowledge and worship of God as Trinitarian Creator. The idol of money is worshipped, in part, because it seems to offer security to the individual from dependence on relations with other creatures and persons for health and well-being. By contrast, God as Trinity is 'God in relation' and, from the second century, when theologians affirmed the Trinitarian character of the being of God, they affirmed that the compassion, kindness, love and mutuality modelled and taught by Jesus Christ were also intrinsic to the character of God. Hence God who is encountered in Christ is not different from, but rather *of one substance* with, God, known as Yahweh in the Old Testament, who is Creator and Lord of heaven and earth.

In 'Christology', Chapter 3, Niels Gregersen recalls the unconscious character of the life-sustaining exchanges between humans and the atmosphere, climate and weather including oxygen and carbon dioxide in their lungs, and food and water derived from soils watered by clouds and from plants and animals sustained by photosynthesis. The coming of the eternal logos by whom all things were made into creaturely and material life is the moment in human history when these life-sustaining processes achieved their fullest degree of self-consciousness in a person who is uniquely biological, material, personal and Spirit. In this event, Christians come to see that Christ and the divine Spirit 'belong to the nexus of creation for which God the Father is forever present'. In Jesus, the Son of God is revealed to be 'with and for all other creatures in the universe through the workings of the Holy Spirit' and as Anselm of Canterbury put it, 'where God is not, there is nothing. Accordingly, God is present through all things and in all things.'[20] Against the tendencies of Cartesian metaphysics, and post-Newtonian science, to underwrite an absolute ontological distance between God and Creation, God and creature are revealed in the Incarnation as 'one complex reality', for what Christians discover in the revelation of Jesus Christ is that without the life-giving Spirit and the cosmic Christ the material world of creation would lack ontological substance, and 'there would be no creation'.

Gregersen then explores the implications of this approach for the intergenerational challenge of climate change. Actions to either mitigate or fail to mitigate climate change now will have momentous consequences for humans living fifty and a hundred years hence. A 'deep time' perspective on the Incarnation situates Jesus as the 'second Adam' in an intergenerational relationship with humanity's ancient ancestors, and with their distinctive species nature as mammalian persons with complex brains, upright stance and strong social capacities. Christ lived *on earth* both socially and atomistically, as well as spiritually, in connection with persons, and organisms, that endure, yesterday, today and until the end of time. This 'deep incarnation' perspective on the material and organic substrate of his embodied and personal life situates Christ astrally, ecologically and socially in a way which transcends the presentist character of conscious experience of space and time, moment to moment. Hence the New Testament and Patristic vision of the cosmic Christ, who is also appointed as the judge of history at the end of time, is the doctrine which, far more than pragmatic or consequentialist propositions, enables present humans to respond with full existential seriousness to their duty to future persons and creatures to mitigate climate change.

In Chapter 4, 'Holy Spirit', Northcott draws an analogy between the pneumatological cosmology of the Old Testament and the relational nexus, described by climate scientists, which connects human greenhouse gas emissions with changes in the climate, including sets of more extreme weather events. The Hebrew *ruach* describes the creative work of the life-giving divine Spirit in moving the elements of air and water, and the same word is used for the manifestations of this vitalising work in breath, clouds, oceans, rivers, storms and wind. This indicates a relational network between humans and heavenly beings which is analogous to the networks of humanly originated carbon atoms and changing climates described by climate scientists. The interactive spiritual agency of gods, humans and other creatures is represented in the Christian tradition by the doctrine of the Holy Spirit. The Holy Spirit 'overshadows' the womb of Mary and so inspires the Incarnation of God in Christ. And the Spirit dwells in Christ in a unique way. In the gospel of John, the Spirit is 'breathed' by Christ on the Apostles after his resurrection, and in Luke-Acts the Spirit falls on the Apostles at Pentecost. In the Old Testament as in the New, the networks that are sustained by the divine Spirit have an idealized shape that is more egalitarian, participative and symmetric than the networks of kings, princes and merchants that ruled over the peoples of the ancient Near East and, later, of the Roman Empire. Consequently, in the Old Testament, and in Christian tradition until Newton, forms of human politics that express a more symmetric balance of power between strong and weak, ruler and ruled, humanity and the land, are said to mirror the agency of the Creator Spirit, and hence to issue in a benign climate, fertile land and good crops. Hence before Copernicus and Newton, Christians believed that good rule and holy lives were rewarded by Christ as the Lord of heaven with benign weather and productive crops. But the rise of Copernican cosmology and Baconian science sundered this premodern conception of co-agency between heavenly and earthly beings. Consequently, modern humans fail to recognize the moral and spiritual risks, as well as ecological dangers, represented by the asymmetric relation to the planet achieved by fossil fuel enabled industrial humanity. Northcott therefore argues that the climate crisis calls for forms of repair of industrial civilization in which the asymmetry between rich and poor, present and future generations, and between citizens – the majority of whom want action on climate change they cannot deliver from their own resources – and fossil fuel and power companies is reduced. Communities and householders who have used the renewable energy revolution to recover control over their production and use of energy are therefore acting in ways consistent with this pneumatological imperative. So, too, are those communities and householders who are attempting to relocalise the production of food, construction materials and other essential goods and services.

In Chapter 5, 'Creation', Celia Deane-Drummond acknowledges, with Sallie McFague and Anne Primavesi, that climate change occasions a growing suspicion of scientific materialism because it reveals a relational interaction between humanity and the earth which materialist, metaphysical assumptions suppress, under the influence of the metaphor of the earth as mechanism. But Deane-Drummond resists the claims of McFague and Primavesi that the ecological crisis calls for a new, immanent metaphysic which identifies God and Creation more fully than Trinitarian theologians conventionally allow. For Deane-Drummond the inadequacies of scientific materialism require a reaffirmation of *creatio ex nihilo* and of the distinction between, as well as enduring relation of, God and Creation. This is because it is essential to distinguish clearly between 'nature' and 'creation': they are too often elided not just in discussions about climate change, but also in conversations about science and theology and God and evolution more generally. Creation out of nothing is, in a primary sense, about the creation of Being as such, rather than the detailed unfolding of the natural world in natural processes.

Deane-Drummond finds valuable resources for her restatement of the doctrine of Creation in the little known *Sentences of Peter Lombard* by Thomas Aquinas. In this work, Aquinas situates the material cosmos in a divinely originated space-time continuum which uses the philosophical notion of Being and is directed from its beginning in God, and towards a return to God. This gives a *relational,* as well as a caused, character to human and other than human being. It also describes a temporal, and graced or salvific, flow of the history of creation which gives material being meaning and moral intentionality, which materialism alone does not provide. The nature of this meaning and intentionality is captured in the sustaining divine relation to creation as love and wisdom. It is also captured in the idea of the Sabbath rest of the Creator, and the call of Jews and Christians to mimic God's rest in their work on creation. In so doing, they acknowledge that there are limits to human work in the world, and that there is a higher value, a higher cause, than the human transformation of creation into monetary wealth which is at issue in the refusal of nations, corporations and consumers to mitigate their pollution of the climate.

The effects of climate change are already being experienced by other than human creatures. This leads us to the most significant innovation in this systematic theological reflection on climate change – the inclusion of a chapter on 'Creatures', Chapter 6, a theme not addressed in traditional systematic treatments of Christian doctrine. The praise of creatures is a core eschatological theme of the Old Testament account of the redemption of creation. Creatures praise God by their nature according to Psalm 148 and human praise joins with the praise of other creatures rather than taking precedence. This points to the value of creatures to the Creator, independent from their utility to human beings. The creatures that Muers first considers in relation to climate change are the heavens. The heavens in the Old Testament are inaccessible and distant from humanity but they mediate divine favour or displeasure since good, or bad, weather determines whether subsistence farmers live well or poorly. That the weather mediates divine favour or displeasure is rejected by post-Copernicans. But the scientific discovery that human behaviours are implicated in growing weather extremes finds analogy in the perception that weather extremes may indicate the influence on the heavens of humanly originated evil. The biblical consciousness that 'ways of inhabiting particular places on earth – virtuous or sinful patterns of life – have something to do with how the heavens are encountered and experienced' affirms that human moral attentiveness to the needs of persons and creatures is both central to finding meaning and purpose in human life, and to sustaining the ecological habitability of earth.

Climate change is already posing habitat challenges to many plants and animals, most of which do not possess the human capacity to migrate to other places when habitability is threatened. The Hebrew name *Adamah* indicates that in biblical anthropology the distinctive and divinely given responsibility of the human is to care for the place-specific capacities of the earth to sustain life. Again, there is an analogy between climate change and this biblical vision since the mixing of gases in the atmosphere produces generalized effects in the heavens which are not place specific in the form of raised temperatures. But these have place-specific effects in particular ecosystems which, at even 2 degrees of global warming, threaten the endurance of up to one third of plant and animal species. This means that climate change is a form of human evil that is as universal in its ecological effects as original sin. But it also makes all the more resonant the eschatological vision of *shalom*, in which the creation redeemed is a peaceable community of praise among all creatures. This vision indicates that animals, in particular, are co-subjects, co-creatures, with humans. And it indicates the mutual dependence of humans on animals and plants as well as their dependence on us. It is precisely this refusal of ecological situatedness and dependence which constitutes human sin: against the Creator, against persons, against other creatures and against the earth and the heavens.

In Chapter 7, 'Humanity', Scott argues that only a dynamic Trinitarian account of creation can situate humanity in the network of agencies in such a way as to adequately describe the relational complexities revealed by the science of climate change. While philosophers such as Stephen Gardiner tend to isolate the human as the principal agent in the spatio-temporal reality of climate change, a theological description is more open to the hybrid forms of agency that characterize the behaviours and practices responsible for destabilizing the climate. Hence the energy production network is mechanical while it also depends on conscious decisions to initiate actions that draw on mechanical energy. Analogously, human-species relations, as manifest in decisions to eat meat, recruit the co-agency of domestic animals in generating greenhouse gas emissions. Finally, decisions to cut down old growth forests cause soils to emit carbon to the atmosphere which would otherwise stay in the ground. These interfaces all reveal that the conventional modern division between nature and culture is inadequate to describe the networked character of agency in the causation of climate change. Instead, Scott argues for the descriptive power of the 'postnatural' as a metaphor which situates human agency among both divinely created beings such as species and soils, and among humanly created mechanisms such as power stations, electricity grids and mobility machines.

The adoption of a Trinitarian, postnatural approach requires resistance to descriptions of climate change as originating in an intrinsic conflict between 'natural limits' and human freedom. Instead this approach acknowledges the centrality to anthropology, *and* to creaturely relations, of the divine command to humanity 'to create his own history and culture, creatively to transform the world and make it into his own.'[21] Hence there is no form of human agency which does not also implicate the agency of what is sometimes called 'nature'. If climate science reveals the influence of human beings on the atmosphere, this reveals what a Trinitarian anthropology also indicates – which is the situatedness of human agency in networks with other creatures, conscious and non-conscious. Recognition of this situatedness should generate 'relative norms' for human institutions and practices that, at appropriate scales in human-creaturely relations, honour the human duty not only to transform the earth towards a more habitable earth but also to make the earth more richly relational, and hence more fertile, for nonhumans as well as humans.

In 'Sin and salvation', Chapter 8, Messer begins from the Augustinian claim that the essence of sin is the refusal to worship God as the ground of human and creaturely being. This refusal results in the worship of what is not God, which is idolatry. From a refusal of moral, physical and spiritual relatedness to God spring distorted relationships with other persons and other creatures. Given the historical and social character of sin, salvation should also be narrated in historical and social as well as individual terms. Hence what some theologians call 'structural sin' is not alternative but intrinsic to the intergenerational character of sin. And hence the Christian practice of justice in communities of word and sacrament should resist and reverse the accumulated inequities manifest in most economic and political structures and institutions.

Cooperative international action to mitigate climate change is corrupted by structural sin. National representatives at climate negotiations claim to do their duty when they pursue their perceived national self-interest by resisting restraints on climate damaging activities. In so doing, they mirror the sinful tendencies of individuals to refuse their original relatedness to the divine Creator; they refuse that their interests coincide with the interests of other created beings and may deny them their legitimate being when this refusal results in the destruction of a stable climate or other ecological conditions essential to the well-being of others. By contrast, a salvific response to climate change will begin with an acknowledgement of the complicity of nations and individuals in climate-damaging activities. From confession of sin, repentance becomes a graced possibility and hence the theological acknowledgement of sin makes possible a more hopeful, and even salvific, engagement in climate mitigation than a more humanistic account of moral corruption. This approach also brings grace and hope to climate change activism, and resists a tendency to self-righteous scapegoating. Instead it narrates responsible, mitigating actions by 'eco-congregations' and others as forms of witness to the divine destiny for the salvation and *shalom* of the whole creation; this destiny is first revealed in the salvific events of Christ's life, death and resurrection in which real guilt is forgiven at the same time as a new salvific way of being is opened up.

This account of sin and salvation sets the place of the Church centre stage in the theological response to climate change. In 'Church', Chapter 9, Grzelidze argues that the Church 'was founded by Christ himself for the salvation of the created order following the broken covenant between God and human beings'. The Fall into sin affects the whole created order, and climate change is an atmospheric illustration of the ecological effects of sin. The intrinsic relationship of climate crisis and human sin accentuates the Church's salvific role as the *mediator* of divine grace to Creation. The Church carries the destiny of the cosmos declared in the divine promise to 'make all things new' (Rev. 21. 5). The Church is therefore required by this vocation to witness liturgically, and in her own life, to human-creaturely relations which symbolize the graced destiny of creation in Christ. This witness finds moral force when Christians reduce their consumption of climate-damaging goods and services and seek to live more lightly on the earth. And this witness also has economic and political implications for secular power; in particular, in relation to the excess consumption and greed which are implicated in the refusal of rich and powerful nations and corporations to restrain their greenhouse gas emissions. The connection between the inner life of the Church and the secular powers that rule the world is underwritten by the liturgical cosmology of Maximus the Confessor for whom the Church images the covenantal relationship of God and the sensible world. The sacramental life of the Church participates in the life-giving and sustaining *energeia* of the Holy Spirit, and hence it reconciles in the performative nature of the liturgy the reconciliation of created and uncreated life begun in the revelation of the Incarnate Christ as the divine *logos*. *Logos* is also crucial to understanding the human vocation to draw the cosmos towards its destiny of participating, alongside humanity, in the life of God. Hence the divine image in humanity places humanity, and more especially the Church, as the 'new creation' in a priestly relation to creation in which the Church represents the Creation as an Offering to the Creator. As Zizioulas argues, for the Greeks *ratio* refers not only to the human capacity to reason but also 'to the human capacity to achieve the unity of the world and to make a cosmos out of it'.[22] The divine priesthood of the Church towards all creation also has political meaning for the secular powers. The Church in her life and worship potentially displays a political apocalypse – or revealing – which anticipates the union of all things with the Creator at the eschaton.

At the core of Christian eschatology, as Skrimshire summarises in Chapter 10, 'Eschatology', are two beliefs: that the earth has a good destiny divinely intended for it from before time but whose full character is ultimately unknowable to human beings; and that human beings are called to act towards and out of hope for that good in the time before their own mortal end, and before the temporal end of the currently knowable space-time continuum. Put like this, Christian eschatology at first seems to sustain ecological pessimism. But the earliest roots of Christian apocalyptic, in the book of Isaiah, indicate that the 'new heaven and new earth' will be characterized by a *shalom* between beings which the appearance and reign of the messiah will bring into history as a possible route map for humans and other species even before the end. Christian messianism situates hope for a new heaven and a new earth in a radical, this-worldly hope for a levelling between persons, and even between persons and species, which is first anticipated in the birth of the messiah in a stable among other animals in the Christian story. Hence, for Pannenberg, the ethical life of Christ, and by extension of Christ's followers, is a forerunner of the state of things that will transpire in and after the eschaton or end of all things.[23] And it is precisely this narrative sense of a connection between the time between the times and the end of time which is the essence of Christian hope, not only for progress in human flourishing and salvation before the end but for ecological redemption. How, though, might such hope have purchase in a time of extensive cultural and political refusal to respond to the urgent threats of extreme climate change to human and other than human flourishing? The first implication is that Christian hope does not excuse Christians from identifying with the suffering of the victims of climate change and other ecological disasters, human and nonhuman. Second, it is essential to read Christian apocalyptic, like the Jewish, as a re-reading of present reality which calls for an alternative, messianic way of living in the present. The messianic alternative appears weak and ineffective from the perspective of the powers that still usurp authority over the earth, and over future climate states.[24] But it is this very weakness which makes it all the more a true sign of the promised in-breaking of *shalom* after a levelling of earthly powers by a final event of divine judgement. Christian eschatology, then, underwrites a range of climate activisms.

The essays presented here provide ample evidence of the cultural work we set out to achieve in this volume. As theologians concerned about the future of the planet, and more especially the impacts of climate change on present as well as future humans and species around the world, we restate and develop Christian doctrines in the chapters that follow in ways which rebalance the relationship between contemporary humanity and the fragile and wondrous ecological networks that constitute life on earth. We do not expect ready agreement with all of the arguments advanced here, but we hope to at least persuade the reader of the fruitfulness of systematic theology in developing and undergirding the Christian response to anthropogenic climate change.

Notes

1 The phrase was first coined by Anselm of Canterbury in *Proslogion*.
2 Daniel W. Hardy and David F. Ford, *Jubilate: Theology in Praise* (London: Darton, Longman and Todd, 1984) and Geoffrey Wainwright, 'The praise of God in the theological reflection of the Church', *Interpretation* 39 (1985): 34–45.
3 Kevin Rudd, 'Faith in politics', *The Monthly* 17 (2006): 22–30.

4 Rudd, 'Faith in politics'.
5 See further Dieter Helm, *The Carbon Crunch: How We're Getting Climate Change Wrong and How to Fix It* (New Haven, CT: Yale University Press, 2012).
6 Intergovernmental Panel on Climate Change, *Climate Change 2013: The Physical Science Base*. Available online at www.ipcc.ch/report/ar5/wg1/#.UpRRXmRg6yf (visited 25 November 2013).
7 Will Steffen, Paul Crutzen et al., 'The Anthropocene: are humans now overwhelming the great forces of nature?' *Ambio: A Journal of the Human Environment* 36 (2007): 614–21.
8 Timothy Gorringe, 'Climate change is a confessing issue for the churches?' Operation Noah Annual Lecture 2011. Available online at www.operationnoah.org/sites/default/files/Tim_Gorringe_lecture_0.pdf (visited 23 October, 2013).
9 Dipesh Chakrabarty, 'The climate of history: four theses', *Critical Inquiry* 35 (2009): 197–222.
10 For a fuller discussion of the nature–culture divide and its role in suppressing human consciousness of, and responses to, climate change see Michael S. Northcott, *A Political Theology of Climate Change* (Grand Rapids, MI: Wm. B. Eerdmans, 2013).
11 On the theological challenges involved in the rising influence of technology on modern human life and society the most influential theologian writing in the existentialist tradition of the theology of crisis is Jaques Ellul: see in particular *The Technological Society* (New York: Random House, 1954) and *The Technological Bluff* (Grand Rapids, MI: Eerdmans, 1991); see also Brent Waters, *From Human to Posthuman: Christian Theology and Technology in a Postmodern World* (Aldershot: Ashgate, 2006) and Peter Scott, *Anti-Human Theology: Nature, Technology and the Postnatural* (London: SCM Press, 2010).
12 Dietrich Bonhoeffer, *Creation and Fall: A Theological Exposition of Genesis 1–3* (Minneapolis, MN: Fortress Press, 2004).
13 See for example Philip Sherrard, *Human Image, World Image: The Death and Resurrection of Sacred Cosmology* (Ipswich: Golgonooza Press, 1992).
14 Will Steffen, Paul Crutzen et al., 'The Anthropocene'.
15 Sallie McFague, *Models of God* (London: SCM Press, 1987), pp. 29–30.
16 McFague, *Models of God*, 30.
17 David Michael Steffes, *The 'Eco-worldview' of Charles Birch: Biology, Environmentalism and Liberal Christianity in the 20th Century*, PhD thesis, University of Oklahoma, 2008, 5.
18 See further Paul Albrecht, L. C. Birch et al., *Faith, Science and the Future* (Geneva: Church and Society, WCC, 1979).
19 David G. Hallman, 'Ecumenical Response to Climate Change, A Summary of the History and Dynamics of Ecumenical Involvement in the Issue of Climate Change', *Ecumenical Review* 49 (1997): 131–42.
20 Anselm of Canterbury, *Monologion* 14.
21 J. M. Bonino, *Doing Theology in a Revolutionary Situation* (Philadelphia: Fortress Press, 1975), p. 166.
22 John Zizioulas, 'Proprietors or priests of creation?' Keynote address at the Fifth Symposium on Religion, Science and the Environment (Baltic Sea), 1 June 2003. Available online at www.orthodoxytoday.org/articles2/MetJohnCreation.php (accessed 29 October 2013).
23 See further Wolfhart Pannenberg, *Metaphysics and the Idea of God* (Grand Rapids, MI: Wm. B. Eerdmans, 2001).
24 For a fuller discussion of messianic climate politics see Northcott, *A Political Theology of Climate Change*.

Bibliography

Albrecht, Paul, L. C. Birch et al. *Faith, Science and the Future* (Geneva: Church and Society, WCC, 1979).
Anselm of Canterbury. *Monologion*.
——*Proslogion*.

Bonhoeffer, Dietrich. *Creation and Fall: A Theological Exposition of Genesis 1–3* (Minneapolis, MN: Fortress Press, 2004).

Bonino, J. M. *Doing Theology in a Revolutionary Situation* (Philadelphia: Fortress Press, 1975), 166.

Chakrabarty, Dipesh. 'The climate of history: four theses', *Critical Inquiry* 35 (2009): 197–222.

Ellul, Jacques. *The Technological Society* (New York: Random House, 1954).

——*The Technological Bluff* (Grand Rapids MI: Eerdmans 1991).

Gorringe, Timothy. 'Climate change is a confessing issue for the churches?' Operation Noah Annual Lecture 2011. Available online at www.operationnoah.org/sites/default/files/Tim_Gorringe_lecture_0.pdf (visited 23 October 2013).

Hallman, David G. 'Ecumenical Response to Climate Change, A Summary of the History and Dynamics of Ecumenical Involvement in the Issue of Climate Change', *Ecumenical Review* 49 (1997): 131–42.

Hardy, Daniel W. and David F. Ford. *Jubilate: Theology in Praise* (London: Darton, Longman and Todd, 1984)

Helm, Dieter. *The Carbon Crunch: How We're Getting Climate Change Wrong and How to Fix It* (New Haven, CT: Yale University Press, 2012).

Intergovernmental Panel on Climate Change. *Climate Change 2013: The Physical Science Base.* Available online at www.ipcc.ch/report/ar5/wg1/#.UpRRXmRg6yf (visited 25 November 2013).

McFague, Sallie. *Models of God* (London: SCM Press, 1987).

Northcott, Michael S. *A Political Theology of Climate Change* (Grand Rapids, MI: Wm. B. Eerdmans, 2013).

Pannenberg, Wolfhart. *Metaphysics and the Idea of God* (Grand Rapids, MI: Wm. B. Eerdmans, 2001).

Rudd, Kevin. 'Faith in politics', *The Monthly* 17 (2006): 22–30.

Scott, Peter Manley. *Anti-Human Theology: Nature, Technology and the Post-Natural* (London: SCM Press, 2010).

Sherrard, Philip. *Human Image, World Image: The Death and Resurrection of Sacred Cosmology* (Ipswich: Golgonooza Press, 1992).

Steffen, Will, Paul Crutzen, and J. R. McNeil. 'The Anthropocene: are humans now overwhelming the great forces of nature?' *Ambio: A Journal of the Human Environment* 36 (2007): 614–21.

Steffes, David Michael. *The 'Eco-worldview' of Charles Birch: Biology, Environmentalism and Liberal Christianity in the 20th Century*, PhD thesis, University of Oklahoma, 2008.

Wainwright, Geoffrey. 'The praise of God in the theological reflection of the Church', *Interpretation* 39 (1985): 34–45.

Waters, Brent. *From Human to Posthuman: Christian Theology and Technology in a Postmodern World* (Aldershot: Ashgate, 2006).

Zizioulas, John. 'Proprietors or priests of creation?' Keynote address at the Fifth Symposium on Religion, Science and the Environment (Baltic Sea), 1 June 2003. Available online at www.orthodoxytoday.org/articles2/MetJohnCreation.php (accessed 29 October 2013).

2

THE TRINITY

Timothy Gorringe

Notoriously, Kant believed that nothing whatsoever could be taken, for practical purposes, from the doctrine of the Trinity, though since he spoke of taking it literally one wonders what he understood by it.[1] Twentieth century theologians of all denominations took Kant's complaint as symptomatic of neglect of the doctrine over the centuries and sought to repristinate it. It was now described as 'an eminently practical doctrine with far reaching consequences for the Christian life'.[2] The emphasis on the social Trinity which followed has, in turn, provoked a reaction. Some complain that there are inflated claims for what we can learn practically from the doctrine.[3] Others tell us that we should recognise it for what it is, merely a second order doctrine, which tells us nothing whatever about how God is in Godself.[4] Whichever of these routes we take, we come back to Kant. This would mean, amongst other things, that the doctrine of the Trinity had nothing of importance to say about climate change. I believe this move is deeply mistaken and I shall address it in four stages, responding to the two challenges just mentioned on the way. First I will take a cue from Martin Luther and ask about the way in which the word 'God' functions; I then consider what is meant by 'Trinity', taking issue with the critics of the social Trinity and spelling out, in relation to the previous section, why I think this is important in relation to climate change; I shall then consider the claim that the Trinity relates to the new physics and biology and turn to the claim that there are Trinitarian virtues; before saying something, finally, about the Trinity and eschatology.

Who or what is God?

Commenting on the first commandment, Luther remarked that the faith of the heart makes both God and idol. He went on:

A God is that to which we look for all good and in which we find refuge in every time of need … Many a person thinks he has God and everything he needs when he has money and property; in them he trusts and of them he boasts so stubbornly and securely that he cares for no one. Surely such a man also has a god – mammon by name, that is, money and possessions – on which he fixes his whole heart. It is the most common idol on earth.[5]

Five hundred years before Durkheim Luther saw very clearly that the concept of God underwrites what we today call a 'world view' or an understanding of society. He was led to this by one of the core themes of the biblical narrative: the contest between true and false gods, especially the conflict between YHWH and Baal. These stories invite us to reflect on how the word 'God' functions.

The person who has explored Luther's insight most profoundly in recent years is the Dutch biblical scholar Ton Veerkamp. He argues that a grand narrative is one which the majority of people in a society recognise and accept, through which they make sense of their own story, find their place in society and internalise the social structure with its loyalties and dependencies.[6] All of the great religions constitute such a narrative, and within the narrative the word 'God' is a symbol whose function is to focus all social dependencies. 'It is the cipher of the social ground order which must be accepted and acknowledged by all members of society, rulers and ruled.'[7] We can say this without committing ourselves to a purely Durkheimian understanding of God as *nothing more* than a social symbol. This account of how the concept of God functions is true whether or not God truly exists.

More closely in line with Luther, Veerkamp also describes the word 'God' as providing the fundamental justification for rights of ownership. The story in Daniel 3 exemplifies this exactly. The king has a huge image of gold made before which people have to prostrate themselves. In words which recall Marx, Veerkamp comments:

A means of exchange, a means of preserving value and a measure of value: gold is the centre of gravity for the Hellenistic economy. The king of kings makes an image out of it; he reifies the economy and makes it a cultic object, he fetishes gold. The embodiment of politics (the king) exalts the embodiment of economics (gold) as God of the whole world – that is the process recounted here. So the story describes the unity of politics, economics and ideology in the Hellenistic period. It describes a world economic order.[8]

But this parable applies not just to the Hellenistic world but a fortiori to our own in which neoliberal ideology unites politics and economics and demands absolute obedience. The question, then, is not, as the fool has said in his heart, whether or not there is a God, for there is always a God in this sense. 'The question rather is *who* is God: the one who represents the politically and economically strong or YHWH who frees his people from the house of slavery and protects the weak'.[9]

'Competitiveness for unlimited money accumulation', says Ulrich Duchrow, 'is the objective and subjective structure, the "god" of our market society, which determines the whole'. It is this god, this Ba'al, which is driving the rise in global temperature which could lead to the end of human life on earth, which lies behind the sweat shops, and which can crucify whole nations through debt. 'Accordingly', says Duchrow, 'the core of what we must reject is the absolute value attributed to competition and the total absence of limits set on the cancerous growth of capital'.[10] Absolute value and absence of limits are traditional attributes of deity. Idolatry is not about harmless 'green eyed yellow idols to the north of Kathmandu', or anywhere else, but about making absolute that which is not God. The idol of Nebuchadnezzar is, as Veerkamp describes it, a 'really existing god', with real power, who has to be celebrated in liturgies which internalise its lordship and to defy which means you have to be cast into the fire, as the opponents of Pinochet and the other Latin American dictators were cast into the fire.[11] 'Every generation will be confronted with its own Ba'als, their own strange gods, who grab power over them and seek to devour them.'[12] Our own Ba'al is the doctrine of necessary economic growth, insisted on by the Bretton Woods Institutions and by all governments. Why? It is part of the very structure of capital and is bound up with the centrality of interest to our system. How am I to meet the interest payments on the loans I have taken out? If my business grows there is money available to repay loans and invest in capital stock. Without growth, interest payments have to be met out of existing profits, which means less is available for investment, which in turn leads to job losses, less spending and a downward spiral. 'In our present economic system, the choice is between growth and collapse, not growth and stability'.[13] In order to maintain constant growth the distinction between needs and wants has to be erased. As the American retail analyst Victor Lebow notoriously put it in 1956:

> Our enormously productive economy ... demands that we make consumption our way of life, that we convert the buying and use of goods into rituals, that we seek out spiritual satisfaction, our ego satisfaction, in consumption ... we need things consumed, burned up, worn out, replaced and discarded at an ever increasing rate.[14]

Of course, all citizens of the North, and many in the South, are beneficiaries of the growth which has taken place since 1750. Of course, growth is necessary to raise the living standards of billions of the world's people. But if growth is at the expense of generations yet unborn, and of the earth, then it is idolatrous, and this is the charge. The claim that the insistence on economic growth is our contemporary Ba'al rests on the understanding, as E. J. Mishan argued forty years ago, and as Herman Daly has spent a lifetime arguing, that it is impossible for all of seven or nine or more billion people to enjoy a Western standard of living because we would need five or more planets to make that possible.[15] It overlooks the fact that the planet is finite. The climate scientist James Hansen argues that continued human-made climate forcings spell the possible end of all life, and certainly of human life. This, in his view, follows directly from the carbon emissions produced by the insistence that the whole world economy should grow as fast as possible.[16] This is a theological issue because the living God is known in the giving of life: death is the hallmark of idolatry. If, as I have argued, insistence on growth leads to death, then we are in the presence of idolatry. In this context, theology is, as Veerkamp puts it, about lie detection. Here the biblical understanding of God functions in a unique way. In Exodus 3 we learn that the Name of God is unspeakable. The fact that the voice of God cannot be tied down (*Gestaltlos*), says Veerkamp, is about resistance to colonisation by any Ba'al.[17] This is crucial in response to claims, such as George Gilder's, that humans imitate God most perfectly in creating money out of nothing. For him God is worshipped on the Stock Exchange.[18] The biblical revelation, according to Veerkamp, opposes all such claims.

'Trinity' as the Name of God

If it is the case, as Veerkamp argues, that the concept of God functions to underwrite the social and economic ground order of any society, how does this apply to the understanding of God as Trinity? In his most recent work, Veerkamp follows Miskotte in translating 'YHWH' as 'the NAME', and Robert Jenson insists that the Trinity is the Name of the Christian God.[19] As we know, the eighth century Irish poem attributed to St Patrick also puts the divine NAME at the centre. Written, according to legend, as Patrick prepared to confront the priests and ideologists of the High King, the poem says that the Christian in danger binds to him or herself the strong NAME of the Trinity. What does the Trinitarian NAME stand for? What does it signify?

The habit of trinitarian naming (to use Jenson's phrase) arose as a response to the way in which the Christian community found itself praying. When Jesus taught his disciples to pray 'Our Father' he was praying as taught by the whole Jewish tradition, whilst changing the structure of affect by addressing God as 'Father'. What happened at the resurrection and at Pentecost modified the way in which the earliest community prayed. In the light of these events, Christians found themselves praying to the Father, through the Son, in the Spirit.

The first thing to be said about the NAME, then, is that it is the summary of a narrative. This is powerfully recognised in 'St Patrick's breastplate':

> I bind this today to me forever
> By power of faith, Christ's incarnation;
> His baptism in Jordan river,
> His death on Cross for my salvation;
> His bursting from the spicèd tomb,
> His riding up the heavenly way,
> His coming at the day of doom
> I bind unto myself today.

For Christians the NAME summarises the biblical story: the Father is the one who delivered Israel out of Egypt, the Son is the one whom the Father raised from the dead as 'the first fruits of all creation' (1 Cor 15.23) and the Spirit is sent by the Father in the name of the Son to lead the people of God into freedom (Gal 5.1). This narrative is framed by a contest with the gods of possession, as Veerkamp argues, but positively it is about the establishment of 'a world made otherwise', which Jesus calls 'the kingdom'. God is known in a history which calls into being a community with a particular task in relation to all other gods. The prophetic polemic against idolatry is fundamentally about the creation of another world. How does the doctrine of the Trinity exemplify that? Following John Zizioulas and many others I shall first argue that what is these days called the idea of the 'social Trinity' was in fact implicit in Christian understanding from the very beginning, and is not a projection of our own understanding of relationships. This in turn, I shall argue, bears on our understanding of society, economy and, therefore, climate change.

Trinity as an account of God as relation

What we call the doctrine of the Trinity arose as Christians tried to give an account to their Jewish and pagan neighbours as to why they prayed as they did. Opposing Praxeas, (possibly a nickname), someone who wanted to insist that Christianity was, after all, monotheist, Tertullian, at the beginning of the third century, insisted that it was essential to talk of three because Father, Son and Spirit are distinguished in Scripture and they speak to and about one another.[20] The language he used to speak of the Three became standard: *tres personae in una substantia*, where '*substantia*' quickly lost its Stoic meaning and came to mean 'one reality', and where '*persona*' was 'the everyday term for the human individual, established in his individuality by his social role, by his speaking and responding'.[21] That the Three persons speak to and about one another does, of course, imply relationship and what was meant by that was the centre of later reflection.

It is clear that, from Tertullian onwards, and in both East and West, Christians believed they were saying something profound about God when they spoke of the divine Triunity, and that this had implications for how Christians understood themselves and their world. As Janet Soskice puts it, 'It was of the essence of the earliest defences of the doctrine that the Godhead be understood as life, love, and complete mutuality – the Son is not less than the Father, nor can the Father be Father without Son and Spirit'.[22] In insisting that there were not three Gods, the Cappadocians argued that what constitute the three 'persons' are their relations:

> the Persons of the Godhead are not divided from each other in time, place, will, occupation, activity or any qualification of this sort, the distinguishing marks observed in human beings. The only distinction here is that the Father

is father, not son: the Son is son, not father; similarly, the Holy Spirit is neither father nor son.[23]

The relations between the identities are their being God.[24]

John Zizioulas argues that the Cappadocians followed Ignatius and Irenaeus in identifying being with life, a move made possible by their understanding of the eucharist. 'The Eucharistic experience implies that life is imparted and actualized only in an event of communion, and thus creation and existence in general can be founded only upon this living God of communion'.[25] Athanasius had already implied that *ousia*, substance, had a relational character so that communion belongs not to the level of will and action, but to that of substance. The Cappadocians took this further by identifying hypostasis with *prosopon*, a relational term. This move was then crucially exploited by Maximus the Confessor who believes that the Logos translates his way of being (*tropos hyparxeos*) from the divine realm to that of creation. The world, then, 'owes its relational being to a personal presence which, although in the world, exists in a dialectical relation with it.'[26] Put otherwise, Maximus makes a distinction between the energy and the essence of God. The latter is unknowable, and God's aseity is absolutely affirmed, so we have to understand the relationship between God and the world as one of love, not nature.[27]

In the sixth century the idea of perichoresis, translated into Latin as '*circuminsessio*', originally used to speak of the relation of the divine and human nature in Christ, was applied to the relation of the three divine 'persons'. There is, then, an understanding of the three divine persons 'mutually indwelling' each other.[28]

In the twelfth century, as is well known, Richard of St Victor reflected on the implications of the divine *circuminsessio*. Building on Augustine's analysis, but using it quite differently, Richard argues that we have the doctrine of the Trinity because otherwise we could not understand what it would mean to say that 'God is love'. Caritas, he says, cannot exist where love is not directed to another. 'In order for caritas to be the supreme good, it is impossible that there can be lacking either someone who communicates caritas or someone to whom caritas is communicated.'[29] The pleasures of caritas are the greatest possible and without fellowship God would lack these pleasures. This axiom might yield binity, but, Richard argues, in fact the logic of love requires a third, because for love to be perfect, the two must share their love. 'Each of the two persons, who is supremely loved and ought to be loved supremely, must seek with equal desire a third person mutually loved and must possess him freely with equal concord'.[30] Richard considers objections to the term 'person' but, modifying Boethius' famous definition, believes we must stick with it.[31] The father is the love that is all gift, the Son the love that is both gift and response and the Spirit the love that is all response. For him, if God is love eternally in Godself, the very being of God must be a Trinity.

This extraordinary treatise has to be understood in the context of the twelfth century renaissance which Colin Morris identified as the birth of individualism, the century which saw the birth of the idea of courtly love.[32] Richard's account of person, and therefore his understanding of relations, was rejected in the next century by Aquinas, and this might have something to do with the need of the institutional church to exercise tighter control on movements and theologies which challenged centralised power. Richard's insights only really flowered in the twentieth century, when David Jenkins, for example, could describe the Trinity as meaning that

> it is neither fantastically visionary nor beyond all reason to take the risk and the hope of commitment to a vision which speaks of community and a communion where love fulfils love so that everyone is fully human because everyone is fully human. The vision and understanding of God which is symbolized by the Trinity sets us free to take love absolutely seriously. The symbol focuses the discovery that God is already that pattern and energy of fulfilling and relating love which we require to receive, and to be contributory parts of, if our humanness is to be fulfilled.[33]

Understood like this, the doctrine of the Trinity is, in John Burnaby's words, 'no superfluous piece of theologizing, but an expression of what is most fundamental in the revelation of God in Christ.'[34]

Two objections have been raised against this way of speaking. First, it is alleged that it rests on projection.

> First a concept of perichoresis is used to name what is not understood, to name whatever it is that makes the three Persons one. Secondly, the concept is filled out rather suggestively with notions borrowed from our own experience of relationships and relatedness. And then, finally, it is presented as an exciting resource Christian theology has to offer the wider world in its reflection upon relationships and relatedness.[35]

Second, and relatedly, it is objected that the claim that God is a pattern of mutually fulfilling relationships tells us nothing which we do not know already. We do not need the Trinity to tell us that human beings condition one another by their relationships.[36]

Karen Kilby believes that the mistake arises from an unnecessary search for relevance. The doctrine of the Trinity arose to say certain things about the divinity of Christ and then of the Spirit against the background of the assumption that God is one. We need not go beyond this. The doctrine does not need to be seen as descriptive of the divine, a deep understanding of the way God really is. It is a second order proposition for how to read the Biblical stories, how to deploy the vocabulary of Christianity in an appropriate way.[37] If we accept this, we go back to the distinction between the economic Trinity (God as God reveals Godself) and the immanent Trinity (God as God is in Godself), and, by implication, we are once more returned to Kant's views of the practical significance of the doctrine. But, in the first place, as my brief sketch of the development of the doctrine highlights, understanding the importance of the mutual relationship of the three persons has been a central part of Christian discourse since the second or third century. In a thoughtful exploration of the bearing of Trinitarian thought on feminist theology, Janet Soskice argues that what we learn from the doctrine of the Trinity is that to be is *to be related in difference* and she comments,

> We may now stand at a moment of evangelical opportunity in the West, a time in which people not only need to hear a fully relational account of the trinitarian life of God, but may also be receptive to it.[38]

It seems not to be the case that the claim that equal and mutual relationships (i.e. 'God' as the Cappadocians describe God) are the ground of all reality is an un-illuminating truism. On the contrary, to return to Ton Veerkamp, this challenges most accounts of what is ultimate, most accounts of the fundamental ground order of society. The 'God' (i.e. the beginning and end of all things, the ground of all reality) who is relationship in Godself does not provide the fundamental justification for rights of ownership nor represent the politically and economically strong. This God, whose name is Trinity, challenges the Ba'al which drives climate change because, as feminist theologians in particular have noted, the thoroughgoing exploitation of resources, including human resources, in the name of freedom, growth, progress or any other mantra, implicitly discounts the relational nature of reality. It is thoroughly mon–archical, i.e. committed to one principle only, in our day-to-day growth. This is partly, as I have argued, because capitalism requires growth, but it is also because the only teleology currently available is that of the maximization of comfort or pleasure, often today called 'happiness'.

Secondly, as Karl Rahner exasperatedly insisted, the doctrine simply has to have effects: 'How can the contemplation of any reality, even of the loftiest reality, beatify us if intrinsically it is absolutely *unrelated* to us in any way?'[39]

> The isolation of the treatise on the Trinity *has* to be wrong. There *must* be a connection between the Trinity and man. The Trinity is a mystery of *salvation*, otherwise it would never have been revealed. We should show why it is such a mystery.[40]

Here is the place to mention the famous argument of Erik Peterson that the doctrine of the Trinity undermined political monotheism.[41] The response to this, as Moltmann noted, is that it should have done this but in fact failed to do so, precisely because monarchy was the primary political formation.[42] If we ask, with Karl Rahner, why the Trinity was a dead letter for so long, this is the answer. The revival of the doctrine of the Trinity begins, problematically, with Hegel, which is to say after 1789. At the same time, we can say that the doctrine of the Trinity, along with the incarnation, constituted the bad conscience of the West for two millennia. The return to the doctrine of the Trinity, the understanding of God as relationship in Godself, is profoundly hopeful in that it challenges the ground order of society which has generated, and continues to generate, climate change through the commitment to never-ending growth.

Of course it is true that, as Kathryn Tanner points out, claims that belief in the Trinity supports egalitarian communities, whilst monotheism supports authoritarian rule, overlook the fact that monotheism can support progressive polities and Trinitarian belief reactionary ones. Such arguments, she says, 'overlook the complexities of theological claims, their fluidity of sense, and complications in their application for political purposes.'[43] Whilst this is quite true, it does not mean that what we believe ceases to matter. Rather, as Wittgenstein put it, 'Practice gives words their sense'.[44] In this remark Wittgenstein refers specifically to the doctrine of the Trinity and David Cunningham comments, 'The way we understand God affects our relation to God and our relations to one another; thus the articulation of a doctrine of the Trinity has concrete ethical implications'.[45] That this is the case has been obscured by the fact that at various periods in church history both Protestants and Catholics have been tempted to regard doctrines as 'timeless, unqualified, absolute truths' unrelated to history.[46] The doctrine of the Trinity, in particular, has been understood in this way. Obviously feeling that this way of understanding doctrine is still around, Tanner notes that Christianity is not simply a body of beliefs but 'a way of living in which beliefs are embedded' and speaks of beliefs as 'helping to make that way of living meaningful and motivated'.[47] This is surely a bizarre way to speak of the relation of belief and practice: it presupposes that act and intention can be disentangled. In the background seems to lie what we can call the Jackson Pollock theory of action, which believes that in painting a picture, for example, it will be all the better if we do not think about it or first have a design. But, in fact, intention is analytic to action. Action is not the automatic threshing about of a nervous system but a set of moves or deeds which embody or express mental processes, intentions or beliefs. You may object that walking is an action which embodies no intention, but in fact we walk to somewhere, or for something, even if we just go for a stroll. There is purpose behind it. Beliefs do not, as Tanner suggests, 'help' to make ways of living meaningful; they are constitutive of ways of living – and this applies to the doctrine of the Trinity as to any other belief (including the belief that we have to have economic growth).

As Cunningham observes, the refusal to draw ethical description from the doctrine of the Trinity represents a failure of nerve. 'If all the hard work required to untangle the complexities of trinitarian doctrine led to nothing more than banal observations about the "dynamic in which we find ourselves" then Christians would be quite justified in dismissing it as irrelevant.'[48] We need, then, to show how faith in the Trinity bears on our practice vis-à-vis climate change.

The Trinity and a relational world

More or less *pari passu* with the rise of the new Trinitarian theology has come the rise of the new physics and biology which, in some quarters though not in all, has been much more open to questions of transcendence than Newtonian physics was. This has suggested to some an analogy, or even a direct connection, between the understanding of God as a pattern of relationships and the manifold relationships of the universe. Thus John Polkinghorne can write that

> [t]he interconnected integrity of the physical universe can be understood theologically as reflecting the status of the world as a divine creation whose intrinsic relationality has been conferred on it through its origin in the will of the triune God.[49]

In response to such ideas, Lewis Ayres draws attention to what he considers to be a fundamental difference between physical and personal relationships. When it is said that relationship is fundamental to being, he writes,

> does this identify basic spatio-temporal features of things or does it identify the complex emotional and psychological content of human relationships as basic to the cosmos? If the former then the features that supposedly identify the cosmos as *imago Trinitatis* are those that all classical theologians agree are not to be predicated of the Trinity. If the latter, then it is not clear how the material structures of our universe exhibit the qualities intrinsic to relationship.[50]

This objection does not seem to me to be fatal because it rests on a false distinction between different kinds of relationship. What Polkinghorne and others appeal to, if I understand them, are not primarily 'spatio-temporal' features but the fact that all reality is related. The 'modern synthesis' in biology, as instanced for example by Theodore Dobzhansky, argued for a metaphysic of levels, so that the chemical presupposed the physical, the biological the chemical, and the social and spiritual all three. Without being reductionist, this understanding wanted to view reality as profoundly whole and refused to make an absolute split between personal and physical realities. This is not pan-psychism, but the claim that it is impossible to think of reality as neatly divided into physical and personal or spiritual parts. We do not have to say that chemical and physical levels of reality manifest emotion but we do have to say that there is a sense in which purely physical or chemical levels of reality are the ground of personal relationship. This is important in relation to climate change because one could plausibly claim that anthropogenic climate change owes a good deal to silo thinking – the belief that actions in one area could not possibly affect actions in another, whereas what we find is that the spiritual (meaning our belief systems, for example, in the necessity of economic growth) affects the economic which affects the biological, chemical and physical (the meteorological) and so forth. Thus a study of the collapse of coral reefs in the Caribbean complains that conventional resource management strategies have failed because 'there is little acknowledgment of the linkages between the social and ecological domains of a system'.[51] Moltmann speaks of the ecological crisis as 'a religious crisis of the paradigm in which people in the Western world put their trust and live'.[52] But this religious crisis manifests itself in particular models of the economy, which in turn bear on farming, forests, the oceans, carbon dioxide levels and so forth. All the different varieties of relationship Ayres distinguishes are involved. The 'entangled world' argument assumes that the relatedness of all things is what we would expect from a creator who is relatedness itself. The universe which God-in-relation creates is set up for infinitely complex patterns of relationship, in which distinctions between physical, mental, spiritual and so forth are made, at best, for analytical convenience.

It could be said that behind this is an unargued assumption that the created will resemble the creator – an assumption which Aquinas finds unproblematic but which is less so for us, given the notorious difficulty of inferring anything from works of art about their creators.[53] However, the 'entangled world' argument in some respects looks back to understandings of divine immanence, and to the idea that *all* reality, in all its complexity, is kept in being by God. So Aquinas tells us, appealing to Gregory the Great, that 'the *esse* of all creaturely beings so depends upon God that they could not exist even for a moment, but would fall away into nothingness unless they were sustained in existence by his power'.[54] The question is how to understand this in the light of the Trinity and in the light of what we understand about the hierarchy and interrelatedness of all reality. Moltmann argues (and Aquinas would not question this) that it is God's Spirit which holds all things in being. He then goes on,

> [t]he Spirit preserves and leads living things and their communities beyond themselves. This indwelling Creator Spirit is fundamental for the community of creation. *It is not elementary particles that are basic, as the mechanistic world view maintains, but the overriding harmony of the relations and of the self-transcending movements, in which the longing of the Spirit for a still unattained consummation finds expression.* If the cosmic Spirit is the Spirit of God, the universe cannot be viewed as a closed system. It has to be understood as a system that is open – open for God and for God's future.[55]

This could be thought of as pure gnostic speculation but it seems to me a proper gloss on the older understanding, expressed by Aquinas, that all things whatsoever are held in being by God. It seems to me to answer Ayres' objection, for the work of the Spirit in this sense transcends, as Paul in Romans 8 quite explicitly says, all merely physical and personal boundaries.

Sarah Coakley puts a more fundamental objection in pointing out that if the relation of the Trinitarian God to the physical universe is *sui generis*, then we should beware of expectations of straightforward mirrorings of such relationality in the physical universe. 'Relationality may be all around us but the conceptual task of marshalling and analyzing different forms of such relationality is formidable and not easily constrained into consistent patterns directly redolent of God'.[56] This is essentially the reminder that God is not a member of any genus, or is Wholly Other, and therefore a warning against natural theology. This is important, but, in the first place, we have already seen Maximus' argument that the relationship of God to creation is one of love not of necessity, which Zizioulas takes as affirming the very relationality Coakley queries. Second, let us suppose that God as relationship in Godself is, as Rahner suggests, a datum of revelation. Then, at the very least, something follows in respect of the fact that human beings are said to be in the image of God, and something follows about what would constitute constructive and destructive, or grace-filled and sinful behaviour. Karl Barth argued that the *Imago Dei* meant relationship, but he restricted it to human relationships. But could we not say, in the light of the doctrine of the Trinity I have been arguing for, that we are encouraged to understand ourselves as coming from and going to the God who is relationship in Godself, the One who creates out of relationship, and that therefore the true relationships to which we are called go beyond the human to all other creatures? In other words, does not our understanding of ourselves and the world as the product of the God who is relationship call us to an ecological understanding, practice and ethics? To go back to Veerkamp, the problem with our contemporary Ba'al, the doctrine of necessary economic growth, is that it does not respect the relationships in difference of which Moltmann speaks. One vision of the human good is proffered and pursued with fanatical consistency regardless of the damage to other humans, other creatures or the planet. By contrast, to say that the ground order of our society is relationship in itself calls us to a quite different practice. It is a call to obedience and to discipleship which would decisively bear on our practice in regard to all else created.

Trinitarian virtues and practices

What I have just argued is formulated more systematically by David Cunningham, drawing on the revival of virtue ethics. He argues that Christians should be formed by trinitarian virtues which issue in practices. The virtues he has in mind he calls polyphony, the good of harmonious difference, mutual participation and non-individualistic particularity. In relation to the world in which we live, polyphony calls us to listen to the entire orchestration of creation, and not to allow the apparently minor melodies to be silenced, and this would bear fruit in, for example, ecological work to protect endangered species.[57] Participation underwrites a sense of interconnectedness within the created order, the sense that we are woven into a web of participation, not only with God and with other human beings, but with the entire creation. It also calls us to give up the idea of possession since that is the antithesis of interconnectedness.[58] Particularity calls us to examine our interactions with the created order more carefully than we are normally in the habit of doing.[59] Of course it is true that a non-Christian can cultivate such virtues, but I agree with Cunningham that the virtues which flow from Trinitarian belief are not the sanctification of contemporary mores which Tanner takes them to be. The doctrine of the Trinity, he argues, is a challenge to the modern cult of the individual.

> It teaches us to think in terms of complex webs of mutuality and participation. The practice of Trinitarian theology thus calls us into newness of life – a life

that bears a very different shape from what we have come to regard as ordinary existence.[60]

In his view, human beings are inclined to violence.

> Peace can only be restored by God's gracious act of self giving, through which we come to participate in the peace of God. In this process, God's Triunity plays a key role: in their polyphony, mutual participation and non individualistic particularity, the Three form us – through specific communal practices – into a peaceable and peacemaking people.[61]

In other words, the Trinitarian virtues school us to cherish relationship in difference.

This is a very attractive proposal which shares the weakness of all virtue ethics, namely that the inculcation of the virtues presupposes an ethos and a disciplined community. The specific communal practices Cunningham has in mind are, of course, ecclesial, and it is a question whether the church which we experience – neither one, holy nor catholic – can provide that ethos. And, strangely, what issues from the discussion of the Trinitarian virtues and practices as regards the non-human world is what Cunningham calls 'an ethic of minimal interference with creation'. Here his guard has certainly slipped. If we begin with participation, for example, we will be led much more to an ethic of grateful and respectful practices of, for example, farming, fishing, building and making which would be vastly different from present practices of exploitation. This is not minimal interference but what Wendell Berry calls 'kindly use'. Humans are part of nature, but, as Aristotle argued, their part is to intervene through the use of their intelligence, guided by an understanding of their final goal. The idea of 'minimal interference' buys in to the idea that all human interactions with the non-human part of creation simply mess things up.[62]

The Trinity and eschatological hope

In 1972, Moltmann had already argued that

> the doctrine of the Trinity is no longer an exorbitant and impractical speculation about God, but is nothing other than shorter version of the passion narrative of Christ in its significance for the eschatological freedom of faith *and the life of oppressed nature.*[63]

Building on his work in the *Theology of Hope,* he understands the Trinity eschatologically. The unity of the Father, the Son and the Spirit is not simply a given, but constitutes an eschatological hope for all reality. 'The unity of the three persons of this history must be understood as a communicable unity and as an open, inviting unity, capable of integration.'[64] The uniting at-oneness of the triune God was, he argued, the quintessence of salvation. This meant that its 'transcendent primal ground' could not be either the one, single, homogenous divine essence (*substantia*), or the one, identical, absolute subject, but existed in the eternal perichoresis of the Father, the Son and the Spirit in which Father, Son and Spirit open themselves for the reception and unification of the whole creation.[65] Put another way, 'the habit of Trinitarian naming' understands both the origin and end of all creation (i.e. 'God') as a pattern of mutual love. This is a faith claim in the teeth of much of the evidence, grounded on the resurrection which itself interprets and illuminates the narrative of the exodus.

Speaking of accounts of the social Trinity of love Kathryn Tanner finds such eschatologies 'almost cruelly quixotic … A treasure is dangled before us with no clue as to how we might get to it from the desperate straits of social relations marked by violent conflict, loss and suffering.'[66] This seems to miss precisely what eschatology exists to do, at least when understood in terms of a theology of hope. Eschatology, Moltmann insists, is not a doctrine about history's happy end.

> In the present situation of our world, facile consolation is as fatal as melancholy hopelessness. No one can assure us that the worst will not happen. According to the laws of experience it will. We can only trust that even the end of the world hides a new beginning if we trust the God who calls into being the things that are not, and out of death creates new life. Life out of this hope then means already acting here and today in accordance with that world of justice and righteousness and peace, contrary to appearances, and contrary to all historical chances of success. It obliges us solemnly to abjure the spirit, logic and practice of the nuclear system of deterrence and all other systems of mass annihilation. It means an unconditional Yes to life in the face of the inescapable death of all the living.[67]

Paul's argument in Romans 8 also addresses a world marked by violent conflict, loss and suffering, and precisely because it did so he pointed out that no one hopes for what they already have and went on to insist that faith in the resurrection faced up to death and all the conceivable depths of creation – all the ruling powers, including those of all the actually existing gods which we ourselves worship and are subject to, and which lie behind the melting of the Arctic ice and the rise of global temperature with all the terrible dangers that implies. None of this, he says, can separate us from the love of God in Christ, and this applies, he has already said, to the whole of creation. On these grounds we 'act here and today', and on these grounds we make sense both of our own lives and the course of the world. But these grounds are set out in that brief summary of the whole Christian narrative which is the Triune NAME.

Notes

1 Immanuel Kant, *The Conflict of the Faculties* M. Gregor (trans.) (Lincoln: University of Nebraska Press, 1992), p. 65.

2 Catherine LaCugna, *God For Us: The Trinity and the Christian Life* (San Francisco: Harper Collins 1991), p. ix.
3 So Katherine Tanner, 'Trinity' in Peter Scott and William Cavanaugh (eds), *The Blackwell Companion to Political Theology* (Oxford: Blackwell 2004).
4 See Karen Kilby, 'Perichoresis and Projection', *New Blackfriars* (October 2000).
5 Martin Luther, *The Large Catechism* (Minneapolis: Augsburg 1967), p. 11.
6 Ton Veerkamp, *Die Welt Anders: Politische Geschichte der Grossen Erzählung* (Berlin: Argument 2012), p. 14. I have translated Grosse Erzählung as 'grand narrative' although Veerkamp actually uses 'Grosse Diskurs' to talk about Lyotard's theory.
7 Veerkamp, *Welt Anders*, p. 416.
8 Ton Veerkamp, *Autonomie & Egalität: Ökonomie, Politik, Ideologie in der Schrift* (Berlin: Alektor, 1993), p. 243.
9 Veerkamp, *Autonomie*, p. 101.
10 Ulrich Duchrow, *Alternatives to Global Capitalism: Drawn from Biblical History, Designed for Political Action* (Utrecht: International Books, 1995), p. 234.
11 Veerkamp *Autonomie*, p. 245.
12 Ton Veerkamp, *Die Vernichtung des Baal* (Stuttgart: Alektor, 1981), p. 51.
13 Richard Douthwaite, *The Growth Illusion* (Tulsa: Council Oak Books, 1992), p. 20.
14 Journal of Retailing, Spring 1955 cited in Alan Durning *How Much is Enough* (London: Earthscan, 1992), p. 22.
15 E. J. Mishan, *The Costs of Economic Growth* (London: Penguin 1967); Herman Daly and John Cobb, *For the Common Good* (London: Green Print, 1990).
16 James Hansen, *Storms of my Grandchildren: The Truth about the Coming Climate Catastrophe and Our Last Chance to Save Humanity* (London: Bloomsbury, 2009), p. 2.
17 Veerkamp, *Autonomie* pp. 373–4
18 'Economists who distrust religion will always fail to comprehend the modes of worship by which progress is achieved. Chance is the foundation of chance and the vessel of the divine' George Gilder, *Wealth and Poverty* (New York: Basic Books, 1981), p. 266.
19 Robert Jenson, *The Triune Identity* (Philadelphia: Fortress, 1982), p. 10ff.
20 Adversus Praxeas xxi; xi 9–10.
21 Jenson, *The Triune Identity*, 72 appealing to R. Braun, '*Deus Christianorum': recherches sur le vocabulaire doctrinal de Tertullien* (Paris: Universitaire, 1962).
22 Janet Soskice, *The Kindness of God* (Oxford: OUP, 2007), p. 113.
23 Gregory of Nyssa, *On Common Notions: Against the Greeks*.
24 Jenson, *The Triune Identity*, p. 119. Jenson argues that Augustine failed to see this. 'When the Nicenes called the Trinity as such God, they so named him *because* of the triune relations and differences; when Augustine calls the Trinity as such God, it is *in spite of them*' (ibid.).
25 John Zizioulas, *Being as Communion* (London: Darton, Longman & Todd, 1985), p. 82.
26 John Zizioulas, 'Relational Ontology: Insights from Patristic Thought' in J.Polkinghorne (ed.), *The Trinity and an Entangled World* (Grand Rapids: Eerdmans, 2010), p. 155.
27 Zizioulas, *Being as Communion*, p. 91.
28 Barth remarks that the theologoumenon of the perichoresis is not so far from the necessary biblical basis of genuine dogmatics as might appear because it 'implies both a confirmation of the distinction in the modes of being, for none would be what it is (not even the Father) without its coexistence with the others, and also a relativisation of this distinction, for none exists as a special individual, but all three "in-exist" or exist only in concert as modes of being of the one God and Lord who posits himself from eternity to eternity … It must in fact be regarded as an important form of the dialectic needed to work out the concept of "triunity"' (Karl Barth, *Church Dogmatics* 1/1 2nd edition (Edinburgh: T&T Clark, 1975), p. 370). Cunningham is more cautious, noting that it is difficult to avoid the idea that three actors or agents are involved whereas what we need is to recognise that the Three mutually constitute one another to such a degree that we cannot speak of them as 'individuals' (op. cit., p. 181).

29 Richard of St Victor 'On the Trinity' 3.3 in B. Coolman and D. Coulter (eds), *Trinity and Creation* (New York: New City Press, 2011), p. 249. I use 'caritas' rather than 'charity' because of the well known misleading meanings of the latter.

30 Richard, 'On the Trinity' 3.11.

31 Boethius: 'De persona et duabus naturis', c. ii: Naturæ rationalis individua substantia (an individual substance of a rational nature). PL 64.

32 Colin Morris, *The Discovery of the Individual 1050–1200* (Toronto: University of Toronto Press, 1972).

33 David Jenkins, *The Contradiction of Christianity* (London: SCM, 1976), p. 158.

34 John Burnaby, *The Belief of Christendom* (London: SPCK, 1963), p. 213.

35 Kilby, 'Perichoresis and Projection', p. 442.

36 Tanner, 'Trinity', p. 327.

37 Kilby, 'Perichoresis and Projection', p. 443.

38 Soskice, *The Kindness of God*, p. 119. This connects with Gregory Baum's account of how doctrine develops: 'Every age has its central questions; every age has its special way of being threatened and its own aspirations for a more human form of existence … In every age, therefore, the Gospel is proclaimed with a central message and thrust, which is the saving response of God to the self-questionings of men' G. Baum *The Credibility of the Church Today* (London: Burns & Oates, 1968), pp.152–53. This central message constitutes the focus of the gospel, 'in the light of which the entire mystery of salvation is understood, and which holds together, interrelates, and qualifies the entire teaching of the Church' (Baum pp. 170–71, cited in N. Lash, *Change in Focus* (London: Sheed & Ward, 1973), p. 153).

39 K. Rahner, *The Trinity* (London: Herder & Herder, 1970), 15.

40 Rahner, *The Trinity*, p. 21.

41 Erik Peterson, 'Monotheismus als Politisches Problem' in *Theologische Traktate* (Munich: Kosel, 1951), p. 49ff.

42 Jürgen Moltmann, *The Trinity and the Kingdom of God* (London: SCM, 1981), 197. It is very clear from the representation of the Trinity in medieval art.

43 Tanner, 'Trinity', p. 321.

44 Ludwig Wittgenstein, *Culture and Value* (Chicago: Chicago University Press 1980), p. 85.

45 David Cunningham, *These Three are One: The Practice of Trinitarian Theology* (Oxford: Blackwell, 1998), p. 7.

46 Nicholas Lash, *Change in Focus*, p. 114.

47 Tanner, 'Trinity', p. 319.

48 Cunningham, *These Three are One*, p. 44.

49 John Polkinghorne, 'The Demise of Democritus' in Polkinghorne (ed.), *The Trinity*, p. 12.

50 Lewis Ayres, '(Mis)adventures in Trinitarian Ontology' in Polkinghorne (ed.), *The Trinity*, p. 132.

51 B. Walker and D. Salt, *Resilience Thinking: Sustaining Ecosystems and People in a Changing World* (Washington· Island Press 2000), p. 73.

52 Jürgen Moltmann, *The Coming of God* (London: SCM 1995), p. 211.

53 Aquinas St, 1a, 44.4.

54 Aquinas St, 1a, 104.1.

55 Jürgen Moltmann, *God in Creation* (London: SCM 1985), p. 103, my italics.

56 Sarah Coakley, 'Afterword: "Relational Ontology", Trinity and Science' in Polkinghorne (ed.), *The Trinity*, p. 198.

57 Cunningham, *These Three are One*, p. 262.

58 So the idea that we are 'masters and possessors of the world', and what C. B. Macpherson called 'possessive individualism' both underlie the terrorism of Western colonialism.

59 Cunningham, *These Three are One*, p. 263.

60 Cunningham, *These Three are One*, p. 8.

61 Cunningham, *These Three are One*, p. 248.

62 On this see Anthony O'Hear, 'The Myth of Nature' in Antony Barnett and Roger Scruton (eds), *Town and Country* (London: Jonathan Cape, 1998), pp. 69–80.

63 Jürgen Moltmann, *The Crucified God: The Cross of Christ as the Foundation and Criticism of Christian Theology* (London: SCM 1974), p. 246, my italics.
64 Jürgen Moltmann, *The Trinity and the Kingdom* (London: SCM 1980), p. 149.
65 Moltmann, *Trinity*, p. 157.
66 Tanner, 'Trinity', p. 327. Later in the article she seems to return to the Trinity as an eschatological symbol. 'Yet uncritical complacency is also overcome by knowledge of the heights of relationships above our own in character, heights of relationships that our relationships with one another in themselves can only strive to approximate without ever matching – at the highest, the relations among perfectly equal, perichoretic persons swirling in and out of one another without loss or gain in incomprehensible light. Without ever taking on the character of such perfection in and of themselves human relations will nevertheless gain that height by being united with the Trinity, by coming within the Trinity's own life, as that Trinity graciously comes to us into the world' (ibid. p. 331).
67 Jürgen Moltmann, *The Coming of God*, p. 235.

Bibliography

Aquinas St. 1a Summa Theologiae (London: Eyre & Spottiswoode, 1964).
Ayres, Lewis. '(Mis)adventures in Trinitarian Ontology', in J. Polkinghorne (ed.), *The Trinity and an Entangled World* (Grand Rapids: Eerdmans, 2010), pp. 130–45.
Barth, Karl. *Church Dogmatics 1/1* 2nd edition (Edinburgh: T&T Clark, 1975).
Baum, G. *The Credibility of the Church Today* (London: Burns & Oates, 1968).
Boethius. 'De persona et duabus naturis', c. ii: *Naturæ rationalis individua substantia* (an individual substance of a rational nature). *Patrologia Latina* J. P. Migne (ed.) (Paris: 1844–79), vol 64.
Burnaby, John. *The Belief of Christendom* (London: SPCK, 1963).
Coakley, Sarah. 'Afterword: "Relational Ontology", Trinity and Science' in J. Polkinghorne (ed.), *The Trinity and an Entangled World* (Grand Rapids: Eerdmans, 2010), pp. 184–99.
Cunningham, David. *These Three are One: The Practice of Trinitarian Theology* (Oxford: Blackwell, 1998).
Daly, Herman and John Cobb. *For the Common Good* (London: Green Print, 1990).
Douthwaite, Richard. *The Growth Illusion* (Tulsa: Council Oak Books, 1992).
Duchrow, Ulrich. *Alternatives to Global Capitalism: Drawn from Biblical History, Designed for Political Action* (Utrecht: International Books, 1995).
Durning, Alan. *How Much is Enough* (London: Earthscan, 1992).
Gilder, George. *Wealth and Poverty* (New York: Basic Books, 1981).
Gregory of Nyssa. 'On Common Notions: Against the Greeks' in Anna Silvas (ed.), *Gregory of Nyssa: The Letters* (Leiden: Brill, 2007).
Hansen, James. *Storms of my Grandchildren: The Truth about the Coming Climate Catastrophe and Our Last Chance to Save Humanity* (London: Bloomsbury, 2009).
Jenkins, David. *The Contradiction of Christianity* (London: SCM, 1976).
Jenson, Robert. *The Triune Identity* (Philadelphia: Fortress, 1982).
Kant, Immanuel. *The Conflict of the Faculties* M. Gregor (trans.) (Lincoln: University of Nebraska Press, 1992).
Kilby, Karen. 'Perichoresis and Projection', *New Blackfriars* (October 2000): 432–45.
LaCugna, Catherine. *God For Us: The Trinity and the Christian Life* (San Francisco: Harper Collins, 1991).
Lash, Nicholas. *Change in Focus* (London: Sheed & Ward, 1973).
Luther, Martin. *The Large Catechism* (Minneapolis: Augsburg, 1967).
Mishan, E. J. *The Costs of Economic Growth* (London: Penguin, 1967).
Moltmann, Jürgen. *The Crucified God: The Cross of Christ as the Foundation and Criticism of Christian Theology* (London: SCM, 1974).
——*The Trinity and the Kingdom* (London: SCM, 1980).

——*God in Creation* (London: SCM, 1985).

——*The Coming of God* (London: SCM, 1995).

Morris, Colin. *The Discovery of the Individual 1050–1200* (Toronto: University of Toronto Press, 1972).

O'Hear, Anthony. 'The Myth of Nature' in Antony Barnett and Roger Scruton (eds), *Town and Country* (London: Jonathan Cape, 1998), 69–80.

Peterson, Erik. 'Monotheismus als Politisches Problem', in *Theologische Traktate* (Munich: Kosel, 1951).

Polkinghorne, John. 'The Demise of Democritus', in J. Polkinghorne (ed.), *The Trinity and an Entangled World* (Grand Rapids: Eerdmans, 2010), pp. 1–14.

Rahner, Karl. *The Trinity* (London: Herder & Herder, 1970).

Richard of St Victor. 'On the Trinity' 3.3 in B. Coolman and D. Coulter (eds), *Trinity and Creation* (New York: New City Press, 2011).

Soskice, Janet. *The Kindness of God* (Oxford: OUP, 2007).

Tanner, Katherine. 'Trinity' in Peter Scott and William Cavanaugh (eds), *The Blackwell Companion to Political Theology* (Oxford: Blackwell, 2004), pp. 319–32.

Tertullian. *Adversus Praxeas*. (Oregon: Wipf & Stock, 2011).

Veerkamp, Ton. *Autonomie & Egalität: Ökonomie, Politik, Ideologie in der Schrift* (Berlin: Alektor, 1993).

——*Die Welt Anders: Politische Geschichte der Grossen Erzählung* (Berlin: Argument, 2012).

Walker, B. and D. Salt *Resilience Thinking: Sustaining Ecosystems and People in a Changing World* (Washington: Island Press, 2000).

Wittgenstein, Ludwig. *Culture and Value* (Chicago: Chicago University Press, 1980).

Zizioulas, John. *Being as Communion* (London: Darton, Longman & Todd, 1985).

——'Relational Ontology: Insights from Patristic Thought' in J. Polkinghorne (ed.), *The Trinity and an Entangled World* (Grand Rapids: Eerdmans, 2010), pp. 146–56.

3

CHRISTOLOGY

Niels Henrik Gregersen

Is it not easy to conceive the World in your Mind? To think the Heavens fair? The Sun glorious? The Earth fruitful? The Air pleasant? The Sea profitable? And the Giver bountiful? Yet these are the things which it is difficult to retain. For could we always be sensible of their use and value, we should be always delighted with their wealth and glory.

(Thomas Traherne, *Centuries of Meditations* I.9)

Words of silence

We live more deeply than we are able to think and experience.[1] Every day we breathe in and out thousands of times. Silently the oxygen we are inhaling is transported through our lungs to the blood that runs in our veins, thus removing the surplus of carbon dioxide from our organism. Regulated by automatic systems in our brainstem, these metabolic processes mostly go on below our awareness. Certainly, we can hear our own breathing; we can even control it up to a certain point. But we can't feel the oxygen running in our veins, nor see or smell the carbon that we emit by exhaling. A self-forgetfulness seems built into our constitution, and it is only when we experience an acute air hunger that we become attentive to our embeddedness in biological processes larger than ourselves. We are metabolic organisms.

Yet we are also atmospheric beings. We regularly experience how our moods change in accordance with sun, rain and atmospheric pressure – more than we will ever be able to conceptualize. Natural processes often operate in such pre-reflexive silence. This also applies to global warming trends. For as pointed out by Mike Hulme, 'Climate cannot be experienced directly through our senses.'[2] The 'dispersion of causes and effects' (Stephen Gardiner) makes it difficult for us to perceive the urgency of global warming.[3]

Here the sciences tell us more about ourselves than we can experience from first-hand experience. Certainly, we experience drought, heavy rains, storms and ice melting as never before, with devastating consequences for some parts of the world (in particular the arctic poles and around the equator). But the greenhouse effect still has the status of a 'theory', similar to the way in which we speak of the Big Bang 'theory'. It cannot be otherwise, since the climate sciences track global patterns of local causes and wide-scale effects. Yet as the scientific evidence for the greenhouse effect is piling up, only ignorance or unwillingness can account for the denial of the *fact* of global warming. The next step is then to ask, *why* are the temperatures and sea levels rising on our planet? In science, mono-causal explanations are extremely rare, and the process of weighting the individual factors (fossil fuels, waste products, volcanoes, solar activity, etc.) is an ongoing task. But it is no longer possible to neglect the importance of the human factor in climate change.[4] Since we live in hidden structures fundamental to our existence, not manifest to our natural eye, we need to be informed by the best available sciences about what we cannot immediately perceive or 'feel'.

Global warming has thus come up as a new ecological challenge for the human race. Since the 1960s, human beings living in heavily populated areas have first-hand experiences of *pollution* and *waste*. Moreover, since the 1970s, the human race has been confronted with a *scarcity of resources*, not just of fuel but increasingly also of metals and unpolluted water. Yet, since the 1990s, we have become aware of the emergency of the *global warming* processes – processes predicted already in 1896 by the Swedish Nobel Prize winner in chemistry, Svante Arrhenius. What we still do not know is to what extent the processes are building up incrementally and to what extent they are exponential, due to the 'avalanche-effect' of positive feedback processes, a well-known natural phenomenon. There is much we do not know, and cannot know in detail.

Global warming, however, *differs* from other ecological problems in at least three respects. Firstly, global warming is a *planetary* problem by nature. Secondly, the causes behind global warming are dispersed, hence *silent*. Whereas people can generally smell pollution and waste, and we can identify the exact site of our natural resources, there is something creeping about global warming. The routes from causes to effects appear to be 'theoretical' in nature, since they are at work over long distances and accumulate over time. Political interests in silencing the global warming problem feed on the silence of the global warming processes themselves.

Add to this, thirdly, that whereas there is always something ugly about pollution and products of waste, carbon dioxide and most other greenhouse gasses have the appearance of something 'natural' about them. The exchange between oxygen and carbon dioxide is as old as life. Carbon dioxide (CO_2) is basic to all life and has been a natural and necessary ingredient in the metabolism of living creatures since the dawn of life on our planet. Broadly speaking, carbon dioxide is exchanged for oxygen in animals, while the photosynthesis of plants constantly absorbs carbon dioxide while emitting oxygen. But just as too much carbon dioxide is toxic for individual organisms, so the emission of carbon dioxide causes temperature rises, regardless of whether the emission comes from living organisms, from the burning of fuels or from volcanoes. The same goes for oxygen, which is also toxic in concentrated forms.

Life is never at rest in a steady state of absolutely optimal balance, but works between the boundaries of too much and too little. If we define the 'good' as that which is beneficial for the flourishing of life, carbon dioxide is an irreplaceable good, just as also oxygen belongs to the goodness of creation. But what makes life flourish becomes life-threatening when the bio-chemicals go beyond bounds. It may be hard to realize that something as fundamental for life as CO_2 can constitute a global problem. There is something deep and wide-scale about carbon dioxide emissions, which easily escapes our attention.[5]

Breaking with self-forgetfulness

The Christian tradition is familiar with the problems of silence, denial and all too facile ideas about what is 'natural.' There can be a need to speak up against silence, to deny denial, and to break with common sense notions of the self-evidential. Here a spiritual dimension comes to the fore. We do not only need to know about the facts of life, but also to attune ourselves to reality. We tend to believe that our own centre of perception is the centre of the world itself, while practically ignoring our dependence on the atmosphere for our living and flourishing. Only in states of crisis do we wake up. In his exposition of Psalm 118 (*Das schöne Confitemini*) from 1530, Martin Luther pointed to the fact that if we suddenly experienced that we could not breathe, we would gladly trade all our properties in exchange for the small portion of air that it takes to pray the Lord's Prayer.

> What is a kingdom compared with a sound body? What is all the money and wealth in the world compared with one sunlit day? ... What would our magnificent castles, houses, silk, satin, purple, golden jewelry, precious stones, all our pomp and glitter and show help us if we had to do without air for the length of one Our Father?[6]

Luther is here reminding us that very elementary bodily experiences tend to escape our attention. Later in the seventeenth century, the Anglican poet-theologian Thomas Traherne pointed to our difficulty in 'retaining' the delightful insights of nature that otherwise come easily to us through experience.

We need to differentiate here between two sorts of self-forgetfulness. There is a self-forgetfulness that belongs to the goodness of creaturely existence. We could not thrive and survive if we constantly had to be aware of all our natural states and dependencies. We live by virtue of the silent biological processes at work beneath our awareness in order to focus on the foregrounds of our attention and act in a forwards-oriented manner. Here we should not worry, but live as the birds of the air or the lilies of the field (Mt 6. 25–34). But in the Jewish and Christian traditions there is also a self-forgetfulness that belongs to what is termed sin, or self-centredness (see

Chapter 8 on Sin and salvation). We thus tend to forget that we are not only living by virtue of nature, but also at the expense of nature. We feed on the same resources as others do and, by over-consumption, we destroy the conditions of future generations of human beings and other creatures (see Chapter 6 on Creatures). The optimal climate for all species does not exist, but each creature is nourished by the silent gifts of innumerable natural processes, most of which are limited. By forgetting to attend to climate changes, we seem neither able to interpret 'the appearance of earth and sky' nor to 'know how to interpret the present time' (Lk 12. 56).

Christology in a changing climate

It would be anachronistic to expect that we could, today, derive specific ethical directives or political solutions from the Jesus tradition. Jesus was a teacher, healer and prophet – not a forecaster of far-future ecological disasters.[7] He lived as a 'wandering charismatic'[8] calling for conversion in an era long before ecological disorders came into existence. Jesus, however, required a mental reorientation that has immediate, practical consequences for his followers' relation to God, other people and the environment. Here the Christian confession to Jesus as Christ is inextricably interwoven with what Luther above called the 'beautiful confession' to the world as God's own creation. The relevance of the synoptic Jesus tradition (Mark, Matthew, and Luke) for ecological issues is thus mediated by the theology of creation implied in Jesus' teaching, as well as in his preaching of the kingdom of God to come. He preached this coming kingdom in analogy to the eschatological vision that the Spirit shall be 'poured out on all flesh' (Joel 2. 28, quoted Acts 2. 17–21). In this sense, Jesus' preaching was earth-bound from beginning to end – without ever separating God and world.

Christology is therefore not first and foremost a backwards-oriented remembrance of the teachings of Jesus in his earthly life nearly two thousand years ago. Christology is carried by the conviction that God's eternal Logos has revealed and re-identified itself – once and for all – as Jesus Christ *within* the matrix of materiality that we share with other living beings. 'He himself is before all things, and in him all things hold together' (Col 1. 17). In this way, divine transcendence and radical immanence are held together in Jesus Christ. A simple way of restating the core concern of classical Christology would be to say that just as Jesus eternally belongs to God's own life (together with the Father and the Spirit), so he and the divine Spirit belong to the nexus of creation for which God the Father is forever present. Or more precisely, the Son of God, who is eternally born *out of* the Father, is present *as* the incarnate Jesus Christ, forever living *with* and *for* all other creatures *in* the universe *through* the workings of the Holy Spirit. Jesus Christ is thus not a bygone historical individual, on whom we can look back in historical distance, but synchronous with each creature in time and co-inherent in all that exists in time and space.

In this view, there are not two realities – God and nature – existing alongside one another, as in some medieval and early modern concepts of a 'supernatural

God' on the top of nature. Once God has chosen to create a world, which is not divine itself (see Chapter 5 on Creation), God and creature make up one complex reality. Remove the life-giving Spirit and the cosmic Christ from the world of creation and there will be no creation. Take away God the Father as the source of all reality and there will be no creaturely events flowing out of divine love.

Incarnation: The Trinitarian stretch and reach of God

Classic Christology is here in conflict with another creed that came up in early modernity (say, between René Descartes and Immanuel Kant), and still today rules the imagination of many Western Christians. Typically, this unspoken creed has the following five tenets:

1 God is elsewhere, in principle unknown to us.
2 We ourselves live in a godless world of impersonal forces, though we may have the luck to shape some humanitarian islands in an otherwise ruthless nature.
3 Jesus is a historical figure of the past; speaking of Christ is a mythic ornamentation.
4 The Christian church is the fellowship among those who gather to remember Jesus as a remarkable person from a past civilization whose example might still be inspirational to us.
5 Just as we are each going to die individually, the world of creation is going to dissolve anyway. Whether human life will come to an end through creeping global climate change or through other, humanly induced catastrophes (such as warfare) – that's the end which will also be God's end.

New Testament traditions as well as the later Christology of the Church speak another language about God and the world of creation. They seem to say something like the following:

1 God is not an unknown X existing behind the world, but is revealed and manifest in Christ, who came into the material world to dwell among us (Jn 1. 14), and whose work will be fulfilled by God's Spirit (Jn 16. 12–14).
2 We live in a world created out of the love of God, and so loved by God that he sent his only Son (Jn 3. 16). Even in the hardships of creation the Father is proximate (Mt 10. 29–31). Due to the cross of Christ nothing can separate us from the love of Christ (Rom 8. 35).
3 In Jesus the Father's eternal Logos took bodily form, so that the fullness of divinity found the pleasure of dwelling in him (Col 2. 9), who himself dwelt in our world (Jn 1. 14).
4 The church is more than a place for remembrance and cultivation of tradition. The church is the body of Christ, 'holding fast to the head, from whom the whole body, nourished and held together by its ligaments and sinews, grows with a growth that is from God' (Col 2. 19) (see Chapter 9 on Church).

5 God has promised to hold fast to his creation so that the world will be re-created even through the 'uncreations' provided by chaos and sin (see Chapter 4 on Spirit and Chapter 10 on Eschatology). Therefore, Christians look forward to 'the world to come' (the Nicene Creed from 381).

Christology therefore has unique resources, if not even a mandate, for speaking of a union of creator and creature.[9] Wherever God is present in creation, God is operative. To use a metaphor, God and nature are like fire and iron, which constitute one reality as long as the iron is heated up by the fire, but become two quite different things, when taken apart.[10] Of course, there are different forms and degrees of union between God and creatures, but even our sheer existence presupposes a participation of our life in God. 'Where God is not, there is nothing. Accordingly, God is present through all things and in all things' (Anselm of Canterbury).[11]

The doctrine of the Trinity (see Chapter 2, The Trinity) expresses God as the encompassing reality – the loving source of all reality (the Father), the sustaining bond between all reality (the Son or Logos) and the directing and fulfilling end of all creation (the Holy Spirit).[12] Here comes to the fore the simplicity in this triune understanding of incarnation: God is at home (Jn 1. 14) in the very world, that God has made in the first place (Jn 1. 8–11), and God continues to love his work even under the conditions of sin and disorder. 'For God so loves the world that he gave his only Son' (Jn 3. 16).

This motif of a union between God and world in Christ does not suggest an identification of God and nature, as in pantheism. Love safeguards the otherness of the beloved. Here the subtlety of the Trinitarian view of incarnation comes to the fore. The life of the Triune God is both copious and capacious. There is a stretch within the divine life that is the precondition for God's ability to span from the high and ideal to the low and practical. The Father is routinely described as 'heavenly' insofar as the Father is never incarnate in the world of creation, but remains its 'transcendent' source. But Son becomes 'flesh', just as the Spirit or divine Breath vivifies all living creatures and shall in the end be 'poured out on all flesh'. Yet where the Son and the Spirit is, there is also the Father. It is this *stretch* of Trinitarian life which facilitates the divine *reach* into the depths of creation in incarnation.

The body of Jesus in an intergenerational context

Let us start from the midst of history, though. The evangelists tell how Jesus moves geographically, as he wanders through the landscapes: he stops, speaks, eats and drinks. But his *biological body* has no independent existence in the gospels, for his concrete body is a *social body* as well. Jesus is always living, walking and talking with others. At the same time, he is portrayed as a *personal* agent, though never described as an autonomous 'Kantian' individual. He is acting on behalf of others while representing God to people. He takes ever-new and unforeseeable initiatives and the gospel narratives explain that he does so in communication with his heavenly

Father whilst being moved and led by the Holy Spirit – the real protagonist of the Jesus story. The Spirit was present at his conception; the Spirit descended upon him at baptism; the Spirit drove him into the wilderness to be tested and, coming back from Jordan, Jesus was 'full of Spirit' (Lk 4. 1). He taught with authority and inspiration and used the vivifying powers of the Spirit in his healing practices. On the cross, he gave back to the Father his spirit, when he 'breathed his last' (Lk 23. 46). Finally, he was raised from the dead by the powers of the Holy Spirit. In the gospels, Jesus is thus inscribed in the common history of humanity while portrayed as existing in the interface between the heavenly Father and the mobile presence of the divine Spirit. Just as Jesus' body is never purely biological but also social, so his personal agency is always related to God the Father and the moving agency of the Spirit (see Chapter 4 on Spirit).

A human body is a metabolic organism and each body is a centre of experience that has an 'internal' experiential side even as it interacts with 'external' circumstances. This relation cannot be broken down into something primary and something secondary. Some philosophers even speak of the *extended mind* in order to do justice to the fact that human consciousness is always co-determined by natural environments and cultural artefacts.[13] Also, the body and mind of Jesus appear to be agitated by the life contexts in which he finds himself – in various ecological spaces (deserts, lakes, rivers, hills) as well as in diverse social and cultural contexts (town and country, friends and enemies, Jews and Romans). In this sense, we might refer to Jesus as an *extended body* as well.[14] Jesus' body is described as comprising the three overlapping life-circles – of nature, sociality and personhood. Who Jesus is as a person is shown by his relation to other people; he himself is touched both bodily and spiritually by others, just as he touches others and affects his surroundings. The kingdom of God is the extension of the body of Jesus, just as his body is a crystallization point of the divine reign.

There is also an *intergenerational* aspect to the Jesus story. While Matthew is primarily concerned with the Jewish heritage of Jesus by tracking him back to King David and Abraham (Mt 1. 1–17), Luke is keen to emphasize Jesus' relation to the common stock of humanity, going back to Adam (3. 23–38). These genealogies offer not only genetic accounts but also cultural ones. Jesus is the son of David, Jacob, Isaac and Abraham – according to Matthew. But according to Luke, he is also the son of Shem and Noah in the early history of humankind, and, last but not least, listed as 'son of Adam, son of God' (v.38). Jesus is hereby registered as first in the history not only of the Jews, but of humankind, and indeed as partaker in God's own history.

Obviously, the biblical writers did not have to hand any ideas of evolutionary biology. Even though the authors behind Genesis placed God's blessing of Adam and Eve in continuation with the blessings of the animals (Gen 1. 22.28), Matthew and Luke do not refer to the ancestral bonds of Jesus with other creatures. This is their shortcoming. After Darwin, we have gradually learned to overcome the dissociation between humanity and nature, as well as the wedge between human history and human prehistory. Just as philosophical ecologists, such as Arne Næss, speak of the human embedment in larger ecological systems in terms of *deep ecology*, so recent historians speak of human culture in terms of *deep history* while emphasizing common features such as extended kinship relations, sharing of food and land and the co-evolutionary spirals in the community between humans, animals and plants, thus leading to gradual changes in the ecological systems.[15]

In such a deep time perspective, what is linking Jesus (and us) to the beginnings of humanity also connects him (and us) with the hominids, higher apes and other forms of life. In his own preaching, the lives of foxes and sparrows feature centrally; likewise, Jesus defined his kinship relations by those who do the will of God (adopted by God) rather than by genetic kin (Mk 3. 31–35); he also shared food with Roman tax-collectors and others who were perceived as sinners, in particular. In this sense, Jesus extends the fellowship of sharing and self-identification beyond germ-lines of proximity and distance. This inscription of Jesus in the intergenerational history of the past corresponds to the evangelical promise of his teaching of the kingdom of God, directed at all future generations. Also the more Jewish-oriented Matthew is aware of this broadening of scope from Jewishness to all fellow beings, as stated in the last words of Jesus, 'Go therefore and make disciples of all nations ... I am with you always, to the end of the age' (Mt 28. 19–20). It goes without saying that such a promise to all nations in the future presupposes that there will be future generations to be included in the fellowship with God.

The evangelists do not regard Jesus from a purely horizontal perspective, of course. Jesus is the crystallization point for the reign of God and for the power of the Holy Spirit that fills him and radiates from him to alter his surroundings. The ecological space, the social space and the religious space belong together in the gospel narratives. It is in the midst of *this* world – and not as a supplement or a theological superstructure – that Jesus preached the gospel that 'the kingdom of God is among you' (Lk 17. 21). Similarly, the resurrected Christ returns to be 'among' his disciples (Lk 24. 36). Christ is the *Immanuel* (in Hebrew, 'God with us').

Even if there is a long and troublesome road from the gospels to the later Christological creeds of the Church, there are common points of emphasis. Over against 'Apollinarianism' (named after Apollinarius of Laodicea), the fathers of the late fourth century argued that God's Son has become human flesh and blood *with* a full human mind and spirit. Jesus should not, as suggested by Apollinarius, be understood as a compound being consisting of two separate things, a purely divine Logos-mind and a purely human body. If so, the Son of God would not be really united with the humanity of Jesus. Rather, Jesus would be like a chimera, half-human plus half-God.

As is well-known, this theological concern was also behind the creedal statement of the fourth Ecumenical Council at Chalcedon in 451. The council emphasized that Jesus Christ is 'truly God and truly human, of a rational soul and body'. Likewise, there is a strong affirmation that the two 'natures' of divinity and humanity (as the Council expressed itself) were to be seen as both 'unconfused' yet 'inseparable'.[16] The intention to speak of a personal union between God and humanity in Christ – which does not lead either to an amalgam ('unconfused') or to a chimera ('inseparable') – may be said to explicate a central concern also of the gospel traditions, even though we are placed in very different worlds of imagination.

In two other respects, however, the Chalcedonian settlement has been rightly problematized in contemporary theology. One problem is that the designation of 'two natures' in the one person of Christ was developed within a substance metaphysics that is no longer ours. Hellenic preconceptions about what is suitable and what is not suitable for divine nature might have been Christianized without reflection (for example, the conviction that God cannot suffer). Another problem is more indirect but highly important for an ecological perspective on Christology: inadvertently, the Chalcedonian focus on the relation between 'divine' and the 'human' has led to a severing of the ties between human and non-human nature, whereby the concern for the redemption of other creatures also fell out of sight. Below we shall look at ways to counteract this tendency (see also Chapter 6 on Creatures).

Reading the Jesus story in front of the world: beyond historicism

The coming-together of the horizontal timeline and the vertical dimensions of divine life is essential for Christology. Since the 1960s, prominent theologians such as Wolfhart Pannenberg attempted to develop a Christology purely 'from below'. Pannenberg, however, later retracted this purely historicist approach to Christology, when he realized that one cannot understand the person of Jesus apart from his relationship to his heavenly Father and the moving forces of the divine Spirit.[17] In a historicist view, Jesus (and any other historical figure) will be depicted as an individual in a bygone past. This is the standard method of historical criticism. Often, however, this method of historicism is aggrandized into metaphysics, presupposing the view that all that can count as 'real' must either be indexed in time and space or be evidenced from such indexical identification. But this view sits badly with both science and everyday experience. A living body is a metabolic, social and extended body (in German *Leib*), which is something more than the idea of the body as a particular furniture of the universe with measurable properties such as height, weight and so on (in German *Körper*). As phenomenology argues, when *Leib* is reduced to *Körper* one abstracts the body from the engaged person's self-involvement with his or her environment. Likewise, a biological view of a living body would argue that a purely historicist approach will abstract the living body from the natural flows of metabolism, and from the ecological place of the body. Biologically speaking, there exist no fixed boundaries between a bodily self and its environment. Finally, theology would argue that a human person can't be abstracted from his or her relationship to God, either.

Methods of historical-critical scholarship – when standing alone – will thus preclude us from seeing the nexus between Jesus and the cosmos. What historical scholarship does (and must do) is to situate Jesus in his historical context, to select from the stories of Jesus a supposed 'critical minimum' that might go back to a historical person called Jesus of Nazareth and then, perhaps, extract something of more general interest from his teachings and doings, based on this critical minimum. The task left for contemporary Christology would then be to 'apply' this critical minimum of a historically excavated Jesus figure to contemporary contexts.

This approach is rather narrow, though, and the route pursued here will be different. Our task is to understand Jesus as being in constant exchange with his contemporaries while offering a view of God's presence in the world of creation, and a wisdom practice that makes the reign of God close to anyone affected by his message (now as well as then). What is common to the historical and to the theological interest in the gospel narratives is what we could call 'the world of meaning *in* the text'. What is all-important to the historical approach, but only of subordinate interest for the approach of a contemporary systematic theology, is to reconstruct 'the world *behind* the texts'. What is of little interest to the historical approach, but of so much more interest to systematic theology, however, is the 'world *in front of* the text'. The world in front of the text is inhabited by any prospective reader, much like contemporary approaches of reader-response theory.

What will be attempted here is a more phenomenological approach, according to which the interest of interpretation concerns the typical forms of human engagement with reality as articulated in the gospel texts.[18] The focus on the social body of Jesus, including the intergenerational perspective so important for us, constituted a first attempt in this direction. We now turn to the earth-bound aspects of the Jesus tradition belonging to the wisdom teachings of Jesus.

Mingling 'high' and 'low': earth-awareness in the Jesus tradition

In the Jesus tradition, the connection between Jesus and earth is a persistent theme. As formulated by Denis Edwards, the parables of Jesus as well as his wisdom sayings 'reflect a close observation of and delight in the natural world as the place of God.'[19] Indeed, Jesus is mingling high and low when talking of God's reign and, also, his styles of speech go from the high style of quoting Scripture to low styles of colloquial reasoning, and further on to hyperbolic rhetoric. He can thus compare the coming of God's kingdom to the growth of a mustard seed (Mt 13. 31–32). He instructs his followers to live as unworried as the birds of the air and as the lilies of the field rather than being overly concerned and serious (Mt 6. 25–34). He also teaches his disciples to pray to God the Father by stretching their imagination between the high and the low: 'Your will be done, on earth as it is in heaven' (Mt 6. 10). The disciples, moreover, are required to become 'the salt of the earth' rather than passive lazybones (Mt 5. 13). But Jesus speaks to the tentative people who were not part of the inner circle of the disciples when saying, 'Blessed are the meek, for they will inherit the earth' (Mt 5. 5).

The earth is thus a recurrent motif in the teaching of Jesus. There seems to be a strong affinity between the 'inner' nature of God and God's 'external' work in creation. Jesus is often placed in apparent solitude in nature. The gospel of Mark situates Jesus among 'the wild beasts' while 'the angels ministered to him' – again a stretch between high and low (Mk 1. 15). This passage is open to a variety of interpretations.[20] Does it mean that Jesus had a dominating power over the beasts, just as he later used his authority on the evil spirits (cf. Mk 1. 27)? Or does it rather mean that Jesus was convening with the wild animals in the wilderness, just as he also showed compassion with the meek and the low? It speaks for the latter interpretation that Jesus (who is otherwise well versed in Scripture) never uses the language of human dominion over nature (as in Gen 1. 26–27). It also seems that Jesus usually identifies himself with the earth and the poor. Jesus thus referred to himself obliquely as the Son of Man, in Aramaic most likely *bar 'ænash,* corresponding to the *ben adam* in Hebrew. Thus, Jesus has come as the 'son of Adam' who was the 'son of the earth' (earth, in Hebrew, is *adamah*). In this sense, Jesus was the son-of-the-son-of-earth.

At the same time Jesus is quite often speaking in the vein of the Jewish wisdom tradition (see also Chapter 5 on Creation). Martin Hengel has pointed out that the wisdom traditions, especially from the intertestamental period, provided the 'generative matrix' of early Christology.[21] In general, wisdom has to do with finding the *halakha* or 'the way'; that is, the interpretation of the divine will under the challenges of time and circumstance, inspired by the divine Spirit. Some words of Jesus are clearly spoken in the vein of this tradition, such as the following:

> To what then will I compare the people of this generation, and what are they like? They are like children sitting in the market place and calling to one another, 'We played the flute for you, and you did not dance; we wailed, and you did not weep.' For John the Baptist has come eating no bread and drinking no wine, and you say, 'He has a demon'; the Son of Man has come eating and drinking, and you say, 'Look, a glutton and a drunkard, a friend of tax-collectors and sinners!' Nevertheless, wisdom is vindicated by all her children.
>
> *(Lk 7. 31–35)*

Here Jesus is indirectly describing himself as *God's wisdom in person,* who is vindicated by the children of wisdom. Other passages seem to imply a self-identification with the pre-existing wisdom of God, as when he calls for discipleship of both pressure and comfort:

> Come to me, all you that are weary and are carrying heavy burdens and I will give you rest. Take my yoke upon you, and learn from me; for I am gentle and humble in heart, and you will find rest for your souls. For my yoke is easy, and my burden is light.
>
> *(Mt 12. 28–30)*

In earlier scholarship, such words were routinely taken as a reflex of later Christian confessions, but more recent scholarship suggest that these sayings are fully understandable within the Jewish wisdom tradition available to Jesus and his contemporaries. Jesus is here saying in his own name what God's wisdom said in the Book of Sirach (24. 19 and 6. 24–30).[22]

The parables of Jesus are like the invitations of the divine wisdom to see one's situation in a new light while attuning oneself to do the right thing in the moment. Nature operates on its own (in Greek *automatiké*, Mk 4. 32), but is not therefore depicted as bucolic. Foxes survive not easily though they find holes to hide in (Mt 8. 20), and birds have nests but also fall down from the sky. Yet 'no sparrow will fall to the ground apart from the Father' (Mt. 10. 29).

Human beings do not operate by instinctual reactions only but also have to ponder about what to do. We even have to *learn* to live like the sparrows or the ravens (Lk 12. 24). Jesus here compares the human art of weather forecasting with the need of self-knowledge and of interpreting the signs of their times and circumstances. He is not exactly speaking softly when pointing to our failures in discerning the changing conditions of weather and life:

> When you see a cloud rising in the west, you immediately say, "It is going to rain"; and so it happens. And when you see the south wind blowing, you say, "There will be scorching heat"; and it happens. You hypocrites! You know how to interpret the appearance of earth and sky, but why do you not know how to interpret the present time?
>
> *(Lk 12. 54–57)*

Reading the times is always difficult. But the unwillingness to change one's own life patterns may impede one's willingness to understand. Such denial is often a sign of human self-protection.

God conjoining the material world: from deep incarnation to deep sociality

In his treatise *Cur deus homo?*, Anselm of Canterbury famously asked, 'Why did God become human?' But as a matter of fact, it is nowhere said in the New Testament that God became human, though we in Paul hear that Christ was bearing 'human likeness' (Phil 2. 7). It is rather said that 'the Word (*Logos*) became flesh (*sarx*)' (Jn 1. 14). Accordingly, the first and second Ecumenical Councils in Nicaea in 325 and Constantinople in 381 were careful to say both that God's eternal Son 'was incar-nate' and that he 'was made man.' For that God has a human face can only be maintained if God assumes a real human body, situating him in continuity with the rest of the material world.

The notion of 'all flesh' (*kol-basar*) is familiar to any reader of the Hebrew Bible. In a few distinctive passages, human beings are even likened to grass and flowers to the point of their identification: 'Surely the people are grass. The grass withers; the flower fades. But the word of our God will stand forever' (Isa 40. 8; quoted in 1 Pet 1. 24). Sometimes this is meant critically (as here in Isaiah), but 'flesh' (*basar*) can also have positive connotations, as when Ezekiel prophesizes about the new creation of 'hearts of flesh' that shall replace the old 'hearts of stone' (Ezek 11. 19; 36. 26). At other times, the terms 'flesh' and 'all flesh' are used as neutral descriptions of human beings as psychosomatic unities that share the general conditions of all other forms of creaturely life.

Understood in a Jewish framework, the point of incarnation may be that the presence of God does not dwell (*shekinah*) in the temple of Jerusalem built of stones, but in the living flesh of Jesus. However, the Gospel of John is also a philosophical text saying that the divine Logos and the material *sarx* are co-present in the person of Christ. Divinity does not hide *behind* the flesh (as Platonists would have it), neither did he appear only *in* the flesh in a transitory manner (like in the burning bush of Exodus 3). Rather, the divine Logos genuinely 'became flesh' (*sarx egeneto*) and was present in Jesus *as* flesh, *with* the flesh of others, and *for* all flesh.

The Gospel of John thus uses a polysemantic concept of *sarx*, referring neutrally to the whole nexus of materiality: positively to the living and spirited embodiment, and negatively to the world of sin and decay. Accordingly, the dwelling of God's Word in the world was not confined to his skin and skull. In Jesus Christ, the divine Logos assumed the entire realm of humanity, biological existence, earth and soil.[23] God's Logos/Word/Wisdom shares the conditions of material existence with all the flesh that comes into being in order later to disintegrate. Here we see the basic contours of the meaning of *deep incarnation*. Deep incarnation speaks of a divine embodiment, which reaches into the roots of material and biological existence as well as into the darker sides of creation. The cross of Christ is here both the apex and the depth of incarnation.[24]

Let us now address some *soteriological* implications of deep incarnation. The first point is that in order for human beings to be included in the process of incarnation (from the birth of Jesus to his death and resurrection), the body of human beings must somehow be included in the concrete embodiment of the divine Logos. This corresponds to a classical soteriological principle formulated by Gregory Nazianzus: 'What Christ has not assumed he has not healed, but that which is united to his Godhead is also saved.'[25] This principle already presupposes that the body of Jesus cannot be understood only as a purely physiological body (*Körper*): it must be a living and extensive body (*Leib*) that shares the conditions of biological and social existence with human beings in general. Above, we saw that this requirement is fulfilled in the gospel narratives. So far, the soteriological concerns of the idea of deep incarnation are met in the gospel stories of the extended body of Jesus. Even the concrete body of Jesus cannot be understood as reaching only from his tiptoes to his hair. *Leiber* are not that easily locatable.

Yet in order to share a body with us it is necessary that the body and mind of Jesus – like our bodies and minds – share the same conditions of metabolism and climate-dependence as any other living organism, human or not. This means that even on anthropocentric premises (that is, in the soteriological interests of humanity) there *must* be a healing also of the non-human existence, *if* the whole of humanity is to be healed. As Gregory of Nazianzus argued, 'Keep, then, the whole man [humanity], and mingle Godhead therewith that you may benefit me in my completeness.'[26] What we must add to Gregory's argument is that a holistic understanding of human existence should include also the social relations between human beings as well as the relations of human beings to other creatures within the shared biosphere of planet Earth.

On being a neighbour on planet Earth

The extensive scope of human existence has immediate repercussions for a contemporary interpretation of what it means to be a *neighbour* to one another (see also Chapter 7 on Humanity). In the world of antiquity, neighbour care was about helping the poor who had an urgent need of assistance; accordingly, to become a neighbour for another person was to help her or him as a good Samaritan (cf. Lk 10. 25–35).

In today's world of global interdependencies, our webs of neighbouring are both widening and tightening. My life-styles in Copenhagen will have consequences for the life-conditions of people around the equator just as the diminishing of the rainforests has global effects on our shared climate conditions. Moreover, our generation's human life-styles will unilaterally constrain or facilitate the conditions under which our own grandchildren and other future offspring can thrive, or not. In a sense, non-human creatures have also become our neighbours since we are breathing the same air and using the same resources as they do. We are deeply intertwined with nature through our dependence on fresh air and sunlight for our existence, and also by being doomed to boredom without the existence of bees and bears, dogs and dolphins in the world around us. Their lives depend on us and ours on them.

Granted that we are living as metabolic and atmospheric creatures (constantly in deep exchange with nature) and as social creatures with responsibilities towards future generations (without clear-cut boundaries between 'us' and 'them'), let us then take a look at the future-oriented aspects of the teaching of Jesus. How are we to interpret – in view of the world in front of us – the parable about the Son of Man who will be coming in glory to judge all people (Mt 25. 31–46)? Any prospective reader of this text will have to ask him- or herself, who are the thirsty and needy, in whom the Son of Man claims to have been present in non-visible ways? In light of our contemporary awareness of our co-dependence on all life, our neighbours might indeed live far away from us. Are the creatures belonging to non-human species also our neighbours? And what about the future generations of human beings and other beings? The point of the parable of judgment is that the Son of Man has established kinship relations, even beyond genetic divides, to each and any who is needy, thirsty, and hungry. The Son of Man will say to the righteous as well as to the unrighteous, 'Truly I tell you, just as you did it to one of the least of these who are members of my family, you did it to me' (Mt 25. 40).

It is this unfamiliar extension of the family ties between God and humanity in Christ that may give us reason to work out a Christology which emphasizes the wider dwelling-places or inhabitations of God on the planet in which we live and breathe together. As a matter of fact, whether we are righteous or not, and whether we belong to the human species or not, we actually live as co-dependent neighbours of one another. We are not only sharing a common atmosphere but also a common vulnerability.

Notes

1 As far as I know, the expression 'we live more deeply than we can think' appears first in Bernard E. Meland, *Fallible Forms and Symbols: Discourses on Method in a Theology of Culture* (Minneapolis: Fortress Press, 1976), p. 24. While Meland contrasts experiential faith and religious symbols, my point here is that we, as biological creatures, are embedded in processes and structures far below immediate human experience.

2 Mike Hulme, *Why We Disagree About Climate Change: Understanding Controversy, Inaction and Opportunity* (Cambridge: Cambridge University Press, 2009), p. 3.

3 Stephen M. Gardiner, *A Perfect Moral Storm: The Ethical Tragedy of Climate Change* (New York: Oxford University Press, 2011). There is more on Gardiner in Chapter 7, Humanity.

4 Even the environmentalist skeptic Bjørn Lomborg (a Danish political scientist promoted by *Wall Street Journal* and other economic media) admits that global warming is a reality, that the sea levels are rising, that the development is mostly anthropogenic and will impact the future significantly. See his minimalist view in *Cool It: The Skeptical Environmentalist's Guide to Global Warming* (London: Cyan-Marschall Cavendish, 2007), Chapter 2. He believes that technological counter-measures can be taken, such as building higher dams, sending out a fleet of ships to emit damp to the atmosphere, etc.

5 Cows, for example, emit very high levels of greenhouse gases. It is estimated that cows are responsible for around 30 per cent of Argentina's emission of greenhouse gases, since the methane gas emitted by their faeces is 23 times more potent than CO_2 (www.daily mail.co.uk/science tech/ article-1033656). Of course, since human consumption of meat is the cause behind the number of cows, humans are responsible here, too.

6 Martin Luther, 'The Beautiful Confitemini' (Psalm. 118), Jaroslav Pelican (ed.), *Luther's Works* volume 14 (Saint Louis: Concordia Publishing House, 1958), 48 = *Weimarer Ausgabe* (WA) 31, p. 70.

7 If Jesus were an apocalyptic prophet, as presupposed in the German exegetical tradition from Albert Schweizer to Rudolf Bultmann and Gerd Theissen, he was a short-term apocalyptic who failed in his prediction of a divine glory to come in the imminent future. This may be so. However, contemporary American scholars argue that it is not necessarily so. Markus J. Borg speaks of Jesus' 'sapiential eschatology' in 'Reflections on a Discipline: A North American Perspective', in Bruce Chilton and Craig A. Evans (eds), *Studying the Historical Jesus: Evaluations of Current Research* (Leiden: Brill, 1994), pp. 9–31. John Dominic Crossan writes in a similar vein, 'The sapiential Kingdom … is a style of life for now rather than a hope for life in the future', *The Historical Jesus: The Life of a Mediterranean Peasant* (Edinburgh: T&T Clark, 1992), p. 292. This orientation towards the present does not, of course, exclude a concern for the future.

8 Gerd Theissen, *Sociology of Early Palestinian Christianity*, trans. John Bowden (Philadelphia: Fortress, 1978).

9 Niels Henrik Gregersen, 'Unio creatoris et creaturae: Martin Luther's Trinitarian View of Creation', in Else Marie Wiberg Pedersen and Johannes Nissen (eds), *Cracks in the Wall: Essays on Spirituality, Ecumenicity and Ethics* (Frankfurt am Main: Peter Lang Verlag, 2005), pp. 43–58.

10 The analogy is widespread in tradition, used, for example, by Basil the Great, *On the Holy Spirit* XVI.38, and by Martin Luther, *On the Babylonian Captivity*, WA 6, p. 510.

11 Anselm of Canterbury, *Monologion* 14: 'ubi ipsa [essential divina] non est, nihil sit. Ubique igitur est per omnia et in omnibus.'

12 Compare Basil the Great, *On the Holy Spirit* XVI.38: 'When you consider creation I advise you first to think of Him who is the first cause (*aitia protoarchtiké*) of everything that exists: namely, the Father, and then of the Son, who is the shaper (*aitia demiourgiké*), and then the Holy Spirit, who is the fulfiller (*aitia teleiótiké*).'

13 I here refer to Andy Clark and David J. Chalmers, 'The Extended Mind,' *Analysis* 58 (1998): 10–23.

14 I have pursued this interpretation in more detail in Niels Henrik Gregersen, 'The Extended Body: the Social Body of Jesus according to Luke,' *Dialog: A Journal of Theology* 51:3 (2012): 235–45.

15 See, respectively, Arne Næss, *Ecology, Community and Lifestyle* (Cambridge: Cambridge University Press, 1989) and Andrew Shyrock and Daniel Lord Smail (eds), *Deep History: The Architecture of Past and Present* (Berkeley: University of California Press, 2011). On the relation between these proposals and Christology, see Niels Henrik Gregersen, '*Cur deus caro*: Jesus and the Cosmos Story,' *Theology and Science* 11:4 (2013): 384–407.

16 Chalcedon states that the one and the same Christ should be 'acknowledged in two natures, unconfusedly, unchangeably, indivisibly, inseparably' (in Greek, ἐν δύο φύσεσιν ἀσυγχύτως, ἀτρέπτως, ἀδιαιρέτως, ἀχωρίστως; in Latin, *in duabus naturis inconfuse, immutabiliter, indivise, inseparabiliter*).

17 Compare Wolfhart Pannenberg, *Jesus – God and Man* (London: SCM Press, 2007), pp. 15–20 (German original 1964) with his later insistence on the need to develop a Christology both 'from below' (from the Jesus-history) and 'from above' (from the relation between Christ and God the Father) in 'Christologie und Theologie' (1975), in *Grundfragen systematischer Theologie. Gesammelte Aufsätze Band 2* (Göttingen: Vandenhoeck & Ruprecht, 1980), pp. 129–45. Unfortunately, this text is not in English translation.

18 As phrased by Paul Ricoeur, 'To interpret is to explicate the type of being-in-the-world unfolded in front of the text'; see 'The Hermeneutical Function of Distantiation,' in John B. Thompson (ed.), *Hermeneutics and the Human Sciences: Essays on Language, Action, and Interpretation* (Cambridge: Cambridge University Press, 1981), pp. 131–44 (141).

19 Denis Edwards, *Ecology at the Heart of Faith: The Change of Heart that Leads to a New Way of Living on Earth* (New York: Orbis Books, 2006), p. 51.

20 See Richard Baucham, *Bible and Ecology. Rediscovering the Community of Creation* (London: Darton, Longman and Todd, 2010).

21 Martin Hengel, 'Jesus als messianischer Lehrer der Weisheit und die Anfänge der Christologie,' in *Sagesse et religion. Colloque de Strasbourg* (Paris: Presses universitaires de France, 1979), pp. 309–44, a view later solidified by Gottfried Schimanowski, *Weisheit und Messias. Die jüdische Voraussetzungen der urchristlichen Präexistenzchristologie* (Tübingen: Mohr Siebeck, 1985), pp. 309–44.

22 Ben Witherington, III, *Jesus the Sage: The Pilgrimage of Wisdom* (Edinburgh: T&T Clark, 1994), 143–45 and 155–61. See also Celia Deane-Drummond, *Christ and Evolution: Wonder and Wisdom* (Minneapolis: Fortress, 2009), pp. 95–127.

23 As expressed also by Pope John Paul II in his encyclical letter *Dominum et vivificantem* (Vatican City: Libreria Editrice Vaticana, 1986), § 50.

24 I developed this concept first in the context of evolutionary Christianity ('The Cross of Christ in an Evolutionary World,' *Dialog: A Journal of Theology* 40:2 (2001): 192–207), and then later in theological responses to climate changes (in Danish). See a brief introduction (with literature) in Niels Henrik Gregersen, 'Deep Incarnation: Why Continuity Matters for Christology,' *Toronto Journal of Theology* 26:2 (2010): 173–87. See also the contributions in Niels Henrik Gregersen (ed.), *Incarnation and the Depths of Creation* (Minneapolis: Fortress Press, forthcoming).

25 Gregory of Nazianzus, *Epistula* 101.32, in Edward Rochie Hardy (ed. and tr.) *Christology of the Later Fathers*. The Library of Christian Classics (Philadelphia: Westminster Press, 1954), p. 218.

26 Gregory of Nazianzus, *Epistula* 101.36, p. 219.

Bibliography

Baucham, Richard. *Bible and Ecology. Rediscovering the Community of Creation* (London: Darton, Longman and Todd, 2010).

Borg, Markus J. 'Reflections on a Discipline: A North American Perspective', in Bruce Chilton and Craig A. Evans (eds), *Studying the Historical Jesus: Evaluations of Current Research* (Leiden: Brill, 1994), pp. 9–31.

Clark, Andy, and David J. Chalmers. 'The Extended Mind', *Analysis* 58 (1998): 10–23.

Crossan, John D. *The Historical Jesus: The Life of a Mediterranean Peasant* (Edinburgh: T&T Clark, 1992).

Deane-Drummond, Celia. *Christ and Evolution: Wonder and Wisdom* (Minneapolis: Fortress, 2009).

Edwards, Denis. *Ecology at the Heart of Faith: The Change of Heart that Leads to a New Way of Living on Earth* (New York: Orbis Books, 2006).

Gardiner, Stephen M. *A Perfect Moral Storm: The Ethical Tragedy of Climate Change* (New York: Oxford University Press, 2011).

Gregersen, Niels Henrik. 'The Cross of Christ in an Evolutionary World', *Dialog: A Journal of Theology* 40:2 (2001): 192–207.

——'Unio creatoris et creaturae: Martin Luther's Trinitarian View of Creation', in Else Marie Wiberg Pedersen and Johannes Nissen (eds), *Cracks in the Wall: Essays on Spirituality, Ecumenicity and Ethics* (Frankfurt am Main: Peter Lang Verlag, 2005), pp. 43–58.

——'Deep Incarnation: Why Continuity Matters for Christology', *Toronto Journal of Theology* 26:2 (2010): 173–87.

——'The Extended Body: the Social Body of Jesus according to Luke', *Dialog: A Journal of Theology* 51:3 (2012): 235–45.

——'Cur deus caro: Jesus and the Cosmos Story', *Theology and Science* 11:4 (2013): 384–407.

Gregersen, Niels Henrik (ed.). *Incarnation and the Depths of Creation* (Minneapolis: Fortress Press, forthcoming).

Gregory of Nazianzus, *Epistula* 101.32, in Edward Rochie Hardy (ed. and tr.) *Christology of the Later Fathers* (The Library of Christian Classics, Philadelphia: Westminster Press, 1954).

Hardy, Edward Rochie (ed.). *Christology of the Later Fathers* (The Library of Christian Classics. Philadelphia: Westminster Press, 1954).

Hengel, Martin. 'Jesus als messianischer Lehrer der Weisheit und die Anfänge der Christologie.' In *Sagesse et religion. Colloque de Strasbourg* (Paris: Presses universitaires de France, 1979), pp. 309–44.

Hulme, Mike. *Why We Disagree About Climate Change: Understanding Controversy, Inaction and Opportunity* (Cambridge: Cambridge University Press, 2009).

John Paul II, Pope. *Dominum et vivificantem: On the Holy Spirit in the Life of the Church and the World* (Vatican City: Libreria Editrice Vaticana, 1986).

Lomborg, Bjørn. *Cool It: The Skeptical Environmentalist's Guide to Global Warming* (London: Cyan-Marschall Cavendish, 2007).

Luther, Martin. 'The Beautiful Confitemini', in Jaroslav Pelican (ed.), *Luther's Works* volume 14 (Saint Louis: Concordia Publishing House, 1958).

Meland, Bernard E. *Fallible Forms and Symbols: Discourses on Method in a Theology of Culture* (Minneapolis: Fortress Press, 1976).

Næss, Arne. *Ecology, Community and Lifestyle* (Cambridge: Cambridge University Press, 1989).

Pannenberg, Wolfhart. 'Christologie und Theologie', in *Grundfragen systematischer Theologie. Gesammelte Aufsätze Band 2* (Göttingen: Vandenhoeck & Ruprecht, 1980 [1975]), pp. 129–45.

——*Jesus – God and Man* (London: SCM Press, 2007 [German original 1964]).

Ricoeur, Paul. 'The Hermeneutical Function of Distantiation', in John B. Thompson (ed.), *Hermeneutics and the Human Sciences: Essays on Language, Action, and Interpretation* (Cambridge: Cambridge University Press, 1981), pp. 131–44.

Schimanowski, Gottfried. *Weisheit und Messias. Die jüdische Voraussetzungen der urchristlichen Präexistenzchristologie* (Tübingen: Mohr Siebeck, 1985).

Shyrock, Andrew, and Daniel Lord Smail (eds). *Deep History: The Architecture of Past and Present* (Berkeley: University of California Press, 2011).

Theissen, Gerd. *Sociology of Early Palestinian Christianity*, trans. John Bowden (Philadelphia: Fortress, 1978).

Witherington III, Ben. *Jesus the Sage: The Pilgrimage of Wisdom* (Edinburgh: T&T Clark, 1994).

4

HOLY SPIRIT

Michael S. Northcott

Introduction

Climate scientists describe an invisible network of agency between modern humans and the heavens through which modern industrial rituals, and especially those which rely on energetic inputs from fossil fuels, influence the physical climate.[1] Human greenhouse gases are principally emitted from the burning of buried plants which, over millennia, have turned available carbon in the atmosphere, through photosynthesis, into subterranean solids, gases and liquids.[2] The metabolic process which turns stored sunlight under the earth back into invisible carbon atoms in the atmosphere follows Marx's famous aphorism in that 'all that is solid turns into air'. Carbon atoms from fossil fuels, and from the burning of forests and biomass energy, ascend into the atmosphere. Around 70 per cent of industrial and land use related emissions eventually descend, either into the ocean through the photosynthesis of phytoplankton which feed the ocean food chain, or through terrestrial plants. In the ocean, the carbon fuels calcify in shell fish and end up on the ocean floor. On land, raised levels of carbon dioxide may stimulate additional plant growth and, because of this and related higher temperatures, there is already a greening of land areas in the Arctic Circle.[3]

Despite the fertilising effect of anthropogenic CO_2, the CO_2 that remains in the atmosphere exercises a surprisingly powerful influence on planetary dynamics and, potentially, on human and natural history. Its influence is most directly felt by humans and other animals in droughts and heavier rainstorms, both connected with anthropogenically warmed temperatures. These create more terrestrial condensation, and atmospheric water vapour is presently rising at 1 per cent annually.[4] This is primarily because the oceans are showing more anthropogenic warmth than the land and hence there is more condensation from surface water.

The ecosystem effects of increased warmth, water vapour and CO_2 are unevenly distributed both between and within hemispheres. The Northern hemisphere, between 2000 and 2009, shows a net increase of greening from increased plant photosynthesis and respiration across 65 per cent of vegetated land areas. But, in the same period, the Southern hemisphere shows a net decline of greening over 70 per cent of vegetated land areas.[5] There is also an imbalance in the distribution of the effects of climate change within the Northern hemisphere. Indian cities saw temperatures above 40° Celsius for much of the summer of 2013. In North Africa and the Middle East, significant declines in precipitation since 2009 are causing crop failure and raised food prices. These ecological conditions are implicated in political upheavals and conflicts in these regions, sometimes called the 'Arab Spring', though this phrase hardly captures the death and destruction of the civil war in Syria or the violent religious extremism in Mali that climate change is fuelling.[6]

The relationship between violent conflict and anthropogenic climate change indicates that climate change is not only a scientific theorem. As Bruno Latour argues, climate change challenges the modern boundary between nature and culture.[7] Climate science reveals an agential network of human and nonhuman, earthly and heavenly, beings which is poorly captured by post-Newtonian and post-Enlightenment accounts of nature as governed by mechanical laws, and of culture as governed by reason and law.

There is a significant analogy between the agential network revealed by climate science and the pneumatological cosmologies of Jewish and Christian traditions. The latter describe a network of spiritual agency between terrestrial creatures and celestial forces that can be either beneficent or malign in its effects on human societies. Hebrew descriptions of this relational network suggest that it is characterised by a balance of forces, in which no party should exercise too much power. Where humans, or a small class of humans, attempt to gain too much control over the relational network this is said to produce maleficent effects for all parties. The rise of Copernican cosmology in Europe, following the invention of new optics which revealed that the earth orbited the sun, unseated traditional pneumatological accounts of earth–heaven relationships. Hence in modern theology and scriptural exegesis pre-Copernican traditional cosmology is typically dismissed as magical and superstitious. For one writer, pneumatological cosmology may even be a 'tap root of the ecological crisis' for 'Spirit is valued more highly than matter which, as a lower entrapping element, is meant to be controlled for the sake of spirit.'[8]

I argue in this chapter that the cosmological picture associated with the ancient doctrine of a Creator Spirit represents a more sophisticated account of the relationships between earthly and heavenly orders of being than modernist exegetes often allow, and one which has valuable resonances with the scientific account of climate change. That human beings are now influencing heavenly forces in ways not conceived of by conventional scientific materialism indicates the surprising sophistication of early Jewish and Christian beliefs about the relational networks of earthly and heavenly actors, as described in the doctrine of the Spirit. The doctrine of the Spirit, therefore, has strong synergies with postmodern sensibilities to ecological destruction. As Michael Welker argues, a theology of the Holy Spirit can draw on the 'primary witnesses' of Christian faith in identifying the powers that are at work in destructive interventions in ecosystems and, more especially, the climate.[9] The doctrine of the Spirit is also resistant to the sundering of human communities and peoples which is part of the human face of ecological destruction and climate change.

In Sumatra, for example, indigenous forests are being burned at an unprecedented rate for conversion to oil palm plantations for biofuel, detergent, and cooking oil by urban peoples.[10] Forest burning, and subsequent emissions from drying peat, produce around 20 per cent of anthropogenic greenhouse gas emissions. It also destroys the customary rights to the forests, and hence the homes, farms and water sources, of hunter gatherers and peasant farmers. Urban people use oil palm to make biofuel to drive their air conditioned vehicles and to make electricity to run air conditioners. But this new industrial metabolism pits rural against urban dwellers since it destroys the shared commons of the original forests.

In the biblical traditions, the Spirit is not only the vital life force but also the agency of the overcoming of dissonance and division among human beings.[11] The doctrine of the Spirit therefore provides helpful synergies with ecological consciousness and, in particular, for the claim that the ecological and climate crisis call for deep moral, psychological, political and spiritual changes in the direction of contemporary culture, and not just technical or market adjustments in the management of a growth-oriented industrial consumption economy. The doctrine of the Spirit in the dimensions of charism, indwelling, spiritual experience and infused virtues also provides powerful liturgical, moral and political resources for resisting the culture industries which drive an increasing spiritual as well as material alienation from the ecological roots of life. But at the same time, the global growth of Pentecostalism in the last hundred years is not yet associated with a raised ecological consciousness among the many millions of Christians in the North and South who are drawn to this contemporary transformation of Christian religion.

Pneumatological networks between heavenly and earthly beings

In ancient Mesopotamian cosmologies, the first agrarians of the Ancient Near East understood that, in what scientists now call the Holocene, the agency of the sun, and the air, clouds, waters and winds which mediate its light and heat, are the forces which birth and nurture life, and which, for agrarian and urban humanity, favour good harvests and prosperous cities. Mesopotamian cosmologies link the sky gods and humans in a symbiotic network of influence between the heavens and the earth, from the sun and the clouds to the soil and the seabed. These networks of influence are key to understanding the material as well as the social and spiritual functions and meanings of religious rituals, social codes and agricultural practices, and especially land distribution, irrigation technologies and human–climate interactions, in the ancient Middle East.

There are more than a few traces in the biblical record of the cult of Yahweh of animistic belief in the sun god, who was understood in Ugaritic religion to be the supreme divine Spirit and source of life that dwells in the firmament.[12] But there are a number of distinctive features to the depiction of the earth–human–heavenly network of beings in the Hebrew bible which set Hebrew cosmology apart from aspects of Mesopotamian cosmology, and many of these are captured in the doctrine of the Spirit. The first major difference is that, for the Hebrews, the heavens themselves are created by a higher God who rules over the other gods and heavenly beings. The Hebrew word *ruach* describes the creative work of the life-giving divine Spirit in moving the elements of air and water, and the same word is used for the manifestations of this vitalising work in breath, clouds, oceans, rivers, storms and wind.[13] These moving elements, and their related agencies, are particularly associated with the emergence of life on earth and with the sustaining of the vitality of vegetative and animal life. The Spirit vitalises life in tandem with the life principle resident in creaturely beings and in the elements of air and water. But the Spirit does not rip apart the structure of matter in order to bring life into being, as does the god Marduk in Babylonian mythology when he tears apart Tiamat, the god of gods, and constitutes the cosmos from parts of her body.[14] Instead, the Spirit peaceably draws out and nurtures the emergence of life. In Genesis 1. 2 the *ruach elohim* or breath of God is said to hover or move – *mehrabet* – over the 'darkness of the deep'.[15] The association of the numinous presence of the Spirit with the overshadowing or shrouding effects of clouds is repeated at other significant events in the history of Israel and of Christ. When Moses ascends Mount Sinai to receive the Commandments, the top of the mountain is enfolded in clouds. The Israelites are guided in the day time in the wilderness by the pillar of cloud, and Elijah is taken up to heaven in front of Elishah on a cloud.

The inspiration of the Creator Spirit in nurturing animal and human life is said to be concentrated and perfected when relations between earthly and heavenly powers are peaceable and in harmonious balance and their processual relationships are symmetric.[16] As Welker puts it, 'the pouring out of the Spirit brings about an astounding and ungovernable interaction that cannot be one-sidedly initiated and controlled.'[17] Hence when humanity attempts to exert too much power over creation – as, for example, in the decision of Adam and Eve to eat of the fruit of the tree of life and acquire godlike knowledge over life – the vitalising work of the Spirit in creation is said to be frustrated.

This first story of the human misuse of a special status as the divine image on earth indicates that human actions in creation influence the vitalising agency of the Spirit in ways that may be malevolent or benign. Benign influences on the Creator Spirit are subsequently associated with faithful worship of Yahweh, the eschewal of idolatry, and fidelity to the Mosaic Covenantal ideal of rule which distributes the land and its fruits equitably among the people of God. Just rule is said to cause the heavenly agencies to give favourable weather and to water the crops on earth (Psalm 72). On the other hand, deep and intergenerational inequity in the use of land, and in the distribution of creaturely wealth and political power, are said to be sources of bondage and coercion among humans which offend the heavenly realms. Both Isaiah and Jeremiah attribute drought and crop failure in Israel to injustice and idolatry among the merchants and rulers of the people of God. Hence the Creator Spirit deprived Israel of sufficient rain to water her crops, while also directing the earthly powers of Assyria, Babylon and Persia to ravage her lands and force her people into exile.[18]

The manifestation of the Spirit in the Old Testament is not confined to natural signs such as clouds, storms and wind. It is also concentrated in certain kinds of human charisma including leadership of the people of God by Moses, Joshua, the Judges and Kings David and Solomon. The charisms of temple building, priestly service, prophecy, dreaming, and the creativity of artists, craftsmen, musicians and poets, are also said to be inspired by the Spirit.[19]

For example, the endowment of the Spirit is said to fall on Bazalel, who constructs the Tabernacle as the first dwelling place of the *shekinah* of God's Spirit among the people of God in their wilderness wanderings (Exodus 31. 1–5).[20] King Solomon, like Bazalel, is also said to be particularly endowed with God's Spirit, or wisdom, when he commences the building of the Temple in Jerusalem.[21] Similarly, Hiram, whom Solomon hires from Tyre to oversee the Temple building, is said to be filled with wisdom (1 Kings 7. 14). But this focus of the presence of the divine Spirit in the Tabernacle and Temple, and in particular in the Holy of Holies, turns out to be but a temporary phase in the unfolding revelation of the Spirit in the Old Testament. Writing after the destruction of the Temple, the Hebrew prophets envisage a time when the Spirit will be 'poured out on all flesh' and women as well as men will prophesy, and the old as well as the young will have visions (Joel 2. 28–9). For Ezekiel, the Exile and the destruction of the Temple presage a Messianic era in which the *shekinah* of the Spirit is no longer confined to the Holy of Holies but will be manifest both in the appearance of the four-faced winged 'heavenly man' on earth, and in a new and more palpable presence of spiritual beings moving through the natural world.[22]

In the New Testament, the agency of the Creator Spirit becomes more fully visible in human form in the Incarnation of Christ, who is described as born of the partnership between the creator Spirit and Mary. The word *mehrabet* used for the overshadowing of the primeval waters by the Creator Spirit at the origin of life is translated as *epeskiaso* in the Septuagint which means 'overshadow'. Luke 1. 35 uses *epeskiaso* in the Angel Gabriel's description of the Holy Spirit's creative energy in 'overshadowing' Mary and impregnating her womb with the Christ, creating a link between the original creation and the revelation of the Creator in human form. Luke intends that the overshadowing of the womb of Mary by the Spirit mirrors and recapitulates the overshadowing of the waters of the earth at the beginning of creation, when Mary gives birth to a 'holy thing' which is the 'Son of God' (Luke 1. 35). In Saint Paul's earlier interpretation of this event, the child of Mary is the 'Last Adam', a 'quickening Spirit' who is also 'the Lord from heaven' (1 Corinthians 15. 45, 47).

The Evangelists describe the ministry of Christ as commencing with the 'descent' of the Spirit. Christ is first publicly revealed as the Messiah, the divine Son of God, at his baptism by John in the Jordan when the Spirit descends on Him *hos peristeran*, 'like a dove' (Luke 3. 22). Subsequently the disciples manifest the work of the Spirit when they take up the ministry of Christ in Judea, casting out demons and preaching repentance and the coming Kingdom of God (Luke 10. 1–24). Before this ministry begins the disciples are 'overshadowed', and so empowered, by the Spirit in the form of a cloud that descends on the mountain during the Transfiguration of Jesus when the Messianic Sonship of Christ is revealed to them by the voice that speaks in the cloud (Luke 9. 34).

Jesus directly speaks only twice of his experience of being indwelled by the Spirit. When his disciples return from their first mission to cast out demons and heal the sick in his name, he tells them that 'he saw Satan falling like lightning' (Luke 10. 18). The second is when Jesus is challenged about the authority for his ministry and he replies with a question about the baptism of John, whether or not it was of God (Mark 11. 27–33). It was the normal Jewish practice for prophets to appeal to their experience of the divine call as the authority for their ministry. As James Dunn argues, in referring to his baptism by John as the origin of his divine authority, Jesus indicates that it was at this event that he had the life-changing experience of spiritual call. Hence when the evangelists later describe his baptism, which was not without its problems since one interpretation would have been that Jesus was a follower of John, they describe it as the occasion for the descent of the Spirit on Jesus, and of the affirmation of his call in divine words from heaven 'you are my Son, the beloved' (Mark 1. 9–11).[23] As Mark has it, 'at once' Jesus follows the leading of the Spirit who takes him to the testing of his call in the wilderness. The Apostle Paul makes a similar linkage between the work of the Spirit and his apostolic calling when he indicates that it was not 'flesh and blood' who called him on the road to Damascus and confirmed his call in his sojourn in Arabia (Galatians 1. 16–17). Paul first develops the implications of the presence of the Spirit in Jesus at his conferral of this presence on his disciples. For Paul, the Spirit who indwells Christians after Pentecost is the same Spirit who was in Jesus, and hence the Spirit is the form in which Jesus is now present in the Church.[24]

Perhaps the most momentous moment in which the new presence of the Spirit on earth is recorded in the gospels is the rending of the veil of the Temple which shrouded the Holy of Holies, an event Matthew describes as accompanying the moment of Christ's death, which is also marked by an earthquake (Matthew 27. 51). At the same time, the souls of the dead are said to be revived and to return to their bones in their graves, and the saints who had died 'went into the holy city and appeared to many' (Matthew 27. 53). For Matthew the crucifixion and resurrection of Christ forever change the relations of the Spirit to the bodies of mortals, and the dry bones live again by the reviving breath of the Spirit (Ezekiel 37. 5). At the same time the earth groans and bears witness to the shocking attempt of human creatures to kill the Creator of earth and heaven.

John the Evangelist reads the resurrection of Christ in an analogously pneumatological way when he describes Christ as 'breathing' the Spirit which indwelled his incarnate and risen body to the disciples at the first resurrection appearance (John 20. 22). Luke-Acts locates the gift of the Spirit in the day of Pentecost, a few days after the Ascension.[25] But for both evangelists the Christ events, and above all his incarnation, death, resurrection and ascension, presage the end of the traditional Israelite confinement of the divine Spirit to the Holy of Holies in the Temple. As Christ's body moves towards its risen form, the Spirit moves from the temple of Christ's incarnate form to the new temple which, as Peter has it, is built with the 'living stones' of the people of God (1 Peter 2. 5).

Pentecost and the recapitulation of the cosmos

The Spirit falls on the disciples on the day of Pentecost, which is the day of the first fruits and the fifth most holy day in the Jewish calendar. It is also the day when leavened bread is brought back into the Jewish home after it has been banished for the feast of Passover. At Pentecost, the Spirit is said to 'sit on' and 'fill' the Apostles. They are then empowered to proclaim the Gospel to all nations, not only to the Jews, and hence the Gentile 'god-fearers', who are assembled from cities across the empire in Jerusalem for the Passover week, hear the Apostles speaking to them in their own tongues, as well as the Jewish pilgrims from the diaspora (Acts 2. 8–12). Clearly, Luke-Acts intends that the universalization of the presence of the Spirit, and the empowerment of all peoples to worship God in the Messianic era, has begun in the Pentecost events. Saint Paul subsequently teaches that the agency of the Spirit among the people of God is revealed in the moral 'fruits of the Spirit' (Galatians 5. 22–5) and the economy of the gifts of the Spirit which characterises the worshipping communities of the early Christians (1 Corinthians 14). The descent of the Spirit on the Apostles, and the move towards the conversion of the world through the 'new creature' who is Christ (Galatians 6. 15), begins at the feast of leavened bread, and this is highly significant in the iconography of the new Christian pneumatology. Bread is 'raised' by the fermenting action of gluten which creates bubbles of air; leavened bread is therefore raised by the breath of the Spirit. Similarly, for the early Christians the Pentecostal Spirit was both the leaven who raised up Jesus from the dead (and who raised the spirits of the disciples after his ascension so that they might become witnesses to Christ to the ends of the earth) and, at the same time, is the leaven who raises up the one loaf which is broken and distributed at the eucharistic ritual of the early Church. This 'makes the church', drawing the many into the fellowship of the one and so recapitulating the body of Christ on earth (1 Corinthians 10. 16–17).[26]

Christian pneumatology identifies the agency of the Spirit in the quest for holiness through sanctification. Christians are made holy by the power of the indwelling Spirit who is encountered supremely in the sacraments of baptism and eucharist. This focusing of the work of the Spirit is also realised in the ascetic work of those who seek to discern the spirits by controlling and guiding natural desires, bodily appetites and practices towards holy ends. The indwelling of the sanctifying Spirit in the believer, as already described by Paul, is therefore clarified in the inner life and outward practices of those who dedicate themselves to the life of the Spirit, and is manifest in the richer development in the personality of what Paul called the moral 'fruits of the Spirit' and which Aquinas later called 'infused virtues'. This focusing of the revitalising and sanctifying life of the Spirit on the inner life and sacramental worship reaches beyond these to the creation, fulfilling the expectation of Isaiah and Ezekiel of a coming messianic age which would bring peace among the nations, in human–nature interactions and in creaturely relationships (Isaiah 55. 12–13, Ezekiel 34. 25).[27] There is, therefore, in the history of the Church in both East and West a growing sense of holiness in human actions in, and relations to, creation so that those especially devoted to the religious life achieve a new peace with creatures as, for example, in the many images of Saint Jerome plucking a thorn from the paw of a lion.[28] This sense of redemptive agency in creation is manifest in the emergence of monastic farming and craft techniques which in the Middle Ages are said to be forms of agency which offer the potential restoration of Paradise on earth.[29]

This sense of the work of the Spirit – as moving from the sacraments and the life of holiness to the restoration of creation and of human and creaturely relations – was increasingly attenuated in the West, especially in the second millennium, when a strong contrast between Eastern and Western pneumatology opened up. This contrast is presaged by a change in eucharistic practice which occurs midway through the first millennium. The Pentecostal symbol of the Spirit as leaven plays a pivotal role in this change. The Eastern Fathers develop a pneumatological account of the revivifying power of the Eucharist by analogy with the work of the Spirit as the leaven which raises the loaf which Christians break and share in the Eucharist. However, the practice gradually emerged in the Latin Church of the third and fourth centuries of the use of unleavened bread in the Eucharist. The Latin Church took the view that because the Last Supper took place on the night of the Passover according to the Synoptic Gospels, that Christ used unleavened bread at the first Eucharist. But, in an essay against the use of *matzos*, unleavened bread, at the eucharist, Athanasius argues that John is correct, and not the other evangelists, when he places the Last Supper on the night before the Passover. If it was the night before the Passover, then at the Last Supper Christ would have used *artos* – leavened bread – and not *matzos*, as he had at all other meals with the disciples.[30]

A later writer argues that those who participate in the Eucharist using *matzos* do not participate in a true eucharist for

> the being of our own composition, which the Word of God took up and became substance for, is besouled. Therefore, he who partakes of matzos does not eat the bread 'for-our-being' and 'of-one-being-with' us of Christ our Saviour. For what is without leaven is clearly also without soul, as the nature of the matter clearly shows.[31]

The Orthodox believed that in the New Covenant, living bread – and not unfermented or 'dead' bread – was mandated and that, therefore, the use of unleavened bread in the Latin West invalidated the Eucharist since it is not living and therefore lacks 'soul'.

The 'azymes controversy', as it became known, was one of the sources of the ultimate division between Rome and Constantinople, Western and Eastern

Christendom, together with the Filioque clause and the Primacy of Peter, in the tenth century. It represents a singular struggle over the spiritual significance of material agency after the resurrection of Christ and in the era of the gifting of the divine Spirit to the Church. Behind the controversy are two increasingly contrasting views in East and West about the ways in which the presence of the Spirit is reflected in the material world, in human–nature relations, beyond divine and sacramental worship and the inner life of the Christian.

In Eastern Orthodoxy the liturgy is not only a human drama in which God is present in Word and Sacrament but is also a theurgic reality through which the creative work of the Spirit reaches out from the sanctuary towards the renewal of life in the whole created cosmos. This conception of the cosmic implications of the Spirit's presence in the Church is evoked in Temple theology as elucidated by Margaret Barker, who argues that there are strong analogies between the architectural and ritual shape of Orthodox worship and of the Jewish Temple. In this perspective, Christian worship in the time of the Spirit performs the same renewing and sustaining functions in mediating in the network of earthly and heavenly beings which are part of the Mesopotamian influenced cosmology of the Hebrews.[32]

The same sense of the Spirit of Christ mediating a renewal of creation is evident in many Byzantine mosaics and medieval frescos. This trope is beautifully illustrated in the Apse Mosaic of the Church of Saint Clement in Rome which, although tenth century, is said to be a copy of a much earlier mosaic. In this mandala-like mosaic the vivifying Spirit of God, who hovers over Christ on the Cross, reaches his outstretched arms through green vines, in the circular branches of which are myriad plants and animals who are renewed by the Creator Spirit revealed in Christ, along with the apostles and saints. The same idea is also present in much Western Christian art, both before and even after the Reformation and Counter-Reformation. In the apse of the Catholic Church of Saints Peter and Paul in Potsdam, an eighteenth century fresco depicts Christ as Pantocrator looking down from heaven with outstretched arms. Behind him the light of the sun, representing God the Father, and below him the rays of the sun, a symbol for the work of the Spirit, reach down to the apostles and Christian rulers on earth who, by implication, experience benign weather when they worship God above all things and their rule is symmetrically related to divine authority.[33] This association between Christ and a benign climate is reflected more broadly in the mapping of the liturgical year, and the festivals of Incarnation, Passion, Resurrection, Ascension and Pentecost, onto the agricultural year in the Northern hemisphere. This is also illustrated by the liturgical feast of Rogation Sunday which, from the fifth century in France, takes place before Ascension and involves priests and people going into the fields around the parish calling for a divine blessing, followed by an extended liturgy of offering of tithes of money and produce in the Mass.[34] Some rural and urban parishes in England still 'beat the bounds' of the parish in recollection of this practice even if most priests no longer sprinkle holy water on the fields.

The realisation of the potential of the Spirit's power in the new era of the Church to produce fruitful effects in creation reaches a material high point during the medieval age in the monastic development of new agricultural techniques and new technologies such as clocks, the deep plough, telescopes and windmills. In the growing influence of Christian monks and the Church over agricultural practices, and in the synergy between the Church's liturgical year and the climatic seasons of the Northern hemisphere, there is not only a recovery but a sense of the renewal of the Hebrew idea of an order of beings earthly and heavenly in which right worship and just rule sustain favourable climates and agricultural conditions. Hence, although the Eucharistic symbolism of the Spirit as a vivifying agent flowing out from the sanctuary into all creation is to an extent corrupted by the loss of the symbolism of the *artos* or 'whole loaf' in Western practice, there remained in the Latin Mass, at least until the late Middle Ages, a deep spiritual connection between the bread and wine of the sacrament and the materiality of human work on creation, and an awareness of its spiritual potential to beautify and renew the face of the earth under the lordship of Christ and through the creative inspiration of the divine Spirit.

The theological roots of the Anthropocene

In the late Middle Ages the discoveries of Copernican cosmology advances a new kind of human agency in the creaturely network of invisible and visible influences on nature which resists the symmetric nature of this network in Jewish and Christian pneumatology. Copernicus disabused the Gentile and Jewish descendants of the Yahwists of the idea that the sun rose and fell by divine fiat to warm their crops and their faces. New optical instruments revealed to Copernicus, Galileo and Kepler that the earth moved around the sun and that the perception of the sun's rise and fall in the sky is a sensory illusion, although underwritten by religious symbols and stories. Far from the sun serving the earth, it is the earth's revolutions around the sun and the weight of air refracting and capturing the sun's rays which sustain the earth's uniquely life-favouring habitat.[35] However, there was spiritual and theological risk in the new idea of humanity and the earth as epiphenomenal to the sun and the stars, for it corroded the theological and pneumatological understanding of spiritual mediation between humanity and the heavens in which creaturely as well as human and divine life are also caught up. If the heavens no longer tell the glory of God, and humanity is no longer a little lower than the angels beneath the heavens, then, as Jacob Taubes argues, Copernicanism as cosmology 'not only overthrew an old astronomical theory but also destroyed man's dwelling in the cosmos'.[36]

The increasingly godlike power over the earth that humanity claimed after the Scientific Revolution disturbed the symmetric relationships which Hebrew and Christian traditions had once seen as a guiding principle to cosmic peace and order in the network of earth and heavenly beings. The Copernican displacement of a geocentric cosmology gives rise to a scientific eschatology in which growing asymmetry in relations between human beings and other creaturely forces is said to be the source of human salvation and the restoration of paradise. After Copernicus, the inaugurators of the scientific revolution, such as Francis Bacon, argue that it is through the control and reordering of nature and its subjection to mindful and hence spiritual purposes that human beings draw the material creation towards the remaking of Paradise.[37] Instead of a harmonious balance between humanity and natural and spiritual beings, for Bacon and his heirs the coercive interrogation and reordering of nature by science becomes the source of salvation, and heralds a *novum organum* in which scientists gain understanding and control over the life principle itself. In the related imperial 'age of discovery', human influence over nature reaches to the ends of the earth and Bacon imagined that this great increase in human understanding of, and influence over, the earth would result in the emergence of a 'new Atlantis' in which technology will make men and women like gods in their powers over life.[38]

For the heirs of Copernicus there are no spirits in the air other than the thoughts of men and women which, through scientific experimentation, have the potential to turn the earth into more purposive and hence mindful directions than those which it otherwise follows as brute or 'virgin' matter.[39] For Bacon the scientific re-engineering of the earth becomes the marker of being human and the way in which humans fill the earth and their own history with meaning. Hence, while Copernican astronomy decentres human from earth history, the scientific revolution recasts humanity as the technical controller of the habitat of the earth, although human beings lack the knowledge or the wisdom to use such power wisely.

Since the invention of the steam engine, industrial atmospheric emissions from fossil fuels and burned forests have become so influential on the earth system that scientists now propose that the earth has left the benign Holocene era behind, and is entering the new and more threatening epoch of the Anthropocene. The 'Great Acceleration' in fossil fuel consumption since the 1950s has taken atmospheric CO_2 levels from 320 to 400 parts per million in just sixty years, and humans are now on course to double the quantity of preindustrial carbon in the atmosphere by 2050.[40]

In the era of the Anthropocene, the air is alive with the atmospheric influences of the industry and consumption activities of mindful beings. When a climate scientist slices an Antarctic ice core representing the atmosphere in 1960 they cannot tell whether the frozen gaseous atoms of carbon dioxide preserved in the ice core were emitted by humans or other creatures. For some this is an epoch defining moment. If human beings can no longer easily distinguish their cybernetic influences on the world around them from the natural background to their cultural life, then the Anthropocene has begun. Hans Shellnhuber argues that the Anthropocene represents a second Copernican revolution in which human spiritual and material influences on the earth and the heavens are recognised by modern scientists, and not only Byzantine or Latin theologians, as central to the destiny of life on earth.[41] The influence of anthropogenic gases on cloud formation, a process still little understood by natural scientists, is analogous to biblical accounts of the life-giving and life-changing influence on the unfolding of life, and on human affairs, through the analogy of the presence of the Spirit in overshadowing clouds. But the ascent of industrial greenhouse gas emissions represents a post-Christian subversion of the descent and ascent of the Spirit in the history of Creation, Christ and the Church.

In that history the Spirit, like a dove, responds and sustains gentle and peaceable rule. But in the Anthropocene, humanity has forcibly imposed an energetic will from below the surface of the earth to the heavens and, despite growing evidence that this imposition is endangering the stability of the atmosphere and a benign climate for many humans and other animals, the powerful agencies of this reordering, and in particular national and multinational fossil fuel and plantation companies, are burning more forests and fossil fuels now than at any time in modern history.

Towards a pneumatological politics of climate repair

In Jewish and Christian traditions, the doctrine of the Holy Spirit calls into question the tendency of human rulers, merchants and priests to concentrate agency and power in fewer hands. For the Hebrew prophets, the attempts of a controlling class of Temple priests to mediate the grace of the divine Spirit to the people of God came to an end with the destruction of the first Temple. Christ is equally unrelenting in his criticism of the misuse of power by the priests and rabbis of the Second Temple which he sees as a symbol of the hierarchical power of Rome rather than of the reign of God. With the coming of the Messiah, the Holy Spirit enables all the people of God to experience and express the inspiring agency of the Spirit. After Pentecost, all Christians through baptism in water and the Spirit participate in the new gift economy of love and spiritual worship inaugurated by Christ, and in a new symmetry between earthly and heavenly realms which is the architechtonic petition of the Lord's Prayer, 'thy will be done on earth as in heaven.'

The New Testament and early Christian account of the empowering presence of the Holy Spirit in the lives of Christians, and in the Church as the body of Christ, is a crucial theological matrix for deconstructing resistance by large centralising economic corporations and government agencies to the scientific rediscovery of co-agency between the earth and the heavens. The economy of Spiritual gifts in the body politic of the Church as described by Saint Paul, about which I have written elsewhere, also offers a paradigm for a post-fossil fuel energy economy of distributed renewable power.[42] In the emerging distributed energy economy householders, farmers, makers and traders are creators and conservers of energy rather than receivers and consumers. In Germany as a result of the *energiewende* or 'energy change', half of electric power generation capacity is now in the hands of householders and small businesses rather than large power producers.[43] Similarly, in the United States the extent of take up of solar power is beginning to subvert the grid dominance of private power utility companies. This paradigm of distributed locally-made and renewable power is deeply at odds with the tendencies of borderless global capital to the construction of an invisible, offshore and unaccountable pooling of nature's wealth in a shadow economy. The deep asymmetry of this economy is connected with the refusal of large corporations, both public and private, to reduce deforestation, fossil fuel extraction and cement making and so to begin to rebalance the asymmetric agential relationship between industrial humans and the other beings of earth and the heavens in the climate crisis.

Pneumatological participation in the sacramental life of the Church, and participative communication among those gathered in Christian congregations, are key generative sources of democratic and participative communities in Christian and post-Christian societies.[44] This spiritual origin of modern democracy remains key to the continuing expansion of democratic governance in the global South.[45] A spiritual pneumatology may therefore also sustain a more distributed energy economy of the kind already being pioneered by congregations and religious communities in Europe and North America which have begun to source electric power from sunshine on the church roof or from wind in the community garden.[46]

From the opening metaphor of divine creative action in the Bible, the Spirit is the sustaining breath who gives vitality to life on earth, just as in the New Testament the Spirit is the agent who makes the Incarnation possible and whose subsequent fruit is the birth of the Church. Christian moral theologians from Aquinas and Abelard to Karl Barth and Oliver O'Donovan have also underlined the role of the indwelling Holy Spirit as the divine agency who works with the individual in transforming intentions and actions towards the good,[47] including the good of a sustainable way of living which reduces harms to persons distant in space or time of the presently centralised and fossil-fuelled energy economy. The doctrine of the Holy Spirit is therefore key to the ecclesial response to the moral, as well as the political, project of inter-generational climate care.

Notes

1 For a fuller account of climate science in theological perspective see further Michael S. Northcott, *A Moral Climate: The Ethics of Global Warming* (London: Darton, Longman and Todd, 2007), pp. 1–49. On the relative global carbon emissions of human activities by type see M. R. Raupach, G. Marland *et al.*, 'Global and regional drivers of accelerating CO_2 emissions,' *Proceedings of the National Academy of Sciences*, 104 (2007), pp. 10288–93. On the metaphor of actor-network to describe human–climate interactions see Bruno Latour, *Facing Gaia: Six lectures on the political theology of nature being the Gifford Lectures on Natural Religion*, Edinburgh, 18–28 February 2013, available online at www. bruno-latour.fr/sites/default/files/downloads/GIFFORD-SIX-LECTURES_1.pdf (accessed 19 June 2013).

2 Rolf P. Sieferle, *The Subterranean Forest: Energy Systems and the Industrial Revolution*, trans. Michael P. Osman (Cambridge: White Horse Press, 2001).

3 Richard G. Pearson, Steven J. Phillips *et al.*, 'Shifts in Arctic vegetation and associated feedbacks under climate change,' *Nature: Climate Change* (2013): DOI 10.1038/NCLI-MATE1858.

4 K. H. Rosenlof, S. J. Oltmans, *et al.*, 'Stratospheric water vapor increases over the past half-century,' *Geophysical Research Letters* 28 (2001), pp. 1195–98.

5 Maosheng Zhao and Steven W. Running, 'Drought-Induced Reduction in Global Terrestrial Net Primary Production from 2000 Through 2009,' *Science* 329 (2010): 940–43.

6 The Gravity Recovery and Climate Experiment (GRACE), begun in 2007, uses satellite data on the force of gravity to estimate the presence of groundwater in the Middle East and it shows that the nations most affected by violent upheavals are also suffering from significantly reduced water supplies: see further K. A. Voss and J. S. Famiglietti, *et al.*,

'Groundwater depletion in the Middle East from GRACE with implications for trans-boundary water management in the Tigris-Euphrates-Western Iran region,' *Water Resources Research* 49 (2013): 904–14. On the relationship of climate change and civil conflict in the Middle East see S. Johnstone and J. Mazo, 'Global Warming and the Arab Spring,' *Survival: Global Politics and Strategy* 53 (2011): 11–17.

7 Latour, *Facing Gaia.*

8 Elizabeth A. Johnson, *Women, Earth, and Creator Spirit* (New York: Paulist Press, 1993), p. 11.

9 Michael Welker, *God the Spirit,* trans. John F. Hoffmeyer (Minneapolis, MN: Augsburg Fortress Press, 1994), pp. 39–40.

10 Emily B. Fitzherbert, Matthew J. Struebig *et al.,* 'How will oil palm expansion affect biodiversity?' *Trends in Ecology and Evolution* 23 (2008), pp. 538–545.

11 Welker, *God the Spirit,* p. 40.

12 There is good evidence of the influence of Ugaritic sun worship in the Hebrew bible: see further J. G. Taylor, *Yahweh and the Sun: Biblical and Archaeological Evidence for Sun Worship in Ancient Israel* (Sheffield: JSOT Press, 1993) and Steve A. Wiggins, 'Yahweh: the God of the Sun?' *Journal for the Study of the Old Testament* 21 (1996), pp. 89–106.

13 There are 377 uses of the word *ruach* in the Hebrew bible but these are the primary classes of individual whom the spirit is said to 'inspire' or 'move': see further Strong's Hebrew Concordance. The spirit's active movement in the Old Testament is generally described through the element of air, and hence the use of the same Hebrew word in contexts where it means variously air, breath, blast, storm and wind as well as for divine or spiritual inspiration; there is no association of *ruach* with other life elements such as fire, as Charlie Moule points out in C. F. D. Moule, *The Holy Spirit* (London: Mowbray, 1978), pp. 1–3. Elizabeth Johnson argues that fire is an element associated with Spirit but there are only two biblical instances – the burning bush and the tongues of fire at Pentecost – which can provide evidence for this and I agree with Moule that in neither case is a clear association between *ruach* and fire made: Johnson, *Women, Earth, and Creator Spirit,* p. 47.

14 Walter Wink, *Engaging the Powers: Discernment and Resistance in a World of Domination* (Minneapolis: Fortress Press, 1992), p. 14.

15 According to Saint Basil, the Holy Spirit in Genesis 1. 2 'cherished the nature of the waters as one sees a bird cover the eggs with her body and impart to them vital force from her own warmth. Such is, as nearly as possible, the meaning of these words – the Spirit was borne: let us understand, that is, prepared the nature of water to produce living beings: a sufficient proof for those who ask if the Holy Spirit took an active part in the creation of the world, and above all ensouled life.' Basil of Caesarea, *On the Six Days of Creation: A Translation of the* Hexaemeron *by R. Grosseteste,* trans. C. F. J. Martin (Oxford: Oxford University Press, 1996), II. 7.

16 Welker, *God the Spirit,* pp. 169–70.

17 Welker, *God the Spirit,* p. 170.

18 For an extended discussion of this trope in Hebrew prophetic texts see Michael S. Northcott, *The Environment and Christian Ethics* (Cambridge: Cambridge University Press, 1996), Chapter 5.

19 Wolfhart Pannenberg, 'The doctrine of the Spirit and the task of a theology of nature,' in Carol R. Albright and Joel Haugen (eds), *Beginning with the End: God, Science, and Wolfhart Pannenberg* (Peru, IL: Open Court Publ. Co., 1997), pp. 65–79.

20 For a discussion of the Spirit's indwelling in Bazalel and in Hiram, Solomon's chief builder, and its significance for human interactions with creation through arts, crafts, technology and work see the thesis of my graduate student Jeremy H. Kidwell, 'Drawn into Worship: A Biblical Ethics of Work', PhD thesis, University of Edinburgh, (2013).

21 On the Spirit's inspiration in activities connected with the Temple see Welker, *God the Spirit,* 101–8; on the Spirit and human work more broadly see Miroslav Volf, *Work in the Spirit: Toward a Theology of Work* (Eugene, ON: Wipf and Stock, 2001).

22 Ezekiel's vision of the Heavenly Man and the wheeled cherubim moving about in nature are key sources of inspiration for the Romantic poets and William Blake and their criticism of the environmentally destructive tendencies of industrialism and mechanism: see further Harold Bloom, *The Visionary Company: A Reading of English Romantic Poetry*, revised and enlarged edition (Ithaca, GA: Cornell University Press, 1971), pp. 318–50; Christopher Rowland, *Wheels Within Wheels: William Blake and Ezekiel's Merkebah in Text and Image* (Milwaukee, WI: Marquette University Press, 2007); and Gordon Strachan, *Prophets of Nature: Green Spirituality in Romantic Poetry and Painting* (Edinburgh: Floris Books, 2008).

23 James Dunn, *Jesus and the Spirit* (London: SCM Press, 1975), pp. 62–65. Leander E. Keck describes the history of this rationalist interpretation of the baptism of Jesus in Keck, 'The spirit and the dove,' *New Testament Studies* 17 (1970): 41–67.

24 Dunn, *Jesus and the Spirit*.

25 On the formativity of Christ's post-resurrection absence for the Christian experience and doctrine of the Holy Spirit see G. W. H. Lampe, *God as Spirit: The Bampton Lectures 1976* (Oxford: Clarendon Press, 1977): see also James P. Mackie, *The Christian Experience of God as Spirit* (London: SCM Press, 1983) and Douglas Farrow, *Ascension and Ecclesia* (Edinburgh: T and T Clark, 1999).

26 See further Paul McPartlan, *The Eucharist Makes the Church: Henri de Lubac and John Zizioulas in Dialogue* (Edinburgh: T and T Clark, 1996).

27 Turner, 'The significance of spirit endowment for Paul,' p. 67.

28 See the interpretation of the story of Jerome and the lion, and its extensive artistic representation, in Kyle Van Houtan and Michael S. Northcott, 'Nature and the nation-state: ambivalence, evil, and American environmentalism', in Kyle Van Houtan and Michael S. Northcott (eds), *Diversity and Dominion: Dialogues in Ecology, Ethics and Theology* (Eugene, OR: Cascade Books 2010), pp. 138–156.

29 See further Elspeth Whitney, *Paradise Restored: The Mechanical Arts from Antiquity through the Thirteenth Century* (Philadelphia: Temple University Press, 1989) and George Ovitt, Jr, *The Restoration of Perfection: Labor and Technology in Medieval Culture* (New Brunswick, NJ: Rutgers University Press, 1987).

30 Athanasius, 'Concerning Matzos', cited in Mahlon H. Smith, *And Taking Bread: Cerularius and the Azyme Controversy of 1054* (Paris: Editions Beuchesne, 1978), p. 176.

31 Leo of Ochrida to John of Trani, trans. Smith, *And Taking Bread*, 68, n. 68.

32 Margaret Barker, *Creation: A Biblical Vision for the Environment* (London: Continuum, 2009).

33 For an excellent illustrated survey of human-environment depictions in Christian art see further Susan Power Bratton, *Environmental Values in Christian Art* (Albany, NY: State University of New York Press, 2008).

34 The records of weather conditions kept by priests around Rogation Sundays provide a data set for the reconstruction of weather in Spain in the seventeenth century: Mariano Barriendos, 'Climatic variations in the Iberian Peninsula during the late Maunder Minimum (AD 1675–1715): an analysis of data from rogation ceremonies', *The Holocene* 7 (1997), pp. 105–111.

35 Galileo was not only the most influential advocate of Copernican cosmology but he also conducted the first experiments which revealed the weight of the gases that constitute air: see further Gabrielle Walker, *An Ocean of Air: A Natural History of the Atmosphere* (London: Bloomsbury, 2007), pp. 11–14.

36 Jacob Taubes, *From Cult to Culture: Fragments Towards a Critique of Historical Reason* (Stanford CA: Stanford University Press, 2010), p. 168.

37 Francis Bacon, *Novum Organum or True Suggestions for the Interpretation of Nature* (London: William Pickering, 1844), p. 249: see also William Leiss, *The Domination of Nature*, 2nd edn. (Boston: Beacon Press, 1974) and Caroline Merchant, *The Death of Nature: Women, Ecology, and the Scientific Revolution* (London: Harper Collins, 1990) on the implications of Baconianism for the human–nature relationship.

38 For a fuller discussion of Bacon's recasting of Christian millennialist eschatology as the new age of science and empire see further Michael S. Northcott, *A Political Theology of Climate Change* (Grand Rapids, MI: Wm. B. Eerdmans, 2013).

39 Francis Bacon, *Preparative Toward Natural and Experimental History* (London: 1620): see also Carolyn Merchant, 'The "Violence of Impediments": Francis Bacon and the origins of experimentation,' *Isis* 99 (2008): 731–60.

40 Will Steffen, Paul J. Crutzen and John R. McNeill, 'The Anthropocene: Are Humans Now Overwhelming the Great Forces of Nature?' *Ambio* 36 (2007): 614–21.

41 H. J. Schellnhuber, ' "Earth system" analysis and the second Copernican revolution,' *Nature* 402 Supplement (1999), C19–C23.

42 See further Michael S. Northcott, 'The World Trade Organisation, Fair Trade and the Body Politics of Saint Paul,' in John Atherton (ed.) *Through the Eye of a Needle: Theology, Ethics and Economy*, (London: Epworth Press, 2007), pp. 169–188.

43 Jonas Rest, *Gruner Kapitalismus? Klimanwandel, globale Staaten-konkurrenz und die Verhinderung der Energiewende* (Heidelberg: KunkellLopka Medienentwicklung, 2011).

44 See further Jeffrey Stout, *Democracy and Tradition* (Princeton, NJ: Princeton University Press, 2004), p. 167.

45 See further Samuel P. Huntington, *The Third Wave: Democratization in the Late Twentieth Century* (Norman, OH: University of Oklahoma Press, 1991), pp. 72–8.

46 On North American religious communities and renewable energy see Sarah McFarland Taylor, *Green Sisters: A Spiritual Ecology* (Cambridge MA: Harvard University Press, 2007); on UK Ecocongregations see the movement's self-description at http://ew.eco congregation.org/about and www.ecocongregationsscotland.org (accessed 20 August 2013).

47 On the Holy Spirit in Christian ethics see Oliver O'Donovan, *Resurrection and Moral Order: Outline for an Evangelical Ethics* (Leicester: Intervarsity Press, 1986).

Bibliography

Bacon, Francis. *Preparative Toward Natural and Experimental History* (London: 1620).

——*Novum Organum or True Suggestions for the Interpretation of Nature* (London: William Pickering, 1844).

Barker, Margaret. *Creation: A Biblical Vision for the Environment* (London: Continuum, 2009).

Barriendos, Mariano. 'Climatic variations in the Iberian Peninsula during the late Maunder Minimum (AD 1675–1715): an analysis of data from rogation ceremonies', *The Holocene* 7 (1997): 105–111.

Basil of Caesarea, *On the Six Days of Creation: A Translation of the* Hexaemeron *by R. Grosseteste*, trans. C. F. J. Martin (Oxford: Oxford University Press, 1996).

Bloom, Harold. *The Visionary Company: A Reading of English Romantic Poetry*, revised and enlarged edition (Ithaca, GA: Cornell University Press, 1971).

Bratton, Susan Power. *Environmental Values in Christian Art* (Albany, NY: State University of New York Press, 2008).

Dunn, James. *Jesus and the Spirit* (London: SCM Press, 1975).

Farrow, Douglas. *Ascension and Ecclesia* (Edinburgh: T and T Clark, 1999).

Fitzherbert, Emily B., Matthew J. Struebig *et al.* 'How will oil palm expansion affect biodiversity?' *Trends in Ecology and Evolution* 23 (2008): 538–545.

Huntington, Samuel P. *The Third Wave: Democratization in the Late Twentieth Century* (Norman, OH: University of Oklahoma Press, 1991).

Johnson, Elizabeth A. *Women, Earth, and Creator Spirit* (New York: Paulist Press, 1993).

Johnstone, S. and J. Mazo, 'Global Warming and the Arab Spring', *Survival: Global Politics and Strategy* 53 (2011): 11–17.

Keck, Leander E. 'The spirit and the dove', *New Testament Studies* 17 (1970): 41–67.

Kidwell, Jeremy H. 'Drawn Into Worship: A Biblical Ethics of Work', PhD thesis, University of Edinburgh (2013).

Lampe, G. W. H. *God as Spirit: The Bampton Lectures 1976* (Oxford: Clarendon Press, 1977).

Latour, Bruno. *Facing Gaia: Six lectures on the political theology of nature being the Gifford Lectures on Natural Religion* Edinburgh, 18–28 February 2013. Available online at www.bruno-latour.fr/sites/default/files/downloads/GIFFORD-SIX-LECTURES_1.pdf

Leiss, William. *The Domination of Nature*, 2nd ed. (Boston: Beacon Press, 1974).

Mackie, James P. *The Christian Experience of God as Spirit* (London: SCM Press, 1983).

McFarland Taylor, Sarah. *Green Sisters: A Spiritual Ecology* (Cambridge MA: Harvard University Press, 2007).

McPartlan, Paul. *The Eucharist Makes the Church: Henri de Lubac and John Zizioulas in Dialogue* (Edinburgh: T and T Clark, 1996).

Merchant, Caroline. *The Death of Nature: Women, Ecology, and the Scientific Revolution* (London: Harper Collins, 1990).

——'The "Violence of Impediments": Francis Bacon and the origins of experimentation', *Isis* 99 (2008), pp. 731–760.

Moule, C. F. D. *The Holy Spirit* (London: Mowbray, 1978).

Northcott, Michael S. *The Environment and Christian Ethics* (Cambridge: Cambridge University Press, 1996).

——*A Moral Climate: The Ethics of Global Warming* (London: Darton, Longman and Todd, 2007).

——'The World Trade Organisation, Fair Trade and the Body Politics of Saint Paul', in John Atherton (ed.), *Through the Eye of a Needle: Theology, Ethics and Economy* (London: Epworth Press, 2007), pp. 169–88.

——*A Political Theology of Climate Change* (Grand Rapids, MI: Wm. B. Eerdmans, 2013).

O'Donovan, Oliver. *Resurrection and Moral Order: Outline for an Evangelical Ethics* (Leicester: Intervarsity Press, 1986).

Ovitt, George Jr. *The Restoration of Perfection: Labor and Technology in Medieval Culture* (New Brunswick, NJ: Rutgers University Press, 1987).

Pannenberg, Wolfhart. 'The doctrine of the Spirit and the task of a theology of nature', in Carol R. Albright and Joel Haugen (eds), *Beginning with the End: God, Science, and Wolfhart Pannenberg* (Peru, IL: Open Court Publ. Co., 1997), pp. 65–79.

Pearson, Richard G. and Steven J. Phillips *et al.* 'Shifts in Arctic vegetation and associated feedbacks under climate change', *Nature: Climate Change* (2013) DOI: 10.1038/NCLIMATE1858.

Raupach, M. R. and G. Marland *et al.* 'Global and regional drivers of accelerating CO_2 emissions', *Proceedings of the National Academy of Sciences*, 104 (2007), pp. 10288–93.

Rest, Jonas. *Gruner Kapitalismus? Klimanwandel, globale Staaten-konkurrenz und die Verhinderung der Energiewende* (Heidelberg: KunkellLopka Medienentwicklung, 2011).

Rosenlof, K. H., S. J. Oltmans, *et al.* 'Stratospheric water vapor increases over the past half-century', *Geophysical Research Letters* 28 (2001): 1195–98.

Rowland, Christopher. *Wheels Within Wheels: William Blake and Ezekiel's Merkebah in Text and Image* (Milwaukee, WI: Marquette University Press, 2007).

Schellnhuber, H. J. '"Earth system" analysis and the second Copernican revolution', *Nature* 402 Supplement (1999), C19–C23.

Sieferle, Rolf P. *The Subterranean Forest: Energy Systems and the Industrial Revolution* trans. Michael P. Osman (Cambridge: White Horse Press, 2001).

Smith, Mahlon H. *And Taking Bread: Cerularius and the Azyme Controversy of 1054* (Paris: Editions Beuchesne, 1978).

Steffen, Will, Paul J. Crutzen and John R. McNeill, 'The Anthropocene: Are Humans Now Overwhelming the Great Forces of Nature?' *Ambio* 36 (2007): 614–21.

Stout, Jeffrey. *Democracy and Tradition* (Princeton, NJ: Princeton University Press, 2004).

Strachan, Gordon. *Prophets of Nature: Green Spirituality in Romantic Poetry and Painting* (Edinburgh: Floris Books, 2008).

Taubes, Jacob. *From Cult to Culture: Fragments Towards a Critique of Historical Reason* (Stanford CA: Stanford University Press, 2010).

Taylor, J. G. *Yahweh and the Sun: Biblical and Archaeological Evidence for Sun Worship in Ancient Israel* (Sheffield: JSOT Press, 1993).

Turner, M. M. B. 'The Significance of Spirit Endowment for Paul', *Vox Evangelica* 9 (1975): 56–69.

Van Houtan, Kyle and Michael S. Northcott. 'Nature and the nation-state: ambivalence, evil, and American environmentalism', in Kyle Van Houtan and Michael S. Northcott (eds), *Diversity and Dominion: Dialogues in Ecology, Ethics and Theology* (Eugene, OR: Cascade Books, 2010), pp. 138–56.

Volf, Miroslav. *Work in the Spirit: Toward a Theology of Work* (Eugene, OR: Wipf and Stock, 2001).

Voss, K. A. and J. S. Famiglietti, *et al.* 'Groundwater depletion in the Middle East from GRACE with implications for transboundary water management in the Tigris-Euphrates-Western Iran region', *Water Resources Research* 49 (2013): 904–14.

Walker, Gabrielle. *An Ocean of Air: A Natural History of the Atmosphere*, London: Bloomsbury, 2007).

Welker, Michael. *God the Spirit*, trans. John F. Hoffmeyer (Minneapolis, MN: Augsburg Fortress Press, 1994).

Whitney, Elspeth. *Paradise Restored: The Mechanical Arts from Antiquity through the Thirteenth Century* (Philadelphia: Temple University Press, 1989).

Wiggins, Steve A. 'Yahweh: the God of the Sun?' *Journal for the Study of the Old Testament* 21 (1996): 89–106.

Wink, Walter. *Engaging the Powers: Discernment and Resistance in a World of Domination* (Minneapolis: Fortress Press, 1992).

Zhao, Maosheng and Steven W. Running. 'Drought-Induced Reduction in Global Terrestrial Net Primary Production from 2000 Through 2009', *Science* 329 (2010): 940–43.

5

CREATION

Celia Deane-Drummond

Introduction

The rising tide of political discourse on climate change that is attributable directly or indirectly to human activities, both at global and local levels in the Western world, represents a shift in public consciousness that arguably is on a par with an awakening to environmental consciousness half a century earlier. Of course there are still some sceptical commentators, but in the main the cultural climate is shifting, especially in the Western world. The scientific evidence, however, in identifying both current problems and future projections of escalating impacts, generates cultural anxieties that call for a religious as well as a secular response. It is well known that the window for reducing emissions is now narrowing, and must be reduced by at least 15 per cent by 2020 if global warming is to be kept within the 2 degree Celsius limits.[1] Alongside this, a cascade of anxieties about the certainty of scientific predictions of climate impacts prevails. The scientific predictions are always best estimates based on the best available evidence, but the very latest data to date suggest that the collective effort of IPCC's most recent report seems to have underestimated the rate of sea level rise, even while being about on track for the projection of global temperature increase.[2] A theologian's most immediate response is bound to be an ethical one, dealing with the most immediate issues of human vulnerabilities, biodiversity loss and unjust suffering.[3] Deeper questions about the legacy of modernity have left philosophers such as Jürgen Habermas much more open to a religious voice in key public debates of social importance. Attempts to find solutions through, for example, engineering the climate through technological means are, in one sense, attempts at human agency in a sphere where that agency is clearly found wanting.[4] There is therefore a changing climate in a double sense, in as much as there is a new climate for appropriating religious insights, especially beliefs that foster solidarity between peoples.[5] But even before such negotiations might be achieved, it is important for theologians to consider more deeply how and in what sense the disruptive impacts of climate change impinge on their own basic beliefs about God as Creator.

Secular writers, flailing around for inspiration in order to inform their approach, have been more than ready to co-opt biblical language in order to enhance the metaphorical content of their message for collective action. Hence, we find prominent public spokespersons for climate change action such as Mike Hulme provoking religious sensibilities by naming a need for a return to Eden, and Bill McKibben drawing on the image of God speaking in the whirlwind in Job.[6] Both such approaches show up the vacuum in public debate about a sustained and explicitly theological approach to climate change, one that can go further than simply introducing what might be called biblical sound bites to satisfy those who intuitively sense that something needs to be said from a theological perspective.

Furthermore, the philosophical issues that are on the table are profound. Climate change calls out for a metaphysical approach that will both be satisfying and make sense in such a context. Climate science, unlike Darwinian forms of natural selection, has not yet attempted to attach itself to an aggressive new atheism in the interests of scientific reasonableness. But the challenge to think more carefully about creation and its meaning theologically is no less profound. Both climate change and evolution by natural selection challenge belief in a Creator by destabilising the possibility of its reasonableness. At the same time, both, on their own terms, lead to a sense of meaninglessness and the ultimate threat of the extinction of the human.

I am beginning this chapter, therefore, by returning to the work of Thomas Aquinas, a medieval scholar who was also faced in his day with deep challenges about the reasonableness of belief in God as Creator, and whose philosophical and theological reflections still, I suggest, are highly relevant. His work carries what might be termed the strength of a classic, one that speaks into the present by offering imaginative insights that draw on centuries of religious wisdom. One of the difficulties, of course, which any doctrine of creation presents, is the fact that it is not only a pervasive theme throughout biblical literature, but that it also connects with other doctrines, including anthropology and eschatology. I hope to indicate, at least in the form of a sketch, how a classic doctrine of God as Creator is still relevant in relation to specific issues that need to be addressed in climate change. In this, I will be arguing for (a) a retrieval of the philosophical doctrine of *creatio ex nihilo*, creation out of nothing, and (b) a Trinitarian understanding of belief in God as Creator as a drama of Love and Wisdom. I will also briefly consider possible objections to these views in contemporary scholarship. I recognise that this constructive theological account could be filled out by paying more attention to biblically informed theological elements of the space of creation, including beauty, goodness and wisdom.[7] It is, however, crucial to touch on the crown or goal of creation in the sabbath of creation as a sanctification of time, a foundational concept of creation, which indicates the eschatological element that is built into creation from the beginning.

Creatio ex nihilo

For the early Church, the belief that the world was created from nothing was drawn from a particular reading of the book of Genesis.[8] Although some Jewish scholars spoke of 'creation out of nothing', texts such as 2 Maccabees 7. 28 were not intended to be metaphysical. The doctrine of *creatio ex nihilo* emerged early in the history of the Christian church in response to prevailing philosophical alternatives that matter emanated from God, or was coeternal with God.[9] Plato, Aristotle, Heraclitus and Parmenides were all prepared to advocate the view that the universe is eternal and denied an absolute temporal beginning.[10] Although some were tempted by a Platonic view of God forming the world from pre-existing matter, the settled view at the end of the second century was that Christian revelation stood in sharp contrast to this position. Theophilus of Antioch argued that the eternity of matter would compromise the sovereignty of God, since if it was co-eternal it would be equivalent in status and thus be divine. Irenaeus and Tertullian extended this doctrine in order to maintain the ontological distinction between God and all creation, so that nothing is certainly not 'something'.[11] God is therefore not on the same level of being as other creatures, and the creation of the world out of nothing seeks to safeguard this view. Belief in an eternal world was also objected to on the grounds that it seems to indicate a self-sufficiency of the universe that is denied in Christian revelation; namely, one that is radically dependent on the free, creative act of God.

The early Church fathers, therefore, insisted on a temporal view of creation in order to protect the idea that history is linear *salvation history*, rather than cyclical. Augustine, as well as upholding the concept of the universe beginning with time, introduced the idea of the two moments of creation: one in the first phase of creation in the beginning, and the second in the upholding of creatures in the here and now.[12] He viewed the Genesis account of God as creating over the six days as not so much a sequence of time, but in terms of establishing causal connections. The pressure to make matter eternal was also premised on observations that the world seemed evil, so, in order to protect God, eternal matter was considered evil. Marcionites, Manichees and Gnostics all held variants on this theme, so matter became the work of heavenly beings of lower rank, displaying an evil principle.[13] Augustine vigorously opposed such views.

Aquinas builds on and develops these insights on creation from the early Church, interrogating Muslim philosophers, especially Avicenna's conception of essence and existence, and offers a constructive view of creation that I suggest bears relevance to the present discussion on climate change. Aquinas's understanding of *creatio ex nihilo* is arguably the high water mark in the development of this metaphysics.[14] Simon Oliver argues that the idea of creation out of nothing is so radical that to associate it with natural processes is misleading; rather, it needs to be linked primarily with a doctrine of God.[15] Further, objections to the classical view in the contemporary context echo problems associated with the ferment of alternatives that Aquinas sought to address. In order to give some structure to this analysis, and to make it manageable, I am going to draw primarily on Aquinas's *Writing on the Sentences of Peter Lombard*,[16] not only because it provides a clearer portrait of his doctrine of creation compared with other scattered texts on the theme, but also because it gives a clear systematic shape to his understanding of creation out of nothing. It is also a fuller account of this doctrinal aspect compared with the *Summa Theologiae*.

The first article, accordingly, is on whether there is only one first principle of creation. Any doctrine of creation has to contend with the origin of evil as well as goodness in the world, and what this might mean in terms of principles of origin. This is, arguably, also a primary challenge in climate change: does the disruption of the global order indicate a malevolent force is at work, or a belief that God is not really the Creator of all that exists? While the Manichean tendency was prevalent in Aquinas's time, it is no less of a temptation for contemporary scholars who still struggle with belief in a good God as author of all that is. Aquinas argues that while there is more than one principle at work in the world, in absolute terms there is only one principle.

Contemporary philosophers such as Thomas Nagel, in his controversial book *Mind and Cosmos*, in a way that parallels this discussion, may therefore, like the authors Aquinas interrogated, be prepared to recognise a transcendent (non-material) force in the world, but not recognise that there is only one absolute first cause or, as in Nagel's case, that God exists.[17] While he does not write directly on climate change, Nagel presents a secular alternative to the view that materialism is the only reasonable philosophical alternative that can be considered today. My suggestion is that climate change adds to the pressure that already exists against naming materialism as a satisfying philosophical alternative, and may be one reason why secular writers are also turning to religious beliefs for inspiration. Furthermore, if Nagel's argument is followed the basic laws of physics that underlie both the ordering of the cosmos and, I would add, the current observations of a changing climate, point to the intelligibility of the existence of non-material agency as a viable alternative to materialism. While the conclusion that Aquinas draws that the non-material is a single absolute divine source that points to a common end or purpose is not strictly necessary in philosophical terms, it is at least intelligible.

In addition, it could be objected that Aquinas, in drawing favourably on Aristotelian philosophy about the eternity of the universe, is using an out of date cosmology that needs to be updated with reference to modern physics. But does objection to his use of out-dated cosmology necessarily require a rejection of his metaphysics? Further, it needs to be noted that in his historical context Aquinas was deeply conciliatory in that the Aristotelian thesis that the world was eternal seemed to clash head-on with the theological concept of *creatio ex nihilo*, which was first conceived as a defence against Gnostic and pantheistic speculation about the creation of the world. Aquinas, in insisting that *creatio ex nihilo* did not *require* a temporal origin was not rejecting a temporal origin as such, which he believed was a matter of faith, but rather broadening out the possible philosophical scope of *creatio ex nihilo* to its theoretical limits. In other words, attempts by scholars such as

Bonaventure to shore up belief in a temporal universe as tied to belief in *creatio ex nihilo* were not strictly necessary. Later Protestant writers would make the same move; Friedrich Schleiermacher, for example, insisting that *creatio ex nihilo* was more about the world's being held in absolute dependence than about its temporal origins.[18] Aquinas therefore insists on the importance of creation as the initiation and continuation of being considered together, rather than being tied to a specific physical cosmology. Some scholars have been tempted to identify the Big Bang theory with the first moment of creation, but Ernan McMullin is among prominent scholars who have insisted that, strictly speaking, this goes beyond what physical science can predict, quite apart from the hazards of identifying theology with a particular science.[19] The most we can say is that a Christian belief in temporal origins of the universe is consistent with a finite beginning.[20] And, if that is the case, then the laws of physics that apply to climate change originated at the same time but are an aspect of the natural laws of the world, rather than being identified in an absolute sense with creation as such.

Aquinas then develops a hierarchy in the ordering of being, from rocks through to intelligent life, and, ultimately, to humanity. While contemporary feminist scholars may find hierarchy objectionable, the increasing level of consciousness in different creatures is undeniable. More importantly, for Aquinas this points to an absolute Being that is the ultimate source of all such being; in other words, an ultimate Being must be the origin of being and existence *as such*. All things, other than God, have being that exists *by analogy* to the ultimate Being of God. The interconnection of all things that is characteristic of climate change comes through strongly in such an analysis, even if Aquinas's view presupposes a metaphysical approach to creatures that stresses both their accidental and essential character of being.[21] This discussion is relevant for climate change in a further sense, in that on theoretical grounds climate change, or any other change in creaturely existence, cannot on this basis undermine arguments for an absolute first principle of Being itself; namely, God.[22] Finally, while Aquinas believed incorrectly that the movements of the heavenly bodies were moved by intelligent movers to one *telos* or end, contemporary physics does support the idea of a degree of order and intelligibility and fine-tuning in the universe, even advocating an anthropic principle.[23]

The second article then builds on the idea of what it means for the first principle to give being, and this is explained through a reference to creation out of nothing. Objections to this idea are premised on the basis that creation concerns a change, which Aquinas rejects. Creation out of nothing, understood philosophically in metaphysical terms, means God makes things exist that are radically distinguished from God's being yet dependent on God for their existence. Given the lack of material causality, the natural character of the creature is non-being. For Aquinas the theological concept of creation out of nothing adds the idea of finitude to the philosophical idea of creation out of nothing, but this knowledge comes from revelation rather than reason. For Aquinas the radical dependence of the creature on the Creator is continuous, even after its coming into existence. He also argued, against most of his contemporaries (including, for example, Bonaventure) that *creatio ex nihilo* does not presume a temporal existence after non–being, as if there were a sequence of events prior to being. Rather, it is logically possible to combine the idea of *ex nihilo* and the eternity of the world, but Christian revelation indicates otherwise. Aquinas reasoned that *ex nihilo* means, at its heart, that the creature is ultimately dependent on God, so arriving at the conclusion of the possibility of an eternally created universe. This is also important in that it leads to Aquinas's conclusion that creation is not about temporal change; becoming does not in some fashion precede the creaturely making. This is important as a way of insisting on creaturely being not being dependent on material causes.

Creation is, however, in the category of relation, but this is non–mutual in that God does not undergo accidental change as a result of creation's beginning. He compares this to the relation between knower and what is known; the latter does not undergo any change as a result of what the knower knows.[24] Given this, changes in what is observed in creation, including climate change, do not fundamentally alter the relationship between God and creation and the ultimate dependence of the latter on the former for its existence. In other words, creation's being is still upheld.

In the third article, he concedes that, philosophically, some creatures may be used as instruments in the actual creation of other creatures. In philosophical terms, this is emanationism, giving the power of creating to creatures. Later he changes his mind and only concedes that creatures can conserve creaturely existence, rather than be a source of being. One creature can, therefore, be the cause of well–being for another.[25] The relevance of such a point for climate change is obvious, for we live in an interconnected world where anthropogenic climate impacts are a result of the agency of one creaturely species, *H. sapiens*, even though these impacts are not always recognised or acknowledged. Human beings cannot create the being of other creatures, but they are capable of conserving or destroying the well–being of another, as testified through anthropogenic impacts on the flourishing of all life, not just human life.

The fourth article stresses that the being of a creature, although originating from God, expresses a creature's actual existence and desire for existence. Bonaventure, unlike Aquinas, held that due to *creatio ex nihilo* the creaturely tendency, even after coming into existence, was toward an inherent emptiness, instability and mutability; only grace conserves creatures in being.[26] Aquinas, by contrast, insisted that creatures and the whole of the universe, and, we might add, the earth as a climate system, has its own being and that creaturely being tends to continue in being. This distinction is relevant in the context of climate change, for if the possibility of continuing in being is inherent in the natural world then creatures are autonomous causes. Creatures are causes in the sense of being determinants of that continued being. Here we find an elaboration of secondary causation; namely, that substantial and accidental changes are creaturely, but God is the ultimate source of being. The formal cause, or the inner shaping principle, does not need to be directly caused by God, but by creatures themselves. In Aquinas, forms do not pre–exist in matter except by potential but at the same time do not appear from nothing, as if God was a supernatural agent intervening and responsible for new forms. Becoming presupposes creation, but involves natural agency.

The importance of distinguishing creation from nature cannot be overstated, for it safeguards not only the discovery of real causes in the natural world but also the possibility of genuinely free agency.[27] On this basis, climate change represents changes in secondary causation as an outcome of free human acts, rather than representing God's abandonment of the world. Hence, it is possible to speak both of the dependence of the creaturely world on God, while affirming the significance of the impacts of human action. Further, such a view does not require God to withdraw from the world in order to leave room either for the action of creatures or even the creation itself.[28] Instead, the autonomy of creatures is an expression of God's goodness, as I will elaborate further below.

The fifth article takes up the theme of the temporal beginning of the world, and Aquinas resists the idea that the world is either necessarily temporal or eternal. For Aquinas, the idea of the time of the beginning of the universe has to be constructed in human imagination in order to make sense, but there cannot be a 'before' time. This paves the way for him to argue in the sixth article his theological account of creation in Trinitarian terms. So that on theological grounds creation can be claimed as being finite and out of nothing, but God as Father is the efficient cause, God as Son is the exemplar cause; that is, that which exists in the mind of the Creator, and God as Spirit is the one who conserves creation in being, as I will elaborate further below.

What possible contemporary objections might there be to the theological concept of creation out of nothing? Theological debates around the validity of *creatio ex nihilo,* especially those inspired by feminist theology, focus on whether this amounts to an oppressive *creatio ex potestas.* But the power that Aquinas speaks of is certainly not oppressive and would amount to a misreading of the tradition, since according to him creatures are also given their own autonomy, so their being is genuinely theirs, even if originating from God. As I will develop below, the fundamental movement in God's act of creation is one of love, rather than oppression. Replacing *nihilo* with the watery deep as in Catherine Keller's *creatio ex profundis,* drawing on process theology, weakens the concept of God so that God is no longer primary cause or Being as such. It turns, in other words, the *nihilo* into 'something' rather than 'not something'.[29] One of the arguments Keller uses for resisting the idea of *creatio ex nihilo* is that Genesis 1. 1–2 does not support or even imply this interpretation. Further, the passage in Genesis implies the presence of a watery chaos that is also supported by biblical scholarship that seems to superficially cohere with chaos theory.[30] Keller therefore rejects the idea of an omnipotent Creator and argues instead for a much messier beginning, arising from a 'churning complicating darkness' from which arise an infinite number of possibilities.[31] Her view of God seems inspired by a pluralistic account, showing a messy lack of uniformity even in the Godhead. Here the deity is envisaged as luring the creation into existence and the end envisaged is far from singular, but represents a multiple of possibilities. One reason for her resistance to a single *telos* is her view that such approaches can foster politically violent means for a single end. Her approach rests in stark contrast to, and is almost a mirror image of, that found in Aquinas, but is it necessarily more convincing or even appropriate in the context of climate change? A seemingly emasculated plural deity(s) that has little or no power of being seems to lack investment in creation; what does the lure of divine love really mean where the deity is so bound up with the process itself? Further, as I indicated above and will develop further below, God for Aquinas creates from an overflowing love; the power is the power of love, not the power of a tyrant. The 'single' end or *telos* that Keller finds offensive is one that promotes the flourishing of all creatures, rather than their demise, so it would be a misappropriation to justify violence as a means to this end. In the context of climate change, a lack of goal would undercut hope for the future, whereas clarity in a final goal or end of creation restores a sense of the reality of divine providence over creation and God's ongoing covenantal relationship with God's creatures.[32]

The apparent lack of support from Genesis 1. 1 for the systematic concept of *creatio ex nihilo* may be troubling for some, but other commentators have argued that overall the vision of God as radically distinct from creation is presupposed, so it would certainly be more consistent with the classical view of God and creation compared with the process view that Keller draws on for inspiration. Claus Westermann's monumental commentary on Genesis also concedes that *creatio ex nihilo* may not be spelt out in the text, but it does not exclude such an interpretation.[33] Paul Copan and William Lane Craig go further and argue that creation out of nothing is *demanded* by cumulative analysis of the Hebrew scriptures as a whole, as well as being presupposed in the New Testament.[34] Their position, however, seems untenable, given the textual uncertainties. Further, Keller's views are more like the emanationist views that Aquinas successfully argues against in his treatise. In her treatment, the clear distinction that Aquinas maintains between 'creation' and 'nature' is lost in a way that seems, ironically, to *undermine* creaturely agency, rather than to reinforce it. Hence, it not only collapses the distinction between God and creation, it also undermines the movement towards the hoped-for future that is inherent in a Trinitarian reading of creation.[35]

Jürgen Moltmann, on the other hand, in his doctrine of creation seems to position himself somewhere between the classic framework of creation out of nothing and process thought. On the one hand, he affirms the idea of *creatio ex nihilo*; on the other hand, he argues that this means that creation is also out of chaos, merging the idea of *nihilo* with *chaos*. This is philosophically and theologically unsatisfying in that once *nihilo* is equated with something rather than nothing, it compromises the sovereignty of God and undercuts the very dependence of all being on God as the deepest meaning of creation in the manner I have argued for above. This then leads to an equally problematic notion of the necessity for divine withdrawal in God in order to 'give those he has created space, time and a relative freedom, and he awaits their response'.[36]

The difficulty of Aquinas's account so far is not so much its rational cogency, assuming of course that a metaphysical philosophical starting point is still a reasonable one to hold, but its analytical approach does not readily include a portrait of how God acts as emerging from the rest of the tradition. In other words, God as Creator also needs to be thought of as an act of divine Love and Wisdom, rather than simply building on principles established through an analytical philosophy. In this respect, both Moltmann and Keller are correct to stress the fundamental importance of the love of God in the origin of creation and its continued sustaining. The difficulty in Keller's case is that there is a removal of any sense of God's transcendence, which for Moltmann is largely pushed into the temporal future, thus undercutting the profound metaphysical argument from the analogy of being that is integral to the classic tradition. Furthermore, Aquinas does not just restrict an account of creation to metaphysical arguments, he also provides a sketch of how God's love and wisdom can become incorporated into an understanding of creation. Though it is not as well developed or as well-known as the philosophical aspects of his thought, it is worth considering these aspects in order to develop a systematic approach to creation in more detail.

Creation through Love and Wisdom

In retrieving a classical account, a clear distance between God and creaturely being safeguards belief in God as the ground of all being, but does not develop the idea as to why God created the world in the first place. While Keller objects to the idea of *potestas* in *creatio ex nihilo*, what is more to the point is what appears to be a lack of *amore* when such accounts are treated in isolation from the rest of the tradition. Moltmann's solution to the perceived difficulties with *creatio ex nihilo* through *creatio ex amore* comes perhaps closest to the kind of position I am supporting here, except that it is not immediately clear how that love is shaped, nor does it necessarily improve on Aquinas's classical account.[37] In the case of the Trinity, creative power is 'common to them all', but at the same time the creative power of the Son is derived from the Father, and that of the Spirit from them both, so that

> to be the Creator is attributed to the Father as to one not having the power from another. Of the Son we profess that through him all things were made … Then of the Holy Ghost, who possesses a power from both, we profess that he guides and quickens all things created by the Father through the Son.[38]

He also acknowledges that it is 'Wisdom, though which an intelligent cause operates', and therefore is specially related to the Son, while *goodness* comes particularly from the Holy Spirit, who guides things to their proper end or purpose. The idea of goodness, as concerning a proper end or *telos* of things, is particularly significant, as it detracts from the idea of goodness as equivalent to moral perfection.

Given that the creative act of God involves all three persons of the Trinity, it is logical that a trace of the Trinity is also found in creaturely beings. Hence, Aquinas, drawing on Augustine, elaborates, so

[i]n all creatures, however, we find a likeness of the Trinity by way of trace in that there is something in all of them that has to be taken back to the divine Persons as its cause. For each created thing subsists in its own existence, has a form which makes it the kind of thing that it is, and bears on something other than itself.[39]

The fact of it being created speaks of the Father, its form speaks of the Logos, but in as much as it 'goes out from itself', it speaks of the work of the Holy Spirit as love. Creation is therefore not so much an exercise of divine power, where power is thought of as an imposition of God on matter, but rather an expression of simple dependence, so 'God's sovereign purpose is what the world is becoming'.[40]

There is a hint here, then, of the theology of Irenaeus, where salvation is inextricable from a theology of creation, and who spoke of the two hands of God, the Son and the Spirit understood as the Word and as Wisdom. But in this context Colin Gunton is quite incorrect to oppose Irenaean and Thomistic theology as sharply as he does when he states that Platonic forms are dominant in Aquinas's doctrine of creation and that 'Aquinas's trinitarianism is not strong enough to extricate him from the danger of a slide into pantheism'.[41] Aquinas's *Commentary on the Sentences* discussed above shows up another facet of his Trinitarian theology that strongly disputes such a view.[42] Here Aquinas carefully teases out the relationships between inner relations in God and that in creatures. In God, the term relation has the meaning of the 'being of the divine nature'. But, as Gilles Emery has suggested,

> Thomas does not only treat the divine relations in their efficient causality, but also as exemplar causes. The divine relations, and thus the distinctions which flow from these relations, are the cause of the procession and the diversification of creatures.[43]

There can be little doubt, then, of the strong role of the Trinity in the creative process. Furthermore, the first distinction between the persons of the Trinity is the cause of the distinctions that are found in creation. The plurality of persons in the Trinity provides a fundamental basis on which the abundant variety of life issues forth, including the plurality of genus and species amongst creatures and the multiplicity of individuals within species that was apparent even in the medieval era. What is significant, also, is that Aquinas linked this variety and multiplicity with the variety and multiplicity within history, both finding their ultimate source in the Trinity.

Creation and grace in Aquinas's *Commentary on the Sentences* therefore works through a double movement of coming out of God (*exitus*) and going back to God (*reditus*), so that God is the fulfilment of all life. He certainly distinguishes spiritual beings from other creatures, but whereas all creatures share in the life of God in terms of goodness, in spiritual creatures there is participation in the very *happiness* of God.[44] It is therefore wrong to interpret Aquinas as either excluding material beings from the life of God in a dualistic Neo-Platonism or, its opposite, failing to distinguish adequately between God and creation in Neo-Pantheism.[45]

The name that Aquinas gives to the ultimate purpose at work in the universe as a whole is the final cause. Further, the exemplar cause, or what is in the mind of the Creator, is not arbitrary, but the result of God's wisdom. He elaborates this further in the third article in the *Summa* where the first cause of things is discussed, so the 'configuration' of forms can be traced back to its

> original source in divine wisdom which contrived the world order consisting in the distinctiveness of things. Hence, we should say that divine wisdom holds the originals of all things, and these we have previously called the Ideas, that is, the exemplar forms existing in the divine mind.[46]

Aquinas clearly wants to hold onto the idea of an analogous relationship between creatures and Creator, while maintaining that creatures are 'never so perfect as to be like God according to likeness of nature ... nevertheless, they touch his likeness'.[47] Further, ideas and concepts can never be direct objects of human knowledge, but only exist in particular cases as exemplars. This is important, as it resists the reification of ideas, including even those forms existing in the divine mind, as substantive objects of human knowledge. The partial knowledge of causes and their impacts is equally important in relation to scientific theories and representations about climate change. Humanity's ability to abstract what appear to be universal trends from particular embodiments always needs to be qualified by suitable modesty as to its substantive nature. In this sense, wisdom is always accompanied by appropriate humility in the face of the unknown and unknowable.

If creation originates in the love of God, since it is not so much an act of need but is 'supremely generous' in order to share in goodness, then the ultimate purpose of creatures is 'a resemblance of divine fullness and excellence'.[48] When Aquinas speaks of the power of God, it is the power to create in love and in accordance with this goal in mind. Hence,

> power, which is supremely manifest in creation, is especially the Father's, so we stress that he is Creator. Wisdom, through which an intelligent cause operates, is especially the Son's and so we declare through him all things were made. Goodness is especially the Holy Ghost's, and so we acknowledge that he vivifies them and guides things to their ends: life is an inner spring, and the source is the end and the good.[49]

The goal of creation is therefore drawing creation towards its own life; its inner dynamism reflects the inner dynamism of the life of the Trinity.

One of the strengths of Aquinas's systematic approach to the relationship between the Trinity and creation is that he has managed to envisage a close intimacy between them, without weakening their distinction. The collapse of the immanent Trinity into a social Trinity is therefore not necessary if the full scope of his position is taken into account. He hints, also, at the idea of a dramatic relationship, where creation is the first moment in the overall drama of salvation history, rather than simply the stage or background on which that history develops. While there is insufficient space to discuss this in any detail here, the dramatic start of creation points to a hoped-for end, but it is one where human creatures as free agents in the drama also play a vital role.[50] Current reports indicate that there needs to be an increase in human ambition for taking action in climate change.[51] I suggest that Aquinas's map of the place of humans in creation, and his vision of creation as issuing in the free agency of creatures that are both autonomous yet vitally connected to the life of God, provides both the vision and incentive needed for such action. Such a view is premised on faith in God, but, as indicated earlier, philosophical reflection has also pointed up the paucity of materialist answers to meet contemporary social challenges.

If the natural world can be thought of as good in terms of its divine end, and as displaying beauty in a profound sense of an inner depth to things arising from its exemplar cause, then the space of creation is sanctified. In this context, as noted above, there is no need for a divine withdrawal of God in order to make space for creation in the way that Moltmann has envisaged. However, his reflections on sabbath rest warrant further elaboration, for they point to the sanctification of not just space, but also time. Both are relevant aspects of creation to consider in the context of climate change: space, as climate denotes the space of flourishing or demise of all creatures, and time, because through time climate change will progress towards an end according to the actions of human beings. What might it mean, therefore, to make time holy according to the sabbath of creation, which is the goal of the whole creative process in the book of Genesis?[52]

Moltmann used this idea to good effect in developing his ecological doctrine of creation. In the first place, he points out that God did not just rest from God's works, but rests in the *face of* those works.[53] It is, in other words, an appreciation of what those works are in themselves, a co-existence between God and works so that 'a finite, temporal world co-exists with the infinite, eternal God'.[54] The created order is, in a sense, vulnerable before and with God, but the mode of God's approach is one of enabling rather than intimidation. So, '[i]n his present rest all created beings come to themselves and unfold their own proper quality. In his rest they all acquire their essential liberty'.[55] But Moltmann goes further than simply suggesting that creaturely beings come to their fullness and most abundant form of life in God in the sabbath. Rather, he suggests, echoing process elements, that God

> allows the beings he has created, each in its own way, to act on him ... God begins to experience the beings he has created ... he "feels" the world, he allows himself to be affected, to be touched by each of his creatures.[56]

The crucial, critical, systematic question is whether such impact on God's being as such is really necessary in order to reinforce the concept of a loving, responsive God. The creaturely world is therefore not simply 'outside' God in some way, but creation becomes incorporated into God, so that 'He adopts the community of creation as his own milieu'.[57] But lest we think that he has verged rather too close to pantheism, he qualifies this by suggesting that the close intimacy suggested here does not do away with tensions or even opposition between created things and the Creator, or between created things themselves. Moltmann still insists on the Creator's transcendence over creation, but is this still coherent? If the works express transcendence, then the sabbath expresses God's immanence, so the eternal presence is joined to temporal creation. He goes further and expresses this philosophically, so that while the works of creation are a manifestation of God's will, the sabbath is a manifestation of God's being. Here we find that, in contradiction to Aquinas, who joins God's will and being both in the beginning and end of creation, Moltmann's development separates them. But Moltmann is not content just to leave the topic here; rather, he moves to express sabbath as consummation in the glory of God, the future hope of the whole creation:

> But the sabbath, in its peace and its silence, manifests the eternal God at once esoterically and directly as the God who rests in his glory. Creation can be seen as God's revelation of his works; but it is only the sabbath that is the revelation of God's self ... That is why the sabbath of creation is already the beginning of the kingdom of glory – the hope and the future of all created being.[58]

One of the reasons for promoting the glory of creation as a future sabbatical consummation is that Moltmann reads creation through an eschatological key. But this could weaken a sense of the profound ability of creation, as it is now, to express God's glory that we find in Aquinas. For Moltmann, the abundance of that life is not simply infused by God; rather, the fertility of creation arises from within and this activity receives God's blessing. But this shows up the systematic consequences of the divine withdrawal prior to creation that Moltmann advocates; for him, space has to be emptied of God prior to creation, which puts a distance between God and creatures that then needs to be filled or not. In Aquinas, no such space is needed, for he has a more sophisticated account of divine causation. But Moltmann is correct to point to the significance of the sabbath as a *time* that is blessed by God, hence inaugurating holy time into the rhythm of the week.[59] In blessing time, the sabbath blessing is available to *all* creatures, not just those who are intellectually predisposed towards attaining union with God. In this sense, his views are rather more palatable than the traditional, classical view of Aquinas in the beatific vision where only humans are capable of union with God. Nonetheless, in Moltmann's speculative rendition of the sabbath as a resting place where we find the unmediated presence of God, has the sabbath motif, while being constructively connected with the land and so in that sense grounded in ancient practices of cultivation and rest, become too detached from the historical basis of its emergence?

Some tentative conclusions

The increasing vulnerability that climate change presents is one that at first sight undermines the very possibility of the reasonableness of belief in God as Creator. If evolutionary theory did away with the necessity for belief in God in an evolved world, climate change seems to undercut the rationality, even for Christian believers, of a God-given created order. I have argued in this chapter that while such concerns are understandable, and a retrieval of systematic elements for a constructive theology of creation is certainly extremely challenging, the classic tradition represented by the writing of Thomas Aquinas holds up in the face of such concerns. His arguments are focused on what it means for God to be Creator, rather than on creaturely being as such, which is developed elsewhere in this volume. I have argued that of profound importance is his belief in *creatio ex nihilo*, where nothing represents non-being rather than something. While somewhat parallel to the arguments for the existence of God, his metaphysical position is still reasonable, even if its apologetic function is not crucial to consider in any detail. Prominent atheistic philosophers, such as Thomas Nagel, are currently open to the idea of a non-material cause in the universe. But given belief in God, an approach to God as primary cause is consistent with the basic laws of physics from which climate change can be deduced. Further, while his parsing out of creation in terms of efficient, material, formal, and final cause echoes Aristotelian philosophy, his inclusion of an exemplar cause brings a Trinitarian wisdom that I suggest is vital for a more systematic treatment of God as Creator. *Creatio ex nihilo* therefore protects, as it did in Aquinas's day, the transcendence of God over creation without losing sight of God's immanence, for without God all being would cease to exist. The life that we have is, therefore, gratuitous and flows from the overflowing love of God as Creator, expressed through wisdom and love in a dynamic and dramatic movement of the Trinity. Creation, therefore, incorporates the relation between God as Trinity and creatures; it is the first act in the overall drama of salvation. But, at the same time, creaturely being has its own real autonomy and that means that the responsibility for anthropogenic climate change rests squarely with humanity.

If God is argued to be an ever-present process in the lure of creation to its uncertain end, as in process thought, then the basis for God's action in the world and for God as a source of hope in the future becomes blurred. Where Aquinas's account arguably needed further development was in his eschatological hope for creation that still tended to be truncated according to a beatific vision restricted to humankind. Here I have drawn on Moltmann's account of the sabbath of creation in order to suggest, in line with biblical scholarship, that the crown of creation is the sabbath rest, rather than humanity. While I have not developed this aspect here, the rest of the sabbath is also one, arguably, that would instil an attitude towards the created order that would be beneficial in terms of resource use, and therefore help mitigate against the more damaging trends of climate change. Recent research suggests that local action on climate change has a cumulative impact on climate adaptation and mitigation, even where large-scale international

agreements break down.[60] The sabbath motif is about a localising rest and celebration of the creation that points to a hoped-for future. Furthermore, hope in
creation and in the value of that creation, as affirmed by belief in God as Creator,
will foster those attitudes and increase the resilience that will be needed in an
adaptation to the challenges that will be almost inevitable as we move into the next
phase of earth's history.

Notes

1 Marion Vieweg *et al.*, '2^0 Be or not 2^0 Be,' *Climate Action Tracker*, 30 November 2012.
  Available online at http://climateactiontracker.org/assets/publications/briefing_papers/
  2012-11-30_Briefing_paper_Doha.pdf (accessed January 28 2012).
2 European Environmental Agency Report, *Climate Change, Impacts and Vulnerability in
  Europe 2012*. An indicator-based report, No. 12/2012 (Copenhagen: EEA, 2012).
3 As in, for example, Michael Northcott's, *A Moral Climate: The Ethics of Global Warming*
  (Maryknoll: Orbis Books, 2007), and Sallie McFague, *A New Climate for Theology: God,
  The World and Global Warming* (Minneapolis: Fortress Press, 2008). McFague argues for
  her well-known systematic approach to the God/creation relationship where the world
  is envisaged as the body of God, which is built into the arguments in this book. But,
  notably, her argument for a different way of thinking about God, against the tradition of
  transcendence, is premised on ethical grounds; we have destroyed the earth as we have,
  she believes, imitated the God of transcendence understood in terms of power. While I
  share McFague's identification with those that are suffering the impacts of climate
  change, and the need to reflect carefully on the tradition in the light of that change, it is
  the premise of this chapter that a retreat to immanence without transcendence undercuts
  belief in creation just as much as belief in a Creator. Further, transcendence does not
  have to be parsed out through the language of oppressive power but through love and
  wisdom. It is, therefore, the misappropriation of the tradition that is the fundamental
  problem, rather than the tradition as such. Similar comments could be made with respect
  to Anne Primavesi, *Gaia and Climate Change: A Theology of Gift Events* (London: Routledge,
  2009). Primavesi also argues for a re-thinking of who God is, this time through the
  language of James Lovelock's Gaia hypothesis, combined with a post-modern development of life as gift. But, as I will argue in this chapter, the idea of life as a gift is also
  integral to classical interpretations and does not suffer from the systematic drawbacks
  associated with pantheistic approaches to the relationship between God and the world.
  Such challenges were just as rife when Aquinas first composed his treatise on God as
  Creator, so they are only 'new' theologies in the sense that they represent philosophical
  approaches that were not adopted by the early Church.
4 Serious discussion about climate engineering is starting to escalate. However, it seems to
  me that given that this is perceived as a response to a global emergency, this is just as
  likely to generate even deeper anxieties as to allay fears about climate change. See, for
  example an article supported by the National Academy for Sciences, Ken Caldeira and
  David Keith, 'The Need for Climate Engineering Research,' *Issues in Science and Technology* (2010) Available online at www.issues.org/27.1/caldeira.html (accessed 29 January
  2013).
5 For further discussion of this aspect, see Celia Deane-Drummond, 'Ecological Conversion
  in a Changing Climate: An Ecumenical Perspective on Ecological Solidarity,' *International
  Journal of Orthodox Theology* 3 (2012): 78–104.
6 Climate scientist Mike Hulme has identified four mythologies around which climate
  change discourse orientates itself: namely, Edenic, Apocalyptic, Promethean and The-
  misian. Where Eden is the orientation the language is one of lament, nostalgia and a
  return to a simpler and more innocent era, where climate is viewed as part of a fragile

natural world that is in need of protection. The theme of lament is taken up in Rachel Muers' chapter in this volume. But is the understanding of original creation as innocent and fragile correct from a systematic point of view? This chapter will consider frameworks for a classic belief in God as Creator and challenge such an interpretation of original creation. Mike Hulme, 'Climate Change: No Eden, No Apocalypse,' *Homepage Daily*, 30 July 2012. Available online at www.homepagedaily.com/Pages/article7820-climate-change-no-eden-no-apocalypse-by-mike-hulme.aspx (accessed 30 July 2012); Bill McKibben, *The Comforting Whirlwind: God, Job, and the Scale of Creation* (Cambridge: Cowley Publications, 2005).

7 Unfortunately, I do not have the space to develop this aspect in any detail, but see Celia Deane-Drummond, 'The Good, the Bad and the Ugly: Wonder, Awe and Paying Attention to Nature,' in *Aesth/ethics in Environmental Change,* Sigurd Bergmann and Irmgaard Blindow, and Konrad Ott (eds) (Berlin, Münster, Wien, Zürich, London: LIT Verlag, 2013), pp. 71–84.

8 Most notably in authors writing on Genesis 1. 1, such as Basil the Great, *Hexaemeron* 2:2–3, and Nemesius of Emesa, *On the Nature of Man*, 26, but also Ephrem the Syrian, *Commentary on Genesis 1. 14. 1; 15. 1* in *Ancient Christian Commentary on Scripture: Genesis 1–11*, Thomas Oden and Andrew Louth (eds) (Downer's Grove: IVP, 2001), pp. 2, 8–9.

9 See Gerhard May, *Creatio ex nihilo: The Doctrine of 'Creation out of Nothing' in Early Christian Thought*, trans. A. S. Worrall (Edinburgh: T&T Clark, 1994).

10 By the sixth century, the Alexandrian, John Philoponus, argued that the Aristotelian concept of infinity was incompatible with the idea of an eternal universe. See Richard Sorabji, 'Infinity and Creation', in *Philoponus and the Rejection of Aristotelian Science*, Richard Sorabji (ed.) (Ithaca: Cornell University Press, 1987), pp. 164–78.

11 David Fergusson provides a helpful summary of this development in the second section of his discussion on creation. He traces the emergence of the doctrine to the latter half of the second century, but Gerhard May puts indications of its presence rather earlier than this. However, in Fergusson's summary account of creation he rather too readily marries the evolutionary, scientific account labelled as asking the 'how' questions, with the 'why' questions addressed in theology. In as much as science cannot be anticipated to answer the 'why' questions this is correct, but it would be a mistake to presume that metaphysical presuppositions are not built into a scientific account of the way the world is. Further, in the biblical record at least, the quest for meaning is interlaced with an account of human origins and cosmic origins, even if the latter is not a primary objective. David Fergusson, 'Creation,' in *Oxford Handbook of Systematic Theology*, Kathryn Tanner, John Webster, and Iain Torrance (eds) (Oxford: Oxford University Press, 2009), pp. 72–90.

12 Augustine, *De Genesi ad litteram* 5.11.27, in *The Literal Meaning of Genesis*, trans. John Hammond Taylor, Ancient Christian Writers, 41–42, 2 Volumes (New York: Newman Press, 1982), vol. 1, p. 162.

13 Augustine, *De Genesi ad litteram* 5.5.12, vol. 1, 154.

14 See Rudi te Velde, *Aquinas on God* (Aldershot: Ashgate, 2006). Janet Soskice argues that Aquinas's discussion can seem remote from the loving God of the Hebrew bible, but, as I will show later, there are other aspects of his thought that ameliorate this criticism, and there are specific reasons why it is necessary to have a strong view of creation out of nothing. See Janet Martin Soskice, 'Creatio ex Nihilo: Its Jewish and Christian Foundations,' in *Creation and the God of Abraham,* David Burrell *et al.* (eds) (Cambridge: Cambridge University Press, 2010), pp. 24–39.

15 Oliver develops the relationship between creation out of nothing in Aquinas and his understanding of motion in a Trinitarian perspective. His linking of the creative process with God as Trinity echoes to some extent my own perspective, in that he argues that creation is the intrinsic basis of all causality, rather than causality as such. But he then takes this in a different direction, viewing Aquinas's position as pointing to a further elaboration of the Trinity. I prefer in the present context to see the practical implications for how to interpret climate change, since a doctrine of God is dealt with elsewhere in

this volume. See Simon Oliver, 'Trinity, Motion and Creation *Ex Nihilo*,' in *Creation and the God of Abraham*, David Burrell *et al.* (eds) (Cambridge: Cambridge University Press, 2010), pp. 133–51.

16 Explicitly, Aquinas, *Writing on the Sentences of Peter Lombard, Book 2*, Distinction 1, Question 1. This question is developed over six articles and the sixth article culminates the argument preceding in the first five, and elaborates in theological terms the concept of creation out of nothing. I am indebted to the commentary and the translation of this text in Steven E. Baldner and William E. Carroll, trans., *Aquinas on Creation: Writings on the Sentences of Peter Lombard 2.2.1* (Toronto: Pontifical Institute of Mediaeval Studies, 1997).

17 Thomas Nagel, *Mind and Cosmos: Why the Materialist Conception of Nature is Almost Certainly False* (New York: Oxford University Press, 2012).

18 Friedrich Schleiermacher, *The Christian Faith*, eds H. R. Mackintosh and J. S. Stewart (Berkeley: The Apocrophile Press, 2011), pp. 148–55.

19 William R. Stoeger, 'The Big Bang, Quantum Cosmology and *Creatio ex Nihilo*', in *Creation and the God of Abraham*, David Burrell *et al.* (eds) (Cambridge: Cambridge University Press, 2010), pp. 152–75. See also Ernan McMullin, 'How Should Cosmology Relate to Theology?,' *The Sciences and Theology in the Twentieth Century*, Arthur Peacocke (ed.) (Notre Dame: University of Notre Dame Press, 1981), pp. 17–57.

20 See further discussion in McMullin, 'How Should Cosmology'. The clash between predictions about the future in physics and standard eschatology that includes the idea of redemption of this earth is striking, as Robert Russell discusses in *Time In Eternity: Pannenberg, Physics, and Eschatology in Creative Mutual Interaction* (Notre Dame: University of Notre Dame Press, 2012), see pp. 53–70.

21 Joseph Owens, 'The Accidental and Essential Character of Being,' *Mediaeval Studies* 20 (1958): 1–40. An accident only exists in a subject or substance, such as colour, shape, relation etc., but it is accidental because it is said to possess accidental form. There are nine categories of accidents: quantity, relation, quality, being active, being passive, when, where, position, and possessing. There is only one category of substance. Substances are composites of prime matter and substantial form, while accidental forms inhere in substances. A thing's essence, quiddity or nature, however, is a composite of form and matter, so human beings have a body (matter) and soul (form), both of which are principles of things. Existence as such, on the other hand, contrasts with essence in that it expresses being. To make matters more complicated, there are ten basic categories of being.

22 The idea of an analogy of Being is developed in the thought of Hans Urs von Balthasar, but he proposes a double analogy of Being, so that God is only analogously related to Being as such, rather than equivalent to that Being. The use of analogy is helpful in as much as it provides a way of thinking about the connection, yet distinction, between God and creaturely kinds understood in terms of the speech of creation and the speech of revelation. See Hans Urs von Balthasar, *Explorations in Theology, Vol. 1, The Word Made Flesh*, trans. A. V. Littledale and A. Dru (San Francisco: Ignatius, 1989), p. 84.

23 There is insufficient scope to discuss this in full, but see the discussion in Russell, *Time In Eternity*, pp. 32–34. Russell also acknowledges that the Big Bang is consonant with the idea of *creatio ex nihilo*, rather than an absolute identification, p. 3. But, significantly, in modern physics the concept of an absolute beginning of the universe is now beginning to be challenged. Russell's concern in his book is about the destiny of the universe according to the laws of physics in a 'freeze or fry' scenario. Extreme climate change is more short term but just as threatening to life on the planet.

24 Paul Copan and William Craig object to Aquinas's view that God does not stand in real relation to things on the basis that this 'is to make the existence or non-existence of creatures in various possible worlds independent of God and utterly mysterious,' Paul Copan and William Lane Craig, *Creation Out of Nothing: A Biblical, Philosophical and Scientific Exploration* (Grand Rapids: Apollos: Baker Academic, 2004), p. 179. In view of Aquinas's insistence on the dependence of the creature on the Creator, and the act of

creation as one of love and wisdom, such a conclusion is somewhat astonishing. The authors are also concerned to conserve the temporal aspect of *creatio ex nihilo* and object to Aquinas considering that this is not necessarily required philosophically. What they do not appreciate adequately is that Aquinas does assert that *creatio ex nihilo* is temporal, but that this judgment is reached on *theological grounds*. Hence, to name the (optional) non-temporal philosophical requirement as 'the core doctrine of creation' for Aquinas (p. 148) is an unfortunate misreading of his position.

25 Aquinas, *Summa Theologiae, Divine Government, Vol. 14, 1a 103–109*, T.C. O'Brien (ed.) (London: Blackfriars, 2006), 1a Qu.104.2.

26 Baldner and Carroll, *Aquinas on Creation*, pp. 48–49.

27 Aquinas develops this thread in other works, such as *Questiones Disputatae de Potentia Dei*, Qu. 3.8, which addresses the distinction between nature and creation, and where he discusses twenty possible objections, including the idea that form is imposed on pre-existing matter by supernatural agency. That powers by which nature operates have their ultimate origin in God does not take away from the possibility of efficient causality in the natural world. As applied to human beings, this means that ensoulment is necessarily God's act, but it is not apart from a body and does not permit the possibility of pre-existing disembodied souls (Qu. 3.10). Nonetheless, plants and animals other than humans do not require a specific act of God for their ensoulment (Qu. 3.11).

28 This is one reason why Jürgen Moltmann's understanding of a prior withdrawal of God in Godself through a metaphysical *zimsum* is ultimately unsatisfying, even if he has, unlike many of his contemporaries, given much more weight to the significance of creation in his theology. He does, nonetheless, support the idea of creation out of nothing, but views *zimsum*, incorrectly it seems to me, as a deepening of this concept. See Jürgen Moltmann, *God in Creation* (London: SCM Press, 1985), pp. 74–86.

29 Catherine Keller, *Face of the Deep: A Theology of Becoming* (London: Routledge, 2003).

30 Joseph Blenkinsopp is unusual in arguing in his commentary on Genesis that the residual chaotic matter that seems to be presupposed in the Genesis account is also a menacing presence that is permitted some presence even after the work of creation. While fascinating, this implies a split between God and chaos that feeds into an unfortunate dualistic metaphysics. It does, nonetheless, cohere with Keller's account of creation out of the watery deep, though dualism is the opposite of her intention. See Joseph Blenkinsopp, *Creation, Uncreation and Re-creation: A Discursive Commentary on Genesis 1–11* (London: Continuum, 2012), pp. 20–53. Blenkinsopp also argues that Wisdom is created before the six-day account in primordial space, but he attests, controversially, that personified wisdom is modelled on the Egyptian goddess Isis. While I fully support the importance of the wisdom motif in accounts of creation, Blenkinsopp seems to be more enamoured by resonances with the cultural context rather than with seeing the Hebrew development of Wisdom in some respects as counter to such views. See further discussion of this topic in Celia Deane-Drummond, *Creation Through Wisdom* (Edinburgh: T&T Clark, 2000).

31 Keller, *Face of the Deep*, p. 9.

32 For further development of systematic theology for a changing climate in relation to creatures, see Rachel Muers, this volume.

33 Claus Westermann, *Genesis 1–11* (London: SPCK, 1984).

34 Copan and Craig, *Creation Out of Nothing*, pp. 71–146.

35 Keller, *Face of the Deep*.

36 Although Moltmann developed these ideas in *God in Creation*, he reiterates them in his latest book, *The Ethics of Hope* (Minneapolis: Fortress Press, 2012), p. 122.

37 For example, are the loving relationships envisaged for God founded by analogy on human relationships? For discussion of this and other issues connected with the social Trinity, see Tim Gorringe, this volume; and Moltmann, *God in Creation*, pp. 86–93. Moltmann's preference here for a kabbalistic notion of self-limitation (*zimsum*) and withdrawal in God as prior to creation seems an odd way to solve the problem, filling *nihil* with 'God-forsakenness'

and 'hell absolute death' (p. 87), even though I agree with his theological instinct to safeguard the distinction between God and creation, and with his intention to link original creation with new creation and to link that nothingness with the cross.

38 Aquinas, *Summa Theologiae, Creation, Variety and Evil, Vol. 8, 1a 44–49*, Thomas Gilby (ed.) (London: Blackfriars, 1967), 1a Qu. 45.6.

39 Aquinas, *Summa Theologiae, Creation*, 1a 45.7

40 Aquinas uses the word 'power' (*potentiam*) in ascribing the creative act of God the Father. Rowan Williams is correct in interpreting the language of power here as non-oppressive, for its ultimate origin is in the love of God. Rowan Williams, *Christian Theology* (Oxford: Wiley/Blackwell, 2000), p. 69.

41 Colin Gunton, *The Triune Creator: A Historical and Systematic Study* (Edinburgh: Edinburgh University Press, 1998), 102. He also states that Platonic forms or Aristotelian and Stoic *rationes* tend to replace Christ as the framework for creation. In making this claim he clearly has confined his reading to the first book of the first part of the *Summa Theologiae* and ignored the third part altogether.

42 Gilles Emery, *The Trinitarian Theology of St Thomas Aquinas* (Oxford: Oxford University Press, 2007).

43 Emery, *Trinitarian Theology*, 357. Material, formal, efficient and final causality bear an analogous relationship with each other (p. 344). While efficient causality is appropriated to the Father, formal causality is appropriated to the Son (335). Aquinas draws on Aristotle who understood the formal cause is what a thing is, the material cause is the matter from which something is made, the efficient cause is how a thing is made, and the final cause is the purpose to which it is made. However, Aquinas adds a fifth cause, namely, the exemplary cause, because he believed in the possibility of immaterial being in a way that Aristotle did not. The exemplary cause is the idea in the mind of the artist that exists prior to the work of art being made. In the case of creation, God is the exemplary cause.

44 Emery, *Trinitarian Theology*, p. 359.

45 Gunton accuses Aquinas of being in danger of both a 'slide into pantheism' and adopting Neo-Platonism, a criticism that seems somewhat incongruous as well as being a misrepresentation of Aquinas's thought. Gunton, *The Triune Creator*, pp. 102–20.

46 Aquinas, *Summa Theologiae, Creation*, 1a Qu. 44.3.

47 Aquinas, *Summa Theologiae, Creation*, 1a Qu. 44.3.

48 Aquinas, *Summa Theologiae, Creation*, 1a Qu. 44.4.

49 Aquinas, *Summa Theologiae, Creation*, 1a Qu. 45.6.

50 I have discussed the relationship between creation, Christology and anthropology in more detail in Celia Deane-Drummond, *Christ and Evolution: Wonder and Wisdom* (Minneapolis: Fortress Press, 2009). For further development of Christology, see Niels Gregersen, this volume, and for anthropology, Peter Scott, this volume.

51 Vieweg *et al.*, '2^0 Be or not 2^0 Be.'

52 Westermann, *Genesis 1–11*.

53 Moltmann, *God in Creation*, 279. He also reiterates these ideas in his most recent book, *The Ethics of Hope*, pp. 231–34.

54 Moltmann, *God in Creation*, p. 279.

55 Moltmann, *God in Creation*, p. 279.

56 Moltmann, *God in Creation*, p. 279. This raises intense debate about the passibility of God that is outside the scope of this chapter. Moltmann goes rather too far in spelling out what God may or may not experience in speculative terms. The point is that while this could arguably be hinted at in mystical writing, his work here is strictly systematic, implying that humanity does indeed have open access to such insights about God's inner workings in a way that is somewhat unconvincing.

57 Moltmann, *God in Creation*, p. 279.

58 Moltmann, *God in Creation*, p. 280.

59 I have discussed this aspect of the sabbath in other articles, notably, Celia Deane-Drummond, 'Living from the Sabbath: Developing an Ecological Theology in the

Context of Biodiversity.' In *Biodiversity and Ecology as Interdisciplinary Challenge, Interface 7/1*, Denis Edwards and Mark Worthing (eds) (Adelaide: ATF Press, 2004), pp. 1–13.

60 'Beginning at Home: Domestic Laws and Not a Global Treaty, Is the Way to Fight Global Warming,' *The Economist*, January 19, 2013, accessed January 22, 2013, http://www.economist.com/news/international/21569691-domestic-laws-not-global-treaty-are-way-fight-global-warming-beginning-home. While I agree that the local is likely to be vitally important, to give up on global treaties is not sensible, since, as the article itself admits, such attempts at global treaties foster local action, even where they fail to generate the desired political agreements.

Bibliography

Aquinas, Thomas. *Summa Theologiae, Creation, Variety and Evil, Vol. 8, 1a 44–49.* Thomas Gilby (ed.) (London: Blackfriars, 1967).

——*Summa Theologiae, Divine Government, Vol. 14, 1a 103–109.* T. C. O'Brien (ed.) (London: Blackfriars, 2006).

Baldner, Steven E., and William E. Carroll, trans. *Aquinas on Creation: Writings on the Sentences of Peter Lombard 2.2.1* (Toronto: Pontifical Institute of Mediaeval Studies, 1997).

Balthasar, Hans Urs von. *Explorations in Theology, Vol. 1, The Word Made Flesh*, trans. A. V. Littledale and A. Dru (San Francisco: Ignatius, 1989).

'Beginning at Home: Domestic Laws and Not a Global Treaty, Is the Way to Fight Global Warming'. *The Economist*, January 19, 2013. Available online at www.economist.com/news/international/21569691-domestic-laws-not-global-treaty-are-way-fight-global-warming-beginning-home (accessed 22 January 2013).

Blenkinsopp, Joseph. *Creation, Uncreation and Re-creation: A Discursive Commentary on Genesis 1–11* (London: Continuum, 2012).

Caldeira, Ken and David Keith. 'The Need for Climate Engineering Research', *Issues in Science and Technology* (2010). Available online at www.issues.org/27.1/caldeira.html (accessed 29 January 2013).

Copan, Paul, and William Lane Craig. *Creation Out of Nothing: A Biblical, Philosophical and Scientific Exploration* (Grand Rapids: Apollos and Baker Academic, 2004).

Deane-Drummond, Celia. *Creation Through Wisdom* (Edinburgh: T&T Clark, 2000).

——'Living from the Sabbath: Developing an Ecological Theology in the Context of Biodiversity', in Denis Edwards and Mark Worthing (eds), *Biodiversity and Ecology as Interdisciplinary Challenge, Interface 7/1* (Adelaide: ATF Press, 2004), pp. 1–13.

——*Christ and Evolution: Wonder and Wisdom* (Minneapolis: Fortress Press, 2009).

——'Ecological Conversion in a Changing Climate: An Ecumenical Perspective on Ecological Solidarity', *International Journal of Orthodox Theology* 3 (2012): 78–104.

——'The Good, the Bad and the Ugly: Wonder, Awe and Paying Attention to Nature', in Sigurd Bergmann, Irmgaard Blindow and Konrad Ott (eds), *Aesth/ethics in Environmental Change* (Berlin, Münster, Wien, Zürich, London: LIT Verlag, 2013), pp. 71–84

Emery, Gilles. *The Trinitarian Theology of St Thomas Aquinas* (Oxford: Oxford University Press, 2007).

European Environmental Agency Report. *Climate Change, Impacts and Vulnerability in Europe 2012.* An indicator-based report, No. 12/2012 (Copenhagen: EEA, 2012).

Fergusson, David. 'Creation', in Kathryn Tanner, John Webster and Iain Torrance (eds), *Oxford Handbook of Systematic Theology* (Oxford: Oxford University Press, 2009), pp. 72–90.

Gunton, Colin. *The Triune Creator: A Historical and Systematic Study* (Edinburgh: Edinburgh University Press, 1998).

Hulme, Mike. 'Climate Change: No Eden, No Apocalypse', *Homepage Daily*, 30 July 2012. Available online at www.homepagedaily.com/Pages/article7820-climate-change-no-eden-no-apocalypse-by-mike-hulme.aspx (accessed 30 July 2012).

Keller, Catherine. *Face of the Deep: A Theology of Becoming* (London: Routledge, 2003).

Martin Soskice, Janet. 'Creatio ex Nihilo: Its Jewish and Christian Foundations', in David Burrell, Carl Cogliati, Janet Martin Soskice and William R. Stoeger (eds), *Creation and the God of Abraham* (Cambridge: Cambridge University Press, 2010), pp. 24–39.

May, Gerhard. *Creatio ex nihilo: The Doctrine of 'Creation out of Nothing' in Early Christian Thought*, trans. A. S. Worrall (Edinburgh: T&T Clark, 1994).

McFague, Sallie. *A New Climate for Theology: God, the World and Global Warming* (Minneapolis: Fortress Press, 2008).

McKibben, Bill. *The Comforting Whirlwind: God, Job, and the Scale of Creation* (Cambridge: Cowley Publications, 2005).

McMullin, Ernan. 'How Should Cosmology Relate to Theology?' in Arthur Peacocke (ed.), *The Sciences and Theology in the Twentieth Century* (Notre Dame: University of Notre Dame Press, 1981), pp. 17–57.

Moltmann, Jürgen. *God in Creation* trans.Margaret Kohl (London: SCM Press, 1985).

——*The Ethics of Hope* trans. Margaret Kohl (Minneapolis: Fortress Press, 2012).

Nagel, Thomas. *Mind and Cosmos: Why the Materialist Conception of Nature is Almost Certainly False* (New York: Oxford University Press, 2012).

Northcott, Michael. *A Moral Climate: The Ethics of Global Warming* (Maryknoll: Orbis Books, 2007).

Oden, Thomas and Andrew Louth (eds) *Ancient Christian Commentary on Scripture: Genesis 1–11* (Downer's Grove: IVP, 2001).

Oliver, Simon. 'Trinity, Motion and Creation *Ex Nihilo*', in David B. Burrell, Carl Cogliati, Janet Martin Soskice and William R. Stoeger (eds), *Creation and the God of Abraham* (Cambridge: Cambridge University Press, 2010), pp. 133–51.

Owens, Joseph. 'The Accidental and Essential Character of Being', *Mediaeval Studies* 20 (1958): 1–40.

Primavesi, Anne. *Gaia and Climate Change: A Theology of Gift Events* (London: Routledge, 2009).

Russell, Robert. *Time In Eternity: Pannenberg, Physics, and Eschatology in Creative Mutual Interaction* (Notre Dame: University of Notre Dame Press, 2012).

Schleiermacher, Friedrich. *The Christian Faith*, H. R. Mackintosh and J. S. Stewart (eds) (Berkeley: The Apocrophile Press, 2011).

Sorabji, Richard. 'Infinity and Creation', in Richard Sorabji, *Philoponus and the Rejection of Aristotelian Science* (Ithaca: Cornell University Press, 1987), pp. 164–78.

Soskice, Janet Martin. 'Creatio ex Nihilo: Its Jewish and Christian Foundations', in David B. Burrell, Carl Cogliati, Janet Martin Soskice, and William R. Stoeger (eds), *Creation and the God of Abraham* (Cambridge: Cambridge University Press, 2010), pp. 24–39.

Stoeger, William R. 'The Big Bang, Quantum Cosmology and *Creatio ex Nihilo*', in David B. Burrell, Carl Cogliati, Janet Martin Soskice, and William R. Stoeger (eds), *Creation and the God of Abraham* (Cambridge: Cambridge University Press, 2010), pp. 152–75.

Taylor, John Hammond, trans., *The Literal Meaning of Genesis*, Ancient Christian Writers, no. 41–42 (New York: Newman Press, 1982).

Velde, Rudi te. *Aquinas on God* (Aldershot: Ashgate, 2006).

Vieweg, Marion, Bill Hare, Niklas Höhne, Michiel Schaeffer, Joeri Rogelj, Julia Larkin, Hanna Fekete and Carl-Friedrich Schleussner. '2^0 Be or not 2^0 Be', *Climate Action Tracker*, 30 November 2012. Available online at http://climateactiontracker.org/assets/publications/briefing_papers/2012-11-30_Briefing_paper_Doha.pdf (accessed 28 January 2012).

Westermann, Claus. *Genesis 1–11* (London: SPCK, 1984).

Williams, Rowan. *Christian Theology* (Oxford: Wiley/Blackwell, 2000).

6

CREATURES

Rachel Muers

Co-creatureliness and climate change

> Ecosystems will be highly sensitive to climate change ... For many species, the rate of warming will be too rapid to withstand. Many species will have to migrate across fragmented landscapes to stay within their 'climate envelope' (at rates that many will not be able to achieve). Migration becomes more difficult with faster rates of warming. In some cases, the 'climate envelope' of a species may move beyond reach, for example moving above the tops of mountains or beyond coastlines. Conservation reserves may find their local climates becoming less amenable to the native species. Other pressures from human activities, including land-use change, harvesting/hunting, pollution and transport of alien species around the world, have already had a dramatic effect on species and will make it even harder for species to cope with further warming. Since 1500, 245 extinctions have been recorded across most major species groups, including mammals, birds, reptiles, amphibians, and trees. A further 800 known species in these groups are threatened with extinction.[1]

> Bless the Lord all you works of the Lord:
> sing his praise and exalt him for ever. ...
> Bless the Lord all you of upright spirit:
> bless the Lord you that are holy and humble in heart.[2]

The use of the Benedicite in Christian worship brings the human being in at the end of the sequence of creation's praise – either, as Karl Barth says, belatedly,[3] or perhaps, as others have argued, as the culmination of the sequence of praises, the one who as priest of creation offers, in diverse ways, creation's praise to God.[4] In either case, the Benedicite, like all the Bible's narratives of creation, locates humanity as creatures-among-other-creatures. It directs attention to the scale, the power, the diversity, the unpredictability and the order of creation beyond the human. Human beings who speak or read these words find, like Job, that their attention is directed, in a sustained way, to every created thing *but* themselves; and only after this redirection of attention are they able rightly to return to themselves, in renewed holiness and humility.[5]

The theme of relocating humanity, and humanity's speech about God, among fellow-creatures who are analogously related to God is relatively familiar from the ecotheologies of the late twentieth and early twenty-first centuries – as well as from numerous strands of earlier Christian tradition. Indeed, it is a commonplace of theological anthropology to characterise the human being primarily as a creature, and from that starting-point to acknowledge, in brief or at length, the presence of other creatures with and to humanity. It is less common, though not unprecedented in recent systematic theology, to devote a separate chapter to 'creatures' alongside chapters on God as creator and the human being as a creature of a certain kind. In this volume, the inclusion of a chapter on creatures is intended to perform the three connected functions alluded to above in relation to the Benedicite and the book of Job.

First, pausing at 'creatures' has a critical function. It forces us to acknowledge nonhuman creation in its needs, desires, interests and relation to God. It precludes or interrupts a solipsism of the human, an exclusive focus on humanity as the source and goal of theological and ethical enquiry – as, in numerous dialogical and personalist theologies, attention to the reality of the other person interrupts the solipsism of the individual ego. This move is in itself theologically and ethically important in a response to climate change. It is theologically important, because (as will be discussed shortly) undermining anthropocentrism is a move towards the formation of a theocentric account of humanity and of the world. It is ethically important, because to recognise the threat of anthropogenic climate change is inter alia to recognise the catastrophic consequences of the exaltation over all else of a particular set of perceived human needs and interests.

Second, pausing at 'creatures' has the positive function of enabling us to attend to them – simply as they are, in their scale, power, beauty, diversity, unpredictability and order. This might, prima facie, seem to add little to systematic theology – rather as the extended attention to particular creatures in Job seems to add rather little to the point of the book.[6] However, recent work on the theology of creation, and in particular on the theological significance of nonhuman animals, suggests that this is too hasty a conclusion. More importantly, as I shall go on to argue, there is an issue here of *justice* in the doing of theology, with important though not exact parallels to the concerns of liberation theologies. If nonhuman creatures are not heard and recognised within theological texts – in their specificity as well as in a general catch-all acknowledgement – theology perpetuates a wrong.[7]

Third, pausing at 'creatures' locates humanity *among* the 'creatures'. We do not attend to the other creatures simply in order to learn who we are; their specific scale, power, beauty, diversity, unpredictability and order exceeds anything we could conveniently integrate into a theological anthropology. It is, however, the case that we only understand ourselves rightly when we know ourselves to be creatures-among-creatures, and can speak from within our particular set of creaturely relationships. Anthropogenic climate change strengthens the theological imperative to locate ourselves as creatures who experience, inhabit, depend upon, use and affect the creation. That said, the task of locating humanity among the creatures is clearly not just, or even not mainly, theological; knowing the multiple specific ways in which we are connected to the rest of creation is a complex scientific task.

It is important that this third task – knowing humanity as co-creature dependent on creation – does not overwhelm the first two, both of which direct attention to creatures in themselves, or better, in their relation to God. It is important, in other words, that theological reflection on creatures does not collapse into anthropology. Creation, in the Benedicite and its parallels (such as Psalm 148), praises God regardless of its utility or otherwise to humanity – or to other creatures. Scorching heat and freezing cold, as well as dews and rains, praise God; floods are as much part of creation as are springs. This biblical and traditional feature of 'creation's praise' has led theologians – including proponents of ecotheology – in the recent past to argue that the nonhuman creation praises God fully by being itself, and hence that creation's praise is heard *most* fully when it is – practically and theoretically – left alone and allowed simply to be itself.[8] In its context, this is an important corrective to the anthropocentric theology that allows nonhuman nature to relate to God only through its relation to humanity.

The context of anthropogenic climate change, however, forces us to re-examine or extend the idea of creatures praising God by simply 'being themselves'. This idea does serve to suggest that a theology of creation that starts from, and is limited to, fear for the human future will distort the meaning and value of creation.[9] However, the focus on letting nonhuman creation praise God by being itself makes more sense in the context of a stable 'order of nature', which acts as the relatively unchanging context for human history, than in a situation in which numerous nonhuman creatures are caught up in a process of historical change (catastrophic or otherwise). Our hopes of preserving or 'leaving alone' the nonhuman creation – or at least, those parts of it on which we are capable of having an effect – are called into question by anthropogenic climate change, just as much as are our hopes of improving, fulfilling or perfecting it. If the nonhuman creation that is directly affected by anthropogenic climate change continues to praise God, it does so not through humanity, nor even 'without' humanity, but despite, or over against, humanity. Arguably, in an era of climate change creation's praise carries, as David Horrell and Dominic Coad have noted, a note of judgement on humanity's persistent failure.[10]

In addition, a theology of creatures in the context of climate change must pay attention to the interrelation of praise and lament. Lament – recounting and calling before God the specificities of horrendous suffering and destruction – does not exclude praise. The creatures that praise God 'for ever' are not, themselves, 'for ever'. Praise is said to endure because its object is eternal, not because those who praise have a particular quality of endurance – although particular creatures, in their endurance, may serve as reminders of the fleetingness of human and animal life.

Furthermore, as Bauckham persuasively argues, texts evoking universal creaturely praise of God have an eschatological character; they look forward to the consummation of God's rule. In this context, the praise and exaltation of God points to what is true eternally and in God's future, but lament is a necessary response, in specific times and places, to the inner-historical destruction of creatures formed for God's praise. Hearing only creatures' *praise* of God and not their lament, in the context of anthropogenic climate change, risks another kind of anthropological solipsism – as if anthropogenic climate change were an event only in the history of humanity and not in the history of the inhabited world.

It is an assumption of this chapter, as of much recent theology, that nonhuman creation has a history with God that cannot be reduced to an epiphenomenon of human history. Creatures are the recipients, as well as the subject-matter, of God's promise in relation to both their preservation and their restoration to right relationship. It suggests clearly that the human future should not be considered – whether in fear or in hope – without attention to nonhuman creatures. The 'creaturely' approach to incarnation put forward inter alia by David Cunningham suggests one way to think this through; the lives of other creatures are not merely the backdrop for the human story, but are taken up with human life into God's story.[11]

At this point, however, we need to differentiate among creatures – emulating the texts quoted earlier (both the biblical text and the Stern report) by taking the time to attend to the complexity and specificity of nonhuman creation. Speaking of 'the other creatures' *simpliciter* is useful when the focus is primarily on the relationship between creatures and the Creator, but it is not very useful in an attempt to speak theologically about the creatures themselves.[12] In the rest of this chapter, I examine what can be said about various creatures, or dimensions of the creaturely realm, in the context of anthropogenic climate change.

Heavens, climate and weather

> Bless the Lord you heavens:
> sing his praise and exalt him for ever …
>
> bless the Lord all rain and dew:
> sing his praise and exalt him for ever.
>
> Bless the Lord all winds that blow:
> bless the Lord you fire and heat;
>
> bless the Lord scorching wind and bitter cold:
> sing his praise and exalt him for ever.
>
> Bless the Lord dews and falling snows …

The context of anthropogenic climate change invites theologians to pause in their account of 'creatures' where very few have previously paused – with theological reflection on the weather. In the Benedicite the weather – in its extremes as

susceptible to some degree of investigation or control.[19] As Welker notes in relation to the biblical concept of 'heaven', thinking about the creaturely interactions of these universal and relatively inaccessible forces challenges any attempt to definitively separate the natural and the cultural. We know that in the context of anthropogenic climate change and other forms of environmental degradation it is harder and harder to make the clear distinctions – beloved of earlier theodicies – between natural and anthropogenic disasters.[20]

Richard Bauckham, in one of the relatively few recent theological discussions of climate change to deal directly with weather, argues in an exegesis of the stilling of the storm (Mark 4. 35–41) that climate change reveals the inability of humanity to master the forces of nature – such as the storm – and the tendency of any attempt to do so to unleash destructive natural forces.[21] In Bauckham's analysis, the modern scientific-technological project is a sinful and failed attempt to 'still the storm' – or to control the weather (see God's challenge to Job, 38. 34–35). For Bauckham, then, a strong insistence on the common creatureliness of humanity and the weather is primarily the basis for a reaffirmation of humility. The problem with this analysis is that 'failed attempts to control nature' does not fully name the causes of climate change. Indeed, it is only since the problem of anthropogenic climate change has been identified that there has been much talk about concerted efforts to exert human power in relation to the weather (for example, through geo-engineering). It seems equally plausible to analyse climate change as the result of a failure rightly to inhabit and care for particular places – and to see the resulting 'storm' as an indication not simply of our inability to control the weather, but of our inability to perceive our connections to it.

What, having said all this, of the location of *God* 'in heaven' – a theme not only of biblical texts but also of centuries of Christian liturgical and theological reflection? What of the designation of events that are caused by relatively inaccessible and unpredictable creaturely forces as 'Acts of God'?[22] And what, in this context, of the relatively common contemporary belief, particularly among people whose worldview is not primarily shaped by the scientific paradigm, that the weather events associated with climate change are specific acts of God that can be recognised as divine punishment for human sin?[23]

On the more general point, God's dwelling 'in heaven' can be understood (as Welker argues), firstly through the relationship between 'the heavens' and God. Characteristics that the heavens possess in a relative and creaturely way – universal and differentiated relation to all earth's inhabitants, experienced presence and effectiveness combined with inaccessibility to prediction or control, formative power in relation to all life and history – are characteristics of God. The heavens, in certain respects, image God. It makes at least some sense, in theological terms, to say that God (as, for example, in the first whirlwind speech in Job) is encountered in and through encounters with the heavens and their events – at least by way of counterbalance to the well-established claim that God is encountered in and through the encounter with the fellow human being. Saying this does not, of course, compromise scientific understanding of 'the heavens'; the heavens (like the fellow human being) remain creaturely, and as such relatively accessible to human investigation.

This insight must, however, be separated clearly from the association of 'heaven' with creation's God-given direction, or, to be precise, with the *telos* of created reality insofar as that *telos* can be understood as a dimension of creation.[24] Theologically, the claim that events come 'from heaven' does not – as Welker makes clear – merely say that they are the result of universally effective, and significantly unpredictable, creaturely forces; it says that they make sense within the story of God with creation.

We can see, in this context, that the interpretation of extreme weather events and of the disruption of previously-expected seasonal patterns as divine judgement makes more theological sense than might at first appear to many Westerners. For example, this interpretation holds to the goodness and the God-directedness of weather, even in the context of anthropogenic climate change; it calls burning heat and freezing cold to 'praise the Lord' (even in the face of human lament). It makes the heavens and their events something more than impersonal and remorseless powers of fate. It locates evil, moreover, not in the created powers of 'the heavens' but in human action. And it expresses, at the very least, scepticism about the ability of humans to invent or reason their way out of the perceptible consequences of wrongdoing.

Moreover, on some level the attribution of extreme weather events to divine punishment acknowledges the shared creatureliness, and unpredictable interrelation, of earth and heaven within the creaturely realm. It calls humanity back, as it were, to earth, because it suggests that ways of inhabiting particular places on earth – virtuous or sinful patterns of life – have something to do with how the heavens are encountered and experienced, and should, in any case, be the main focus of human life and action. We now turn our attention, therefore, to the earth. Anthropogenic climate change affects, in different ways, the earth, the plants and all the inhabitants of the earth. We should pause to note that this is also true of various other anthropogenic wrongs that have commanded more extensive theological responses – such as warfare and economic injustice. It is, however, clear that anthropogenic climate change affects, universally but differently, all who live on earth and under heaven, to an extent that does not apply to many, if any, other anthropogenic wrongs.

The earth and the plants

> O let the earth bless the Lord:
> bless the Lord you mountains and hills;
>
> bless the Lord all that grows in the ground:
> sing his praise and exalt him for ever.

The ability visually to contemplate the earth as a whole as 'home planet', arising with the beginnings of space flight and coinciding with renewed global ecological consciousness, marks the latest shift in human imaginings of what it means to be *placed* on the earth. It is a long way, as Theodore Hiebert notes, from the 'placedness' of the Israelite hill farmers in their relatively small areas of fertile land surrounded by a threatening wilderness.[25] In both contexts, however, theology is done from a particular lived and imagined habitat – from 'earth'. The insight that humans (*'adam*) are made of cultivable soil (*'adamah*) has been picked up in recent ecological theology, not merely to inculcate the kind of 'humility' that should arise from being made of 'humus', but more positively as a starting-point for reflection on our creaturely dependence on fertile soil and habitable earth.[26] It is now relatively well established in scholarship that the picture that dominated late twentieth-century theology, of a Bible created by nomads for whom land, place and the cycle of the seasons were of relatively minor importance, is a distorted or exaggerated one;[27] and there is a growing body of research on the theological significance of land, understood as the particular habitat within and from which humans and other creatures live.

The fertility and fruitfulness of the earth – which 'brings forth' vegetation – is often identified in theological accounts of creation, and rereadings of the biblical narratives of creation, as a distinctive sign of divine blessing.[28] The sustainability of inner-worldly ecologies is a gift, at the heart of which is the capacity of the earth to 'bring forth' plant life as the basis for other forms of life. The close association between earth and the production of plant life, particularly food plants for humans and domestic animals, in numerous biblical texts could be seen as presuming a thoroughly anthropocentric account of the earth's value. In some ways it is not, however, significantly different from the contemporary naming of the earth as the 'blue planet', the earth's anthropomorphisation as Gaia, and other ways of associating earth and life. There is a persistent sense in human reflections about 'earth' – whether the specific land on which we live, or the specific planet on which we live – that the earth in some way *makes no sense* without life. This is not to deny the contingency either of the emergence of life as such or of the particular forms of life that emerged.

Barren or lifeless earth, both in the biblical literature and in contemporary ecological sensibility, is no longer earth that 'makes sense'. In numerous biblical texts, in the context of a disruption of the conditions of life and the increase of desert, the earth mourns.[29] This image is in part to be read through the close association of the earth's fecundity with the fecundity of women – the barren woman, in a context in which women's status is closely tied up with her childbearing, mourns her lack of social meaning and economic stability, and the barrenness of land is interpreted through this lens.[30] A theological account of earth need not take up the personification of 'the earth' as feminine – with the associated risks of gendered dualism and the essentialisation of female being. It can, however, recognise the importance of the capacity to bring forth life, to generate (relative) novelty and to replenish loss, as an aspect of creaturely flourishing. The loss of particular habitats – desertification, multiple extinction and so forth – is not only the loss of animals and plants but also the loss of capacity for the land.[31]

The prominent biblical theme of earth's praise and lament is also picked up in recent ecotheology, perhaps most notably in the Principle of Voice identified by the Earth Bible commentators: 'Earth is … capable of raising its voice in celebration and against injustice'.[32] Again, however, the personification of the whole of 'earth' may not be helpful on its own (suggesting as it does a common voice for the entire planet and everything that inhabits it – which risks again the unhelpful hypostasisation of nonhuman creation over against humanity). It is possible to think of laments raised by specific lands and places, that is, by 'earth' understood as multiple specific habitats. The effects of cataclysmic 'heavenly' events are, as discussed above, universal but differentiated. In the contemporary context, the lament and mourning of the Arctic and the lament and mourning of the tropical rainforests may relate to the same events, but they may also merit attention in their specificity, and in their different relationships to the particular places we inhabit.

Placedness is, clearly, a condition of creaturely life (including and especially, as the Stern Report extract above recalls, the life of plants, which are 'brought forth' to flourish in particular places). Being given a place to live, as a creature, entails being given particular relationships to other creatures – and firstly to the earth and to land – as the means of survival and flourishing. Co-creatureliness, for earth and its creatures at least, is not merely the incidental shared possession of a certain characteristic (being created), but rather, as *co*-creatureliness, a determining feature of proper creaturely being.[33] It is worth recalling here the other side of humanity's relationship to the earth as suggested in the Genesis narratives and in the name *'adamah* – a responsibility towards the land (not merely the whole earth).

Theology for a changing climate needs to reckon, not merely with humanity's and other creatures' reliance on habitat and place, but on the increasingly visible reality of lost habitat and forced displacement. Climate change threatens not the physical existence of the planet Earth or the cosmos, but the habitability of parts of the earth. The causes of anthropogenic climate change, moreover, can be read as a series of displacements; the ongoing 'displacements' of the fossilised deposits of plant life, and the construction and maintenance of ways of life that demand rapid travel and dissociation from the productivity of land.

The (other) animals

> Bless the Lord you whales and all that swim in the waters:
> sing his praise and exalt him for ever.

> Bless the Lord all birds of the air:
> bless the Lord you beasts and cattle;

> bless the Lord all people on earth:
> sing his praise and exalt him for ever.

I have suggested that the earth 'makes sense' – theologically and in other ways – as an inhabited place that nourishes plant life and hence the possibility of animal life. By the same token, animals, including humanity, make sense as the co-inhabitants of the earth. Animals seek, form and constitute habitats; that is, they have places to dwell on earth, they make places to dwell on earth and they are, in different ways that are dependent on location, part of each other's 'places' to dwell on earth, part of the ecosystems within and through which each other live. While there has been extensive and justified criticism of the theological accounts of humanity's creation that imply that the other animals are given primarily for humanity's benefit,[34] there is more to be said (theologically, ethically and practically) for the more general claim that the animals are necessary for one another's life.[35] In inhabiting places we help to make, and unmake, the habitats of other animals; we depend on them to make our places habitable. Complex co-habitation of particular places is such an obvious condition of animal life that it is easy to ignore – either theologically, if we focus on the relationship between humans and 'other animals' as a group, or indeed in popular environmental discourse, if we focus on the fate of individual species of charismatic megafauna.[36]

In considering the theological significance of nonhuman animals in relation to anthropogenic climate change, I continue to make the assumption that nonhuman animals are to be understood as in some sense co-subjects with humanity in the history of God with the world, and not merely as background or context for a human history.[37] This suggests, inter alia, that their theological importance as 'creatures' is not fully exhausted by the fact of their creation or by an account of their given characteristics. As has been pointed out in several recent theological works, nonhuman animals are, at least, partners with God and humanity in covenant (Genesis 9, Hosea 2. 18); apparent bearers of some degree of responsibility before God (Genesis 9); recipients of transformed life – that is not only related to their benefits for humanity – in eschatological visions (Isaiah 11); and prima facie included within the 'flesh' that suffers corruption and evil, is taken on in the incarnation, and participates in new creation. This should not, of course, be taken as an excuse for continuing the unfortunate and now widely discredited theological focus on history at the expense of nature and place, nor for a crude over-extension of the category of 'story' such that human histories provide the overarching framework for understanding nonhuman nature's change and development. The timescales of nonhuman nature's 'story' as a whole, and of the life-stories of particular species, do not lend themselves to easy assimilation into a historical narrative.

This should not be taken as a mandate for ignoring any and every distinction between humanity and the other animals. In fact, anthropogenic climate change draws attention to one rather crucial distinction between humanity and the other animals – humanity's collective capacity to endanger the continued existence of habitable earth, through failures of inhabitation that are also failures of co-habitation. Reflection – theological and otherwise – on ethical responsibility in relation to other animals has tended, for obvious and good reasons, to focus on issues of violence, killing and direct ill-treatment – and to say rather less about the responsibilities of cohabitation. The key exceptions are perhaps the theological and ethical literature on farming and animal husbandry, extending reflections on human 'placedness' to our relations with the animals alongside whom we live.[38]

The challenge in the contemporary context is that, by virtue of the universal and differentiated effects of climate change, human effects on human-and-animal habitats are not limited by physical proximity. We have something to do with the habitats of polar bears and desert tortoises, of clownfish and sea turtles, and of some 6.5 million as-yet-unknown species. It is possible that this expansion in human capacity to affect the lives of other animals at a distance relates to an expansion both of what we know as the 'inhabited world' (the entire 'blue planet' understood for certain purposes as a common habitat) and of the category of the animal neighbour – so that all creatures affected by human actions become 'neighbours'. The risk attached to this rereading, as suggested above, is that it colludes in displacement; it obscures the real differentiated forms of co-habitation with other animals that exist in different human communities, and it invites the pursuit of global strategies at the expense of responsible local action.

At the same time, it is important, as we reach the point of completing our account of earth's creatures, not to assume that recognising co-creatureliness calls for a return to original peace – or, in our present context, for the preservation of 'original' harmonious relationships between creatures in supposedly 'untouched' lands. The reality of anthropogenic climate change is, in fact, a stark and material reminder that (precisely because of the unmappable reality of co-creatureliness, the network of relationships that we exist within and do not control), nothing is 'untouched'. This can be said in relation to the depth of creaturely interrelation as well as its breadth. The co-constitution of habitat should not be seen simply as a matter of interactions between individual creatures and species with relatively stable identities. Against the long-term backdrop of creaturely interactions that shape the evolution of species, human actions and patterns of life have made – and continue to make – at least some of the other creatures what they are, and interactions with other creatures reshape the basic conditions of human being.

It is worth recognising in this context that the core biblical images of peaceable relationships between humanity and nonhuman creatures are eschatological as much as, or more than, protological. Alongside the Isaianic vision of the holy mountain (11. 6–9) we might consider here the important and under-discussed renewal of covenant in Hosea 2. 18–23.[39] Here God is represented as instituting a new covenant between humanity and nonhuman animals – particularly the animals that are *not* humankind's immediate 'neighbours'[40] – in order to restore both human security and the fertility of the land, in the context of a restored relationship between 'the heavens' and 'the earth' (2. 21). In the context of Hosea, the cause of the disruption is human wrongdoing (which, according to at least one strand in contemporary scholarship, can best be understood as socio-economic rather than only, or mainly, sexual or cultic).[41] The promised covenant amounts, on one possible reading, to a *re*-creation that reaches back even before the flood;[42] hence it draws attention, in any particular context of reading, to present failures and problems of co-creaturely existence, and to the impossibility of a final peace. At the same time, it draws attention to the everyday lived needs of humanity and the other creatures for one another, and to the ongoing reshaping of creaturely life by their interactions (for example, in the reference to crops bred and grown for food, Hosea 2. 22). It thus recalls not only the hope for new creation, but the urgent need for interim and local forms of peace-making to enable creaturely life to continue.

In the context of anthropogenic climate change, however, talk either of eschatological peace or of forms of interim peace-making may seem wildly unrealistic. One of the key questions about 'creatures' that is posed by anthropogenic climate change is whether the chorus of creation's praise will continue without many of its members (including, perhaps, without humanity).The history of animal suffering and of extinction has been taken up widely as a problem for theodicy, and hence also for theological accounts of creation, in a post-Darwinian world.[43] The specific problem raised by anthropogenic climate change is rather different, because it does not relate to the seeming necessity of suffering for the ongoing processes of 'creation' (the development of species), but rather to the prospect of the widespread and irreversible disruption of those ongoing processes. A theodicy that 'worked' (if that is an intelligible way to talk about theodicy) for the suffering of animals in natural processes prior to anthropogenic climate change would be in danger of being swept away along with the animals of whose suffering it spoke; evolutionary theodicies do not, prima facie, have much to say about a context of catastrophic mass extinction. True, evolutionary biology and psychology may provide some insights into the patterns of human behaviour that have led to anthropogenic climate change; this invites reflection, not on the role and justification of suffering in the evolutionary process, but rather on the problems that beset any attempt to read that process as progress. Anthropogenic climate change certainly calls into question optimistic narratives of the ongoing processes of creation, but it does so by undermining the presumed goodness of the end towards which the narrative leads.

In terms of a theological response to the suffering of creatures in anthropogenic climate change, perhaps the best that can be done at this point is to recall that theologies of creation – even the summons to creation to praise God – are of necessity developed from a context of fallen and preserved creation. They serve to direct attention both to the inescapable conditions of creaturely being (such as co-creatureliness) and to creaturely being's orientation beyond its own needs and survival (in the praise of God); but in doing so they serve prophetic and hortatory, rather than solely explanatory, functions. The loss of species and habitat is grounds, in the first instance, for lament rather than for theodical explanation. It may be that the furthest it is possible to go with a theodicy for climate change is to recognise that the chorus of creation's praise is a summation of creaturely time, rather than a snapshot of a particular moment within time (as is seen in the Benedicite, for example, with the invocation of the seasons). In this context, the real loss suffered and lamented by the land and its remaining inhabitants – including humans – in the extinction event is not a loss of the meaningfulness of creation per se. The context of anthropogenic climate change does not give us any additional licence to speculate about the ultimate *telos* of nonhuman creation.

Notes

1 Nicholas Stern, *Stern Review on the Economics of Climate Change* (London: HM Treasury, 2006), p. 80.
2 'Benedicite' ('Song of the Three Children' 35–65), version from *Common Worship: Services and Prayers for the Church of England* (London: Church House Publishing, 2000), pp. 778–79.
3 Karl Barth, *Church Dogmatics* 2/1:*The Doctrine of God*, trans. G. W. Bromiley (Edinburgh: T&T Clark, 1957), p. 648.
4 See for example Jürgen Moltmann, *God in Creation: An Ecological Doctrine of Creation*, trans. Margaret Kohl (London: SCM Press, 1985), p. 190.
5 See Celia Deane-Drummond's chapter in this volume for a reading of the book of Job along these lines.
6 I discuss this further in Rachel Muers, 'The Animals We Write On: Encountering Animals In Texts', in *Creaturely Theology: God, Humans and Other Animals*, ed. Celia Deane-Drummond and David Clough (London: SCM, 2009), pp. 138–51.
7 On the long and developing tradition of understanding environmental harm as injustice, see Willis Jenkins, *Ecologies of Grace: Environmental Ethics and Christian Theology* (Oxford: OUP, 2008), chapter 3.
8 See for example Richard Bauckham, *God and the Crisis of Freedom: Biblical and Contemporary Perspectives* (Louisville: Westminster John Knox, 2002), pp. 172–73; and the extended discussion of this approach in David G. Horrell and Dominic Coad, '"The Stones Would Cry Out" (Luke 19. 40): A Lukan Contribution to a Hermeneutics of Creation's Praise', *Scottish Journal of Theology*, 64/1 (2010), pp. 41–43.
9 It might, for example, ground a theological critique of the attitude to climate change evoked by the Stern Report's location of damage to ecosystems in a section on 'How Climate Change Will Affect *People* Around the World' (Stern, *Review*, 56; my emphasis). It could be argued that Stern's focus on the economics of climate change invited or even necessitated a focus on 'people', but the question of the proper scope of 'economic' concern is here begged rather than answered.
10 Horrell and Coad, '"The Stones Would Cry Out", p. 42.
11 David S. Cunningham, 'The Way of All Flesh: Rethinking the *Imago Dei*', in *Creaturely Theology: God, Humans and Other Animals*, Celia Deane-Drummond and David Clough (eds) (London: SCM, 2009), pp. 100–117.
12 Thus, for example, Robert Jenson (*Systematic Theology: Volume 2: The Works of God* (New York: Oxford University Press, 2001)) devotes a significant proportion of his chapter on 'The Other Creatures' to angels, and claims that 'when we have finished discussing them [*sc.* angels and heaven], we have said much of what must be said about the rest of creation' (p. 117). I suggest that this manner of proceeding creates (at least) some oddities in the chapter – for example, when responsibility to the creatures that are 'neither human nor angelic', all of which are dealt with together, is reduced to the aesthetic call to 'delight' in them (p. 130).
13 See, for example, Aloysius Fitzgerald, *The Lord of the East Wind*, Catholic Biblical Quarterly Monograph Series 34 (Washington: Catholic Biblical Association of America, 2002) for a detailed account of the close relationships between biblical theophanies (including, notably, prophetic portrayals of the 'day of the LORD') and the meteorological phenomenon of the sirocco. Theodore Hiebert, *The Yahwist's Landscape: Nature and Religion in Early Israel* (Oxford: Oxford University Press, 1996) observes the enormous significance in the J texts of the Hebrew Bible of the divine gift of rain, and of God's establishment of 'seed-time and harvest' (Genesis 9. 22).
14 Wendell Berry, *The Art of the Commonplace: The Agrarian Essays*, ed. Norman Wirzba (Washington: Counterpoint, 2002), p. 311.
15 Michael Welker, *Creation and Reality*, trans. John R. Hoffmeyer (Minneapolis: Fortress, 1999), pp. 33–44; and *God the Spirit*, trans. John R. Hoffmeyer (Minneapolis: Fortress, 1994), pp. 136–42.

16 Unfortunately, there is no reliable source for Macmillan's supposed reply to a journalist's question about what is most likely to blow a government off course: 'Events, dear boy, events'.

17 Welker, *God the Spirit*, p. 140; emphasis original.

18 Job 38. 26. This contrasts interestingly with Elihu's emphasis on seasonal rain as an available sign for humanity – Job 37. 6–7. See also on the weather in Job, Susannah Ticciati, *Job and the Disruption of Identity: Reading Beyond Barth* (London: Continuum, T&T Clark, 2005), pp. 108–9. For Ticciati, rain and frost, which unlike Job do not come from a womb or go back into the grave, indicate the 'surplus of validity with no meaning' in created reality – the way in which creatures exceed Job's capacity to integrate them into his symbolic world.

19 See, for example, Michael S. Northcott, *A Moral Climate: The Ethics of Global Warming* (London: Darton, Longman and Todd 2007); Stephen M. Gardner, *A Perfect Moral Storm: The Ethical Tragedy of Climate Change* (Oxford: Oxford University Press, 2011). This account of event-producing forces is not quite the same as – although it is related to – Walter Wink's influential characterisation of 'the Powers' (Walter Wink, *The Powers that Be: Theology for a New Millennium* (New York: Doubleday, 1999)). In Wink's analysis, the Powers, like the heavens, are creaturely realities that interact with and shape human (and animal) life, and are affected and shaped in complex and circumscribed ways by human activities. The Powers as portrayed by Wink do not, however, have *universal* (and differentiated) effects; they govern or affect particular places. To the extent to which this is true, they belong more obviously to the 'earth' (see my discussion below).

20 And see Peter Scott's chapter in this volume for a more extended discussion of the relationship between human agency and weather.

21 Richard Bauckham, *The Bible and Ecology: Rediscovering the Community of Creation* (Waco, TX: Baylor University Press, 2010), p. 170.

22 In legal terms, of course, the designation of something as an 'act of God' is intended primarily to indicate that nobody can be held responsible for it. It is a tacit admission of the limitations of human agency, rather than a positive acknowledgement of divine agency. Even this limitation of agency, as we have seen, is an important dimension of the biblical and theological tradition of reflection on 'the heavens'.

23 See, for example, the account given of the responses by villagers in Orissa to rising sea levels, discussed in Barbara Rossing, 'God Laments With Us: Climate Change, Apocalypse and the Urgent *Kairos* Movement', *Ecumenical Review* 62/2 (2010): 119–30. I am grateful to Celia Deane-Drummond for discussions on this topic.

24 As in Jenson, *Systematic Theology: Volume 2*, pp. 120–23.

25 Hiebert, *The Yahwist's Landscape*, pp. 3, 140–62.

26 As for example in Norman Wirzba, *Food and Faith: A Theology of Eating* (Cambridge: Cambridge University Press, 2011).

27 Apart from anything else, as Hiebert notes, nomadic herders generally rely on the existence of settled agricultural communities; very few people live on a diet without grain or fruit, and the main exceptions are not from the Near East.

28 See Welker, *Creation and Reality*, pp. 42–44.

29 As for example in Jer 4. 28 and 12. 4, Hos 4. 3, Joel 1. 10.

30 The classic discussion of the ecological significance (in the West) of the metaphor of the earth as mother is Carolyn Merchant, *The Death of Nature: Women, Ecology and the Scientific Revolution* (New York: HarperCollins, 1980).

31 This obviously recalls Aldo Leopold's argument for a 'land ethic' – see, for example, Aldo Leopold, *A Sand County Almanac and Sketches Here and There* (New York: Oxford University Press, 1949). I am, however, not arguing for the 'land ethic' per se, nor seeking to resolve the complex ethical debates over approaches to environmental management.

32 Earth Bible Team, 'Guiding Ecojustice Principles', in *Readings from the Perspective of Earth*, ed. Norman C. Habel (Sheffield: Sheffield Academic Press, 2000), pp. 38–53. See also the

discussion of the Earth Bible principles in Ernst Conradie, 'What on Earth is an Ecological Hermeneutics?', in *Ecological Hermeneutics: Biblical, Historical and Theological Perspectives*, ed. David G. Horrell *et al.* (London: Continuum/T&T Clark, 2010), pp. 295–313.

33 As becomes particularly clear in studies of the priestly literature (but is not applicable only to that corpus), the 'lists' of creatures that appear (for example) in Genesis 1 and Psalm 148 should be read, not primarily as laundry-lists of juxtaposed but separate items that are in principle extendable, but as diagrams of complex interrelated wholes. These are not 'all the individual things that God happens to have created'; these are 'all the members of creation'.

34 See on this, for example, David Clough's critical account of Luther's reading of Genesis – Luther focuses his account of the non-human creation on God's provision for humanity. David L. Clough, *On Animals: Volume 1, Systematic Theology* (London: Continuum/T&T Clark, 2012), pp. 23–24; see also David L. Clough, 'The Anxiety of the Human Animal: Martin Luther on Non-Human Animals and Human Animality', in *Creaturely Theology: God, Humans and Other Animals*, ed. Celia Deane-Drummond and David L. Clough (London: SCM, 2009), pp. 410–60.

35 Norman Wirzba, *Food and Faith*, describes this interdependence powerfully in terms of animal life's reliance on the *consumption* of other lives. The availability of suitable food (including animal food) is clearly a vital part of what it means to have a habitat; but ecosystems are more than food chains, and there are numerous other ways in which the animals form each other's lives by cohabitation.

36 I am not sure whether there are any charismatic megafauna in the Bible, though I would like to think that Behemoth, who 'eats grass like an ox' (Job 40. 15) and is unthreateningly intriguing – albeit not cuddly – would have made it onto the preservation list. Biblical whales, while mega, are not particularly charismatic.

37 I also assume throughout that there is no prima facie incompatibility between an evolutionary account of animal and plant life and a theological account of animals and plants as creatures, and I assume the accuracy (subject to the normal scientific provisos) of the former. See R. J. Berry and Michael Northcott, ed., *Theology after Darwin* (Colorado Springs, CO: Paternoster, 2009).

38 For examples of theological and ethical reflection on human 'placedness', on animal husbandry, and on nonhuman animals as neighbours, see Wirzba, *Food and Faith*; Christopher Southgate, 'Protological and Eschatological Vegetarianism', in *Eating and Believing: Interdisciplinary Perspectives on Vegetarianism and Theology*, ed. Rachel Muers and David Grumett (London: T&T Clark 2008), p. 256; Daniel Miller, *Animal Ethics and Theology: The Lens of the Good Samaritan* (London: Routledge, 2012).

39 I am grateful to Matthew Barton and Kris Hiuser for discussions of their work on this text.

40 That is, 'the wild animals, the birds of the air and the creeping things of the ground' – Hosea 2. 18.

41 See for example Alice A. Keefe, *Women's Body and the Social Body in Hosea* (Sheffield: Sheffield Academic Press, 2001).

42 The post-diluvian covenant in Genesis 9 does not include the 'creeping things of the ground.'

43 Christopher Southgate, *The Groaning of Creation: God, Evolution and the Problem of Evil* (Louisville, KY: Westminster John Knox Press, 2008). I do not myself see why evolution per se raises many more problems for theodicy than does animal suffering in general. On the wider problem of theodicy in relation to animal suffering, a *locus classicus* is Jay B. McDaniel's discussion of the plight of the 'backup' pelican chick in *Of God and Pelicans: A Theology of Reverence for Life* (Louisville, KY: Westminster John Knox Press, 1989).

Bibliography

Archbishops' Council of the Church of England. *Common Worship: Services and Prayers for the Church of England* (London: Church House Publishing, 2000).

Barth, Karl. *Church Dogmatics* 2/1: *The Doctrine of God*, G.W. Bromiley (trans.) (Edinburgh: T&T Clark, 1957).

Bauckham, Richard. *God and the Crisis of Freedom: Biblical and Contemporary Perspectives* (Louisville, KY: Westminster John Knox, 2002).

——*The Bible and Ecology: Rediscovering the Community of Creation* (Waco, TX: Baylor University Press, 2010).

Berry, R. J. and Michael Northcott (eds). *Theology after Darwin* (Colorado Springs, CO: Paternoster, 2009).

Berry, Wendell. *The Art of the Commonplace: The Agrarian Essays*, Norman Wirzba (ed.) (Washington, DC: Counterpoint, 2002).

Clough, David L. 'The Anxiety of the Human Animal: Martin Luther on Non-Human Animals and Human Animality', in Celia Deane-Drummond and David L. Clough (eds), *Creaturely Theology: God, Humans and Other Animals* (London: SCM, 2009), pp. 410–60.

——*On Animals: Volume 1, Systematic Theology* (London: Continuum/T&T Clark, 2012).

Conradie, Ernst. 'What on Earth is an Ecological Hermeneutics?' in David G. Horrell, Cherryl Hunt, Christopher Southgate and Francesca Stavrakopoulou (eds), *Ecological Hermeneutics: Biblical, Historical and Theological Perspectives* (London: Continuum/T&T Clark, 2010), 295–313.

Cunningham, David S. 'The Way of All Flesh: Rethinking the *Imago Dei*', in Celia Deane-Drummond and David L. Clough (eds), *Creaturely Theology: God, Humans and Other Animals* (London: SCM, 2009), 100–117.

Earth Bible Team. 'Guiding Ecojustice Principles', in Norman C. Habel (ed.), *Readings from the Perspective of Earth* (Sheffield: Sheffield Academic Press, 2000), 38–53.

Fitzgerald, Aloysius. *The Lord of the East Wind*. Catholic Biblical Quarterly Monograph Series 34 (Washington: Catholic Biblical Association of America, 2002).

Gardner, Stephen M. *A Perfect Moral Storm: The Ethical Tragedy of Climate Change* (Oxford: Oxford University Press, 2011).

Hiebert, Theodore. *The Yahwist's Landscape: Nature and Religion in Early Israel* (Oxford: Oxford University Press, 1996).

Horrell, David G., and Dominic Coad. '"The Stones Would Cry Out" (Luke 19.40): A Lukan Contribution to a Hermeneutics of Creation's Praise', *Scottish Journal of Theology* 64/1 (2010), 29–45.

Jenkins, Willis. *Ecologies of Grace: Environmental Ethics and Christian Theology* (Oxford: Oxford University Press, 2008).

Jenson, Robert. *Systematic Theology: Volume 2: The Works of God* (New York: Oxford University Press, 2001).

Keefe, Alice A. *Women's Body and the Social Body in Hosea* (Sheffield: Sheffield Academic Press, 2001).

Leopold, Aldo. *A Sand County Almanac and Sketches Here and There* (New York: Oxford University Press, 1949).

McDaniel, Jay B. *Of God and Pelicans: A Theology of Reverence for Life* (Louisville, KY: Westminster John Knox, 1989).

Merchant, Carolyn. *The Death of Nature: Women, Ecology and the Scientific Revolution* (New York: HarperCollins, 1980).

Miller, Daniel. *Animal Ethics and Theology: The Lens of the Good Samaritan* (London: Routledge, 2012).

Moltmann, Jürgen. *God in Creation: An Ecological Doctrine of Creation*, Margaret Kohl (trans.) (London: SCM, 1985).

Muers, Rachel. 'The Animals We Write On: Encountering Animals In Texts', in Celia Deane-Drummond and David L. Clough (eds), *Creaturely Theology: God, Humans and Other Animals* (London: SCM, 2009), 138–51.

Northcott, Michael S. *A Moral Climate: The Ethics of Global Warming* (London: Darton, Longman and Todd, 2007).

Rossing, Barbara. 'God Laments With Us: Climate Change, Apocalypse and the Urgent *Kairos* Movement', *Ecumenical Review* 62/2 (2010), 119–30.

Southgate, Christopher. *The Groaning of Creation: God, Evolution and the Problem of Evil* (Louisville, KY: Westminster John Knox, 2008).

——'Protological and Eschatological Vegetarianism', in Rachel Muers and David Grumett (eds), *Eating and Believing: Interdisciplinary Perspectives on Vegetarianism and Theology* (London: T&T Clark, 2008), 247–65.

Stern, Nicholas. *Stern Review on the Economics of Climate Change* (London: HM Treasury, 2006).

Ticciati, Susannah. *Job and the Disruption of Identity: Reading Beyond Barth* (London: Continuum/ T&T Clark, 2005).

Welker, Michael. *God the Spirit*, John R. Hoffmeyer (trans.) (Minneapolis, MN: Fortress, 1994).

——*Creation and Reality*, John R. Hoffmeyer (trans.) (Minneapolis, MN: Fortress, 1999).

Wink, Walter. *The Powers that Be: Theology for a New Millennium* (New York: Doubleday, 1999).

Wirzba, Norman. *Food and Faith: A Theology of Eating* (Cambridge: Cambridge University Press, 2011).

7

HUMANITY

Peter M. Scott

'Humanity' as a topic of systematic theology

In systematic theology, the discussion of humanity/human being/anthropology usually occurs after the discussion of creation and in preparation for consideration of the person and work of Christ. Located in this fashion, betwixt and between, the difference between the rest of creation/other creatures and the human creature (for example: reason, language, freedom) is usually noted; the *imago dei* may also be used to affirm this difference. Moreover, the fittingness of the human for incarnation identifies the human as the principal actor in the narrative of redemption. With this consideration of humanity comes a discussion of sin and evil, that is, of the falling away of humanity from its exemplary status, and of humanity's restoration in Christ. In other words, the motifs of creation-fall-redemption or nature-grace function as organising principles in the consideration of theological anthropology. Moreover, in modern European systematic theology, with its strong epistemic drive, anthropology may also be discussed earlier when, for example, considering the readiness or otherwise of human beings for revelation.

None of this seems especially promising in the theological consideration of climate change. Does not climate change press theology away from such anthropocentrism? For theological anthropology, does this not mean the re-consideration of the assumed centrality of the human in creation, reconciliation and redemption? In what follows, I assume that the answer to these questions is a qualified affirmative. Overcoming anthropocentric tendencies seems the most promising avenue to pursue.

In this chapter, I seek to locate the *topos* of humanity in the doctrine of creation – and not, as is currently fashionable, in the doctrine of the Trinity.[1] Nonetheless, the doctrine of creation in which I locate humanity is a trinitarian doctrine of creation and this, as we shall see, has important outworkings in the consideration of climate change. Moreover, I develop the theme and concept of 'the postnatural' to argue within theology that Humanity and Nature are not separate categories and need to be thought together.[2] Furthermore, the assumption that in the terms 'creation' and 'creatures' the human and the non-human are separated is a sort of theological laziness.[3] Not least, I argue that under the conditions of anthropogenic climate change, the weather is a hybrid phenomenon. Recent non-theological writing on climate change has moved towards this position also.[4] In what ways, then, may theological anthropology be extended into the contexts of climate change, in a hybrid thought?

A trinitarian doctrine of humanity in the context of anthropogenic climate change

In this section, I shall set out in a rough and ready fashion what I regard as the vital theological clues offered by a trinitarian doctrine of humanity for engaging a changing climate. That is, I try to present in a sequence – by reference to Father, Son and Spirit – how theological anthropology might be developed comprehensively.[5] What does it mean to say that the human is a creature of the triune God?

In the tracks of the Father, a doctrine of humanity may be understood in the context of God's creative activity *ad extra* that is *creatio ex nihilo*.[6] It is out of *God's* life that creation is called into existence. In that creative activity emerges – but never emanates – out of God's triune life of love, such creative activity is radically generative.[7] Creation is understood as other to God and so as dependent on God. Creation presupposes no materials or agencies other than God's activity. This has important consequences in the theological consideration of climate change. First, it bestows a hermeneutical freedom: in theological interpretation, we do not need to draw heavy, theological lines between trinitarian terms – e.g. person, translating *hypostasis* – and creaturely life. Between creator and creatures, there is a creaturely disjunction. What needs theological exploration is rather the breadth of creaturely life as given by God: the range of creaturely life in the creative activity of God. Theological attention does not need to be restricted to the human; indeed, it would be artificial to do so. Second, if creation is to be understood as the out-working of the reciprocal life of the triune God *ad intra*, then the opening of God to the Other in creation invites a response by that Other to God. Worship is grounded in this relationship of creature to creator but other modes of response may also be possible. Third, as the work of the triune Creator, the goodness of creation may be unambiguously affirmed. In other words, in that the operation is *ex nihilo*, there are no obstacles to God's creative activity, and the triune life is one of love. The affirmation of goodness does not mean that such goodness cannot be distorted – see the discussion of sin in Chapter 8. Also, the goodness to be affirmed may suggest that humanity's goodness may also be discovered or rediscovered in its common life with non-human creatures – see Chapter 6 – and also in non-sentient systems and processes – see Chapter 5. Moreover, vested in the disjunction between Creator and creature may be the implication that the goodness is limited, in a precise sense: spatially and temporally. Contemporary practices that assume that the planet's bounty is unlimited, and so that its goodness is also unlimited, may thereby be shown to be Manichean in origin.

In the tracks of the Son, a doctrine of humanity may be understood in the context of God's creative activity as social. That is, reference to the Son commends some *ratio*, pattern, *logos*, ground or frame by which creation is to be grasped. This is the order, stability or continuity of creation in which humanity participates, and which it represents and reshapes. In that humanity participates in this pattern, it cannot claim to know this pattern fully; it is informed *by* this pattern as well as informing it, and therefore lacks an overview. I have elsewhere argued that this pattern is best understood as social, and, as such, is an important guard against voluntarism.[8] Yet the social pattern, as founded in the *ad intra* love between Son and Father, and as renewed in the resurrection of Jesus Christ, offers important clues in the theological consideration of climate change. First, the pattern includes creatures other than the human. I have introduced the term 'postnatural' as a way of exploring the relationship between the human and the non-human in theological enquiry. Second, human praxis towards living needs to be understood along two dimensions, *bios* and *historia*. *Bios* refers to dependence on laws of nature (for example, gravity) and autopoeitic processes (for example, breathing);[9] *historia* refers to the contextual and relative ways in which human beings make a habitat for themselves. In any particular human society, these two come together in human praxes. Third, reference to the social character of the pattern requires attention to a dominant way in which human beings are social – which I shall refer to by way of an ugly phrase, the 'institutionality of humanity-nature'. The air I am breathing now – a reference to the condition of *bios* – contains pollutants created by (post) industrial society. And the structures in place in every society to meet primary human needs regarding food, shelter, childcare, etc., and the creation of new needs as a result of the historical satisfaction of primary needs – a reference to the condition of *historia* – requires institutional structures. In other words, this order is social in its fullest sense: as a life-ly and historical order that can only be understood in terms of institutions. (In order to measure the changing climate, fresh institutions – e.g. the IPCC – have had to be inaugurated.) In short, this order is not given but it does have specific institutional contours in any period. Fourth, that this pattern is renewed through death may have important implications for thought and practice in the context of climate change.

In the tracks of the Spirit, a doctrine of humanity may be understood in the context of God's creative activity as the practice of the social. In other words, reference to the Spirit invites attention to the re-ordering of the patterning of the social. If the patterning of the social is to be understood in terms of *bios* and *historia* in specific institutional forms, then the task of a theological anthropology is to re-interpret and re-practise the present institutional forms of the social. In addition, all that I have said about goodness above is re-affirmed. Moreover, the agency of the Spirit may be related to the movement of creatures, including human creatures, in response to the creative activity of God. A new theme is here introduced in that the Spirit is also an eschatological agent. The social system in which dependencies are acknowledged or obscured and needs are met is located in a wider framework of a co-operation towards a natural-historical good that may or may not be realised in history – an eschatological good.[10] Such co-operation is of course a political effort and thereby takes us into a consideration of politics. In theological anthropology, we are then confronted with the issue of the vocation of humanity and what might intelligibly be said of that vocation in the context of a warming climate. I shall discuss the matter of vocation later.

The contours of a trinitarian doctrine of humanity emerge: oriented on an extra-historical good, humanity practises its social life within determinate institutions that are also populated by creatures other than humans. These institutions are structured by humans interests in *bios* and *historia* but whether they serve those interests will need to be assessed. These human activities occur in the context of a creation judged good. In what ways might these theological understandings be clarified, extended and challenged by anthropogenic climate change in order to arrive at a more refined understanding of the vocation of the human?

Humanity in the context of anthropogenic climate change

It is tempting to construe my remarks in the previous section as general theological commentary and so to invite a response along the lines that systematic theology abstracts too quickly from its context. I hope that a careful reading of the previous section suggests that the theological anthropology that I am proposing has been fashioned, at least in part, in response to ecological issues as well as being loyal to theological traditions. Moreover, in this section I want to explore some of the issues that climate change raises for theological enquiry. We are in a period of transition and a theological anthropology may help illuminate such a transition. The basis of such illumination – the source of its light – remains *ex nihilo* of course; God's only 'interest' in this matter is out of love.

In his monumental *A Perfect Moral Storm: The Ethical Tragedy of Climate Change*, Stephen Gardiner identifies three clusters of issues by which he characterises the ethical challenges and dilemmas posed by climate change.[11] He calls these the global, the intergenerational and the theoretical. Taken together, they contribute to what he dubs moral corruption – a temptation to conduct moral enquiry about climate change in deeply self-serving ways – and together these are the perfect moral storm of his title. There is a fourth issue that he identifies – the non-human – but he does not discuss this matter in any detail.[12] This work seems likely, as far as I can tell, to set the standard in the field, so I want briefly to explore how Gardiner presents climate change. This will allow the development of my theological enquiry and will test whether the theological anthropology I am developing refuses anthropocentrism, denies instrumentalism, and thereafter encourages the re-institutionalization of humanity-nature and permits the development of an appropriate vocation.

Under the heading of the 'global storm', which is his way of presenting the spatial dimensions of climate change, Gardiner identifies three characteristics: (1)

the dispersion of causes and effects; (2) the fragmentation of agency; and (3) institutional inadequacy.[13] As regards (1), although every cause may be local, its effect is not restricted to its locality; a local cause has a global effect. The causes of climate change are widely dispersed both in terms of actors and places and so are its effects. As regards (2), not only are there many agents causing emissions but there is also no single political structure – for example, a world government – that might respond. Instead, we have round after round of international level negotiation between nation-states. As regards (3), even if agreement was possible between nation-states, no mechanism exists for enforcing sanctions flowing from any breach in an agreement.

Under the heading of the 'intergenerational storm', which is his way of presenting the temporal dimensions of climate change, Gardiner notes that the effects of human-generated climate change will take a long time to be realized fully; they are subject to temporal deferral. This, in turn, creates problems for agents and institutions: sustained action over the long term will be required and it is doubtful whether we have the institutions in place for such an effort. Moreover, the cost of emissions is deferred so the present generation has incentives not to act now and instead to enjoy the benefits that emissions bring to the present generation.[14]

Under the heading of the 'theoretical storm', Gardiner argues that ethical theory is not well placed to address the issues raised above – and some other issues besides. Within ethical theory, he notes the weaknesses of Cost Benefit Analysis; later in the book, he will discuss versions of Utilitarianism. As already hinted, he notes that there may also be an ecological storm in the sense that even efforts to undertake theoretical work seem ruthlessly anthropocentric and casually inattentive to the natural world.

Spatial, temporal and intellectual: this is an impressive set of problems! Taken together, Gardiner argues, they offer the temptation of moral corruption: to find ways within moral theorising of letting the present Northern generation off the hook.[15] Nonetheless, as presented, there are ways in which the analysis already seems incomplete.

Consider the matter of the ecological storm that Gardiner notes and claims has been insufficiently attended to by ethicists. In the lack of attention being paid to ecology, we may note that attention is focussed on humanity – implicitly, humanity as a species. In this, it is difficult, as Gardiner notes, to identify which actors may be linked to which causes. In turn, the ascription of blame, and the acceptance of guilt, is rendered difficult. Curiously, hybridity – the assumption that human and non-human creatures operate in mutually embedded networks mediated by machines – makes identification of human actors, and their causes, even more difficult. The assignment of blame within a network is not easy either. Add to these difficulties the likelihood that, as Clare Palmer points out, climate change will cause some beings to exist that otherwise would not have existed – either individually or through speciation – and we have a very complex picture indeed.[16] Nor is this all: Dipesh Chakrabarty has recently argued that humanity must now understand itself as a geological agent as well as an historical agent: ' … we can become geological agents only historically and collectively, that is, when we have reached numbers and invented technologies that are on a scale large enough to have an impact on the planet itself'.[17] Given that the human species now has something more than an interactive relationship with nature, Chakrabarty concludes that humanity is 'a force of nature in the geological sense'. Now, this is perhaps not quite convincing: to acquire the destructive force of nature is not necessarily to be a force of nature. After all, human beings do nothing without an infrastructure. Yet we shall need to take seriously the current human capacity to disrupt the networks and relations in which it participates.

If the spatial dimension (the 'global storm') as presented thus far by Gardiner seems unduly simplified, what of the temporal? Once more, Gardiner's analysis operates in terms of discrete units. At one point, he ponders how long – that is, how many years – should a generation be considered to be? 'Intergenerational' poses the question: in what manner might a discrete temporal unit be understood to have a duty to, or owe an obligation to, another? Yet this seems to be a restricted way of considering the matter. By beginning only from the present, it fails to notice how the present generation is, so to speak, a gift of earlier generations and is enabled – as well as dis-enabled – by earlier generations. We are already resourced by the past and we are resourced by our imagining of the future. We may in the present ask ourselves the question: how do we wish to resource the future? What satisfaction do we wish to take from our plans to resource the future? In addition, how do we wish future generations to evaluate our resourcing of them? The temporalities in play here involve memory of the past and invocations of the future.[18] Additionally, what is required is a community of memory and imagination that explicitly sets itself the task of remembering and imagining. Moreover, it may be that my presentation here is itself overly sanguine. As Chakrabarty notes, imagining a world without us invites us to an impossible task and thereby invites us to make leaps of historical *discontinuity*.[19]

Warming to the task: profiling humanity in the context of a changing climate

What have we learned about anthropogenic climate change in the previous section that will assist us in profiling humanity in the context of a changing climate? First, we are being pressed on the matter of scale. To be precise, we are being pressed about two scales: the spatial and the temporal. Let us consider each of these in turn. After the consideration of these scales, I shall ponder whether we can arrive at a more systematic profile and thereby offer the first stage in a theological contribution to engaging with the intellectual difficulties regarding climate change that Gardiner suggests that we face.

First, the spatial scale. Gardiner neatly disentangles the dispersal of causes and effects, the fragmentation of agency and institutional inadequacy. In my critical commentary, I wondered whether such a focus on humanity as a species properly identified the entanglements of humanity with its fellow creatures. Whatever we might think of his proposal, Chakrabarty points towards this by reference to humanity as a 'geological agent'. The scale, then, is somewhat different from that offered by Gardiner and closer to that offered by Chakrabarty: it is the scale marked by the tension between *planetary* and *global*.[20] On the one hand, we have the matter of human beings as an interruptive force on a planetary scale. However, the scale of global disruption must not be forgotten either: as Michael Northcott has noted, those in the South are affected disproportionately by the consumption of those in the North.[21]

Second, the temporal scale. Gardiner, as we have seen, was concerned to establish clarity regarding generations and the obligation of the present generation to later generations. In my commentary, I noted that the continuities may be deeper, and the discontinuities more interruptive, than Gardiner acknowledges.

Third, it would be tempting to argue that in anthropogenic climate change, two narratives collide. The first narrative identifies the freedom and autonomy of the human. The second narrative identifies the natural limits given with creaturely living. Somewhere in the tension between freedom and limits is the source of climate change. Any resolution, it might be argued, will require the curtailment of human freedom in the face of natural limits. Because of its investment in concepts of nature that stress givenness and inflexibility, it is tempting for theology to affirm such natural limits by reference to *non-relative normativity* grounded in a concept of nature. Nonetheless, to go this way is a mistake. Such a position is unconvincing if, following R. G. Collingwood,[22] we note that the core analogy for interpreting nature in contemporary study is historical. Just as human beings are natural so is nature historical. Instead, I shall argue for a postnatural position that does not contrast natural limits and human freedom. In sum, as Gordon Kaufman notes, we are biohistorical beings in which both *historia* and *bios* require elucidation.[23] A warming climate is a crisis both in our economic production and in our understanding of life.[24] A theological anthropology will theorise both sides of this duality. Sustained attention must therefore be given to the contrast between *life* and *economy*, in which these are not seen to be in competition. Chakrabarty puts the matter a little differently by drawing a contrast between *species thinking* and *critiques of capitalism*. However, I think that the basic point remains the same: what is the relationship between the conditions of life and securing the means to those conditions?

Fourth, although we are considering alteration of a climate, it is important to notice that what is presupposed by the reference to change is the stability of the climate: that, in sum, for a range of species in the Anthropocene period, including the human, the earth has been hospitable. Moreover, although the temperature of the planet may vary across a range, nonetheless this Anthropocene period remains a habitat for humanity and other creatures. This stability is not abstract but is rather given through hybrid networks of which humanity is a part. It is thereby part of the pattern of creation.

Fifth, and finally, the goodness of creation should also be re-affirmed. A warming climate is proof of the distribution of God's goodness through creation rather than a disproof.[25] That the created order may be damaged is in fact not counter-evidence of its *goodness*: it operates within certain limits and distributes goodness within these limits. If it could not be changed, the created order could not support life; it can be changed, and so can be damaged.[26]

What sort of human society makes a climate change?

In the previous section, I cheated. Although I announced a profile of humanity, it proved impossible to offer a profile only of humanity. Concepts such as 'planetary', 'hybridity' and 'goodness' required a postnatural turn. In this fashion, the dynamics of a trinitarian theological anthropology are beginning to emerge. Still, some account of human agency needs to be given. In this section, I try to address the question, what is the role of human agency? A certain theological temptation lurks here: to invoke limits, to claim settled structures. In what follows, I develop an account of normativity without invoking settled structures. After theological consideration of what sort of human society makes a climate change, I shall in the next section turn to human agency in a political context by considering the vocation of the human.

The human causes of climate change may be traced to human freedom in a specific postnatural configuration: social spheres in 'co-operation' with nature. Human freedom *simpliciter* is not the cause of anthropogenic climate change. Instead, what requires elucidation is the interaction of human freedom, a differentiated society and its interaction with Nature. It is in the interaction of praxis and institutions or spheres that the cause resides. This is the postnatural identification of society that causes the climate to change.

José Míguez Bonino's characterisation of creation is helpful at this point:

> Creation is the installation of a movement; it is an invitation and a command to man [sic] to create his own history and culture, creatively to transform the world and make it into his own house and to explore the configuration of human relationships available to him.[27]

Despite the objections raised by Skillen and McCarthy, who argue that this position is close to the Reformed notion of 'cultural dominion' (see Gen. 1. 26), Bonino's position is helpful. What needs to be grasped, contra Skillen and McCarthy, is not a *non-relative normativity* vested in natural structures or a fixed differentiation of social spheres as a counter-balance to creation as an installation of a movement. As already noted, this is the temptation that theology seems often to succumb to: falsely to identify some perduring structure and confound this structure with the will of God.[28]

In other words, rather than limiting the exercise of human freedom by reference to a *non-relative* 'normative structure of creation', what is required is the identification of *relative normativity*.[29] It is correct to say that this 'cultural dominion' position is inadequate by itself – here I agree with Skillen and McCarthy – but that does not mean that an account of creation order needs to be appended to it. Otherwise, we are simply back to the duality of freedom/limits, rejected above, with the doctrine of creation recruited in the service of the establishment of limits.

Instead, what needs exploration is the differentiation of social spheres in present society and the ways in which these embody, deny or obscure the postnatural *relative normativity* in their configuration. Peter Hodgson calls these 'shapes of freedom'.[30] At this point, we might speak of the requirement to transcend these social or structural spheres. This, however, cannot be correct as freedom, and the operation of the will required, does not extend beyond the human. Therefore, we arrive at a different and more accurate conclusion: the re-institutionalization of Nature within a theological anthropology that is also the re-institutionalization of Humanity. I referred to this earlier at the 'institutionality of humanity-nature'.

To try to theorise both sides, I begin with a concept of human freedom that is practical. By practical, I mean that the practice of human beings is situated, re-directive and yet open to cognitive and moral error. Practice here does not exclude the non-human but instead includes it.[31] In *A Political Theology of Nature*, I affirmed the subject-ivity and agency of Nature. This is not to say that Nature enjoys freedom for non-human animals do not have wills. Instead, non-human animals have intention, purpose and thereby agency. Given the commitments of creatureliness-in-common vested in the common realm, there is no actualization of humanity – no deepening of human freedom – except by way of Nature. The task then is to understand this claim in more detail and thereafter to find and fashion the form of human-and-animal society most suitable to this judgement. Such a co-operative society would be one that inhibits a warming climate.

To develop the claim that there is no deepening of human freedom without Nature, the ontological and practical shape of the human – its (re)productive work or activity – may be understood as irreducibly social. Such social activity encompasses not only the fulfilment of basic needs but also the principles, values, mores/customs and codes of conduct that resource and regulate the actions of individuals and groups in a particular society. The social system in which dependencies are acknowledged or obscured and needs are met is located in a co-operation towards a natural-historical good that may or may not be realised in history.[32] We have encountered this postnatural theme before.

What is the theological significance of the irreducibly social? It is the basis of the *relative normativity* referred to earlier in this section. If there are no transhistorical 'givens' – there are no non-relative normativities – there are nevertheless normativities vested in the densities of irreducible social patterns. These patterns exceed human freedom; they are, against voluntarism, more than instantiations of human willing. As such, they are postnatural dynamics. Thinking theologically about humanity in the context of a warming climate will go awry when attempts are made in theory and/or practice to disentangle humanity from its participation in its wider networks. Humanity exceeds itself not by separating itself from other creatures but by its participation with them.[33]

It is now clear why one of the identifying marks of the human is worship. For in worship the human creature moves beyond itself into the movement of God towards humanity. If creation has its origin in a movement between Father and Son, the opening of God to the Other in creating invites a response from creatures. In its most concentrated form, that response is worship: a recognition that the life of creatures has been received. Life under climate change remains a life that has been received and invites a response from creatures. Not least, such a response is a way of acknowledging that the contexts in which humanity finds itself can be neither fully comprehended nor managed. The theological basis for an affirmation of the precautionary principle resides here.

Becoming human in a common realm: vocation

In the theological profile of humanity offered earlier, there was no mention of the Spirit. The discussion of the Spirit has been deferred until this section because vocation directs us to the exercise of postnatural freedom and thereby to the Spirit. In a previous section I recommended that the task of a theological anthropology is to re-interpret and re-practise the present institutional forms of the social. In turn, this requires the reinterpretation of vocation. It is to this task that I turn in this section.

In earlier work, I have suggested that the vocation of postnatural humanity may be understood by reference to *citizen, representative* and *agitator*.[34] In exploring this novel formulation, I am eschewing other options such as steward and priest. These latter, in my view, are not easily detachable from the anthropocentrism that it is the purpose of this chapter to critique. What is required instead is a more embedded account of the human that nonetheless affirms human freedom and answerability in emphatic yet also limited ways.

In this trinitarian formulation of citizen, representative and agitator, the calling of postnatural humanity is to praxes in which humanity understands itself as *citizen* in a common realm with other creatures. It is only through this social ontology of creatureliness – that I have explored above with reference to institutionality – that the human represents the non-human.[35] As *representative*, the human is the perfect summary of the non-human but not its full substitute. The human may speak for the natural without thereby obscuring – or understand itself as obscuring – the human.[36] The praxis of the *agitator* is then to warn against attempts to understand the human as separate from other creatures and encourage acknowledgement of the multiple ways in which humanity participates in a wider creatureliness. Crucially, the vocational task is the identification of *relative normativities* which, if the argument of the fourth section is persuasive, are – as relative – never given ahead of practical engagement. The practical effort is an eschatological task – realising an eschatological good in history – and there is no guarantee that this task of realisation will be achieved. However, as we have seen, there are some clues as to the character of this good.

This good will be co-operative, while acknowledging the representative role of human beings in institutions. This follows from the stress on the social pattern of creatureliness that understands creatures in a co-operation. Sociality bestows stability; institutionality bestows protection. Theological responses to climate change do not fall behind this insight: anthropogenic climate change may focus on the agency of the human as regards culpability but never overlooks that the human is always already a participatory agent. This suggests especially that remedial action will turn upon epistemological modesty. Nor can it be denied that such co-operation will often be divisive: it may be that political alignments cross species boundaries with some humans sharing some political interests with some non-human creatures.[37]

This good resists the end of species while also accepting that the death of species – including the human species? – is not to be resisted at any cost. This is a delicate matter. I have located the discussion of theological anthropology in its usual home in the doctrine of creation. This has important benefits: the goodness and durability of humanity and its fellow species may be affirmed. The triune God supports creation as that which resists the end. Creation is not simply for consummation but is also for itself, so to speak. However, creation is not its own end – and nor is humanity. Thus it is appropriate for humanity to resist humanity's passing out of existence, as individuals, societies and as a species – but not at *any* cost, however. For the destiny of the human is to be a creature but also to be a redeemed creature, a this-worldly creature and a transformed creature. An at-all-costs defence of *this*-worldly existence is not required.

The matter of the goodness of creation has already been discussed by reference to *creatio ex nihilo*. The vocation of the human, interpreted theologically, will be to practise this goodness, while acknowledging asymmetries and distortions. As already seen, such goodness requires the conclusion that there will be limits within which humans and other creatures can live. Such limits are part of the *goodness* of creation. Present policy and practice that fail to address such limits of habitability are in fact Manichean. Vocation will demand communities capable of sustained anti-Manichean witness.[38]

This good will be ruthlessly attentive to scales, temporal and spatial. Such good is distributed through these scales, and is thereby hard to discern and engage. Some of the scales assume the absence of the human.

A trinitarian theological anthropology for a changing climate

The theological anthropology that I am proposing refers to a construal of the dynamic of creation that is always social and relational. Moreover, it is an account of human being that is inseparable from the relations between human creatures and other creatures. It gives an indication of the distortions of sin and maintains the distinctiveness of the human in creation. The human creature lives before, from and towards the triune God and this living is understood in developed ways both theologically and anthropologically.

Theologically, the locus is the doctrine of creation and the identification of the human creature by reference to Father, Son and Spirit. This permits the relating of the human to a wider creaturely life, the affirming of creaturely life as good and the movement of creaturely life towards its creator. That is, theological anthropology is not anthropocentric, does not derive its goodness from its insulation from the wider creation and is oriented outwards. Creaturely life, I proposed, is best understood as social, institutional and as moving along the two dimensions of life and history. The basic categories for interpreting human life are not restricted to the human and acknowledge the relationship between human history and the history of life. For the human, this requires reference to other species and the economic expropriation of resources. Finally, the vocation of the human is raised in the consideration of the practical effort of re-orientating institutions in ways that enable the realisation of an eschatological good in history-nature. In other words, the eschatological consummation that the vocational work of human beings prefigures is the consummation of creaturely – and not just human – life.

Although this is clearly a proposal of an *imago dei*, it is evidently an attempt to offer a much more capacious version in which trinitarian reference stretches the *anthropos* by reference to source, ground and direction. Anthropologically, this living out of the *imago dei* is understood as a creaturely co-operation. Moreover, it is from this co-operation – this social density – that we may ask after the quality of human living in its many institutional spheres as lived before, from and towards the triune God. Trans-historical norms vested in nature – either a human nature or a wider nature – are not part of the position being developed here. Moreover, from here we may enquire after a theological anthropology that presents the human as a creature that warms the climate and thereafter enquires after its vocation. I suggested that the vocation of the human be understood in terms of citizen, representative and agitator and might not extend as far as defending the interests of the human at all costs.

Throughout, I have shown how the human creature is identified by reference to the triune God and how the actions of the human creature as the agent of anthropogenic climate change, and as an inhibitor of such change, might be specified. Nonetheless, difficult issues – theological and anthropological – remain.

Among these issues are:

1   The achievement of freedom in the West is now a nearly irreversible development and, although not eliminable, is deeply embedded in our institutions. In all its ambiguities, it is one of the bases on which western societies understand them-selves.[39] This comports poorly with the integration of non-human creatures in my theological anthropology via the concept of sociality, for these non-human creatures are not free in the required sense. Clearly, the notion of 'institution' is offered as a way of bridging this gap – but how does it do so? How does the agency of the non-human and the freedom of the human co-ordinate in insti-tutions? The point can be put in terms that are more general: what is the point of contact between human freedom and non-human nature and if, for theology, the matter can no longer be framed in terms of active/passive, how should it be framed?

2   As Alan Weisman has noted, climate change invites consideration of a near future without the human.[40] I noted this above when indicating that the tem-poral scale that climate change requires the theologian to work with contains discontinuities, including a future without the human. Nonetheless, theological

anthropology has often been interpreted as preparatory for the incarnation – and in a fuller presentation of a theological anthropology, discussion of the incarnation would be required. The doctrine of the incarnation is usually interpreted as indicating that the human is a summary of creation – and my account of representation has suggested as much. A future without the human is, theologically speaking, a *different* future. Nor do I consider that such difference is overcome – although it is reduced – if we hold to the view that the redemption of the non-human is not via the human. Alternatively, could it be said that, after the ascension, humanity is never lost to God, and so a world without the human is a world whose future is given by the God who – holding the spiritual body of Jesus Christ – already has humanity's future? A different eschatology now hoves into view: an eschatology of the ascension in which a future of the world without the human is not one of loss but instead one of absence. Wherein lies the difference? To speak of the absence of the human is not to deny the goodness of what remains, so to speak. Although the human is the summary of creation, and speaks for creation, the human does not substitute for the rest of creation nor obscure the rest of creation. Moreover, this has implications for human action: if, by the ascension, God already has the future of humanity, humanity should not understand itself as provoked into efforts to 'save the world'. The survival of the human race is not the ultimate aim as its 'survival' is assured and its absence does not qualify negatively the goodness of creation. This is in strong contrast to an eschaton of the Rapture which also envisages a world without the presence of the human but here the non-presence of the human is understood in terms of loss – with the subsequent devaluing of the 'creaturely remnants'. Additionally, the account of human action that follows is world-denying ('when you've seen one redwood you've seen them all') and, in a secular variant, strongly activist in a desire to 'save the world'.

3 If the politics of vocation sketched above is not to be hopeless, its politics requires further detail in two respects. First, in what precise way does humanity represent the non-human? This seems to me to be a crucial question and must presumably be answered by reference to institutions. At what level of society will these institutions be found, and by which principles will they be organised? Is the nation such an institution or are institutions that are more global or more local required? Second, in order to address the way that the effects of climate change are unequally distributed, should a preferential option be part of vocation? If yes, how might the option be adapted for non-human creatures? Will attention to representation – my first point – be sufficient? To address both these points, new social forms – I shall call them 'critical institutions' – are required. These institutions will be critical in two senses. As postnatural institutions, they will theorise their own 'natural conditions' by indicating how as instantiations of freedom, this freedom is also a construal of nature's 'freedom'. Additionally, these critical institutions will seek to enlarge the freedom of those creatures most restricted by climate change.

4 In the context of a changing climate, what is the meaning and force of the teleological discourse that I employed above in the context of a discussion of goodness? Teleological language in the context of climate change is especially confusing because included in the direction of a warming climate is speciation – should we object to that? A warming climate means that some species will thrive – should we object to that? Some species will pass out of existence quicker – which ones should we mourn, and why? Some individuals will come into existence that would otherwise not have – what is the significance of that? Should the vocation of the human be to side with creation and thereby to resist the end, as I suggested above, and how does that relate to teleological discourse? The matter is made more complex if we attempt to theorise *historia* alongside *bios*. For teleological discourse is not restricted to the conditions of life but also attends to the historicity of the human and the good encountered in history. However, history is no abstraction but is in part the work of human creatures. Production for exchange dominates our understanding of work and is intimately related to a warming climate – how does this relate to teleology?

These questions, and the earlier analysis out of which they emerge, suggest the full response to climate change will be, for want of a better word, cultural. That the climate is warming is a contingent cultural event with deep historical, including theological, roots. I have suggested some resources from theological anthropology – a revised theological anthropology – that may assist in the task of understanding the cultural roots of this event and offer some hope of a new direction.

Notes

1 David Kelsey argues that the doctrine of creation is the traditional location of theological anthropology. However, in his survey, theological anthropology has recently migrated to the doctrine of incarnate grace and then to eschatology and next to the doctrine of the Trinity. See David Kelsey, 'The Human Creature', in J. Webster, K. Tanner, I. Torrance (eds), *The Oxford Handbook of Systematic Theology* (Oxford: OUP, 2007), pp. 121–39 (here pages 122–24).

2 P. M. Scott, *Anti-human Theology: Nature, Technology and the Postnatural* (London: SCM Press, 2010).

3 Cf. Muers, 'Creatures', pp. 91–2, this volume, for a three-fold theological rebuttal of such laziness: acknowledgement of other creatures; attending to other creatures; the co-location of humanity among other creatures.

4 Dipesh Chakrabarty, 'The Climate of History: Four Theses', *Critical Inquiry* 35 (Winter 2009), pp. 197–222; Mike Hulme, 'Cosmopolitan Cultures: Hybridity, Foresight and Meaning', *Theory, Culture and Society* 27, 2–3 (2010), pp. 267–76. I thank Stefan Skrimshire for drawing these articles to my attention.

5 In making this presentation, I draw on David H. Kelsey, *Eccentric Existence: A Theological Anthropology*, volume 1 (Louisville, KY: Westminster/John Knox Press, 2010), pp. 122–25, and Scott, *A Political Theology of Nature*, pp. 20–25 and pp. 173–200.

6 Negatively, *ex nihilo* refuses the eternity of matter and creation as emanation; positively and trinitarianly, it commends the view that creation is related to the triune God and so has a 'shape and character consistent with the divine life', David Fergusson, 'Creation', in

J. Webster, K. Tanner, I. Torrance (eds), *The Oxford Handbook of Systematic Theology*, pp. 72–90 (here page 81).

7 In the last quarter of the twentieth century, *creatio ex nihilo* has been subjected to sustained criticism: does the disjunction of God and world vested in *ex nihilo* somehow undermine the value of the latter? See Whitney Bauman, *Theology, Creation and Environmental Ethics: From Creatio ex nihilo to terra nullius* (New York and London: Routledge, 2009).

8 A different guard against voluntarism is the consistency of God's engagement with the world; on this, see Gorringe, 'Trinity', this volume.

9 See Niels Henrik Gregersen, 'Christology', this volume.

10 P. M. Scott, 'Right out of time? Politics and Nature in a Postnatural Condition', in C. Deane-Drummond and Heinrich Bedford-Strohm (eds), *Religion and Ecology in the Public Sphere* (London: Continuum, 2011), pp. 57–75.

11 Stephen M. Gardiner, *A Perfect Moral Storm: The Ethical Tragedy of Climate Change* (New York: Oxford University Press, 2011).

12 Gardiner, *A Perfect Moral Storm*, pp. 43–44.

13 Gardiner, *A Perfect Moral Storm*, pp. 24–29.

14 Gardiner, *A Perfect Moral Storm*, pp. 32–34. In fact, Gardiner contends that the matter is worse than this but I do not need the detail for my analysis.

15 Cf. Messer, 'Sin and salvation', p. 132, this volume.

16 Clare Palmer, 'Does nature matter? The place of the nonhuman in the ethics of climate change', in Denis G. Arnold (ed.), *The Ethics of Global Climate Change* (Cambridge: Cambridge University Press, 2011), pp. 272–91 (here page 275).

17 Dipesh Chakrabarty, 'The Climate of History: Four Theses', *Critical Inquiry* 35 (Winter 2009): 197–222 (here page 206).

18 P. M. Scott, 'The future as God's amnesty? A public theology of resistance for a changing climate', *International Journal of Public Theology* 4, 3 (2010): 314–31.

19 Chakrabarty, 'The Climate of History', p. 198.

20 Chakrabarty, 'The Climate of History', p. 199.

21 Michael S. Northcott, *A Moral Climate* (London: DLT, 2009).

22 R. G. Collingwood, *The Idea of Nature* (Oxford: OUP, 1960 [1945]), part III.

23 Gordon D. Kaufman, *In Face of Mystery: A Constructive Theology* (Cambridge, MA: Harvard University Press, 1993), p. 97ff.

24 P. M. Scott, 'Thinking like an Animal: Theological Materialism for a Changing Climate', *Studies in Christian Ethics* 24, 1 (2011), pp. 50–66 (here page 54).

25 Scott, 'Thinking like an Animal', pp. 60–62.

26 Cf. Skrimshire, 'Eschatology', p. 161, this volume.

27 J. M. Bonino, *Doing Theology in a Revolutionary Situation* (Philadelphia: Fortress Press, 1975), 166.

28 Here lies the most troubling voluntarism, presented as the form of creatureliness: identifying a concept of nature or creation, and attributing this to the will of God, is a form of voluntarism but of a de-historicising – and thereafter oppressive – kind.

29 James W. Skillen and Rockne M. McCarthy, 'History, the unfolding of society and human fulfilment: an evaluation', in Skillen and McCarthy (eds), *Political Order and the Plural Structure of Society* (Grand Rapids, MI: Eerdmans, 1991), p. 371.

30 Peter C. Hodgson, *God in History: Shapes of Freedom* (Minneapolis: Fortress Press, 1989, 2007).

31 P. M. Scott, *A Political Theology of Nature* (Cambridge: CUP, 2003), Chapters 2 and 7.

32 Scott, 'Right out of time? Politics and Nature in a Postnatural Condition', pp. 57–75.

33 I have defended the priority of the social as a category of theological interpretation elsewhere: see P. M. Scott, *Theology, Ideology and Liberation* (Cambridge: CUP, 1994), pp. 184–88; Scott, *A Political Theology of Nature*, pp. 43–52. The other categories for consideration are the interpersonal, the organic and the systemic. The last two have theological dangers buried in them. The first enjoys theological warrant, to be sure, but

requires migrating anthropology to the doctrine of the Trinity. As will be clear by now, I have taken the more traditional route.

34 Scott, *Anti-human Theology*, pp. 31–35.
35 See Scott, *Anti-human Theology*, pp. 31–35.
36 Scott, *Anti-human Theology*, p. 50.
37 See Scott, *Anti-human Theology*, Chapter 3.
38 Cf. Northcott, 'Spirit', p. 62, this volume.
39 G. W. F. Hegel, *Elements of the Philosophy of Right* (Cambridge: Cambridge University Press, 1991).
40 Alan Weisman, *The World without Us* (London: Virgin Books, 2008).

Bibliography

Bauman, Whitney. *Theology, Creation and Environmental Ethics: From Creatio ex nihilo to terra nullius* (New York and London: Routledge, 2009).
Bonino, J. M. *Doing Theology in a Revolutionary Situation* (Philadelphia: Fortress Press, 1975).
Chakrabarty, Dipesh. 'The Climate of History: Four Theses', *Critical Inquiry* 35 (Winter 2009): 197–222.
Collingwood, R. G. *The Idea of Nature* (Oxford: OUP, 1960 [1945]).
Fergusson, David. 'Creation', in J. Webster, K. Tanner, I. Torrance (eds), *The Oxford Handbook of Systematic Theology*, pp. 72–90.
Gardiner, Stephen M. *A Perfect Moral Storm: The Ethical Tragedy of Climate Change* (New York: Oxford University Press, 2011).
Hegel, G. W. F. *Elements of the Philosophy of Right* (Cambridge: Cambridge University Press, 1991).
Hodgson, Peter C. *God in History: Shapes of Freedom* (Minneapolis: Fortress Press, 1989, 2007).
Hulme, Mike. 'Cosmopolitan Cultures: Hybridity, Foresight and Meaning', *Theory, Culture & Society* 27: 2–3 (2010): 267–76.
Kaufman, Gordon D. *In Face of Mystery: A Constructive Theology* (Cambridge, MA: Harvard University Press, 1993).
Kelsey, David. 'The Human Creature', in J. Webster, K. Tanner, I. Torrance (eds), *The Oxford Handbook of Systematic Theology* (Oxford: OUP, 2007), pp. 121–39.
Kelsey, David H. *Eccentric Existence: A Theological Anthropology*, volume 1 (Louisville, KY: Westminster/John Knox Press, 2010).
Northcott, Michael S. *A Moral Climate* (London: DLT, 2009).
Palmer, Clare. 'Does nature matter? The place of the nonhuman in the ethics of climate change', in Denis G. Arnold (ed.), *The Ethics of Global Climate Change* (Cambridge: Cambridge University Press, 2011), pp. 272–91.
Scott, Peter M. *Theology, Ideology and Liberation* (Cambridge: CUP, 1994).
——*A Political Theology of Nature* (Cambridge: CUP, 2003).
——*Anti-human Theology: Nature, Technology and the Postnatural* (London: SCM Press, 2010).
——'The future as God's amnesty? A public theology of resistance for a changing climate', *International Journal of Public Theology* 4. 3 (2010): 314–31.
——'Thinking like an Animal: Theological Materialism for a Changing Climate', *Studies in Christian Ethics* 24. 1 (2011): 50–66.
——'Right out of time? Politics and Nature in a Postnatural Condition', in C. Deane-Drummond and Heinrich Bedford-Strohm (eds), *Religion and Ecology in the Public Sphere* (London: Continuum, 2011), pp. 57–75.
Skillen, James W. and Rockne M. McCarthy, 'History, the unfolding of society and human fulfilment: an evaluation', in J. W. Skillen and R. M. McCarthy (eds), *Political Order and the Plural Structure of Society* (Grand Rapids, MI: Eerdmans, 1991), pp. 357–376.
Weisman, Alan. *The World without Us* (London: Virgin Books, 2008).

8

SIN AND SALVATION

Neil Messer

Introduction

Among protagonists of recent fiction, Professor Michael Beard, the central character of Ian McEwan's novel *Solar*,[1] must surely be one of the less likeable. As the novel opens, the disintegration of his fifth marriage and the doldrums of his professional life – a long middle age of Government committees and institute directorships, following the spectacular early success of a Nobel Prize in Physics – invite the reader's sympathy. Yet as the story unfolds, the unattractive and even vicious aspects of his character become more obvious. He is a persistent philanderer, and although many women find him attractive, he is in some ways startlingly mis-ogynist. His horror of commitment to human relationships is such that, when he settles into a relatively stable relationship and his partner becomes pregnant, he puts pressure on her to have an abortion even though she makes it clear that she does not expect him to bear any responsibility for raising their child. It is only in the closing stages of the story that his love for his young daughter catches us, and perhaps him, by surprise. He is a glutton, who is more or less incapable of refusing food: on one occasion, he has to end a public lecture rather hastily in order to go and be sick backstage, having gorged himself at the reception beforehand. We watch him grow more and more obese, until the novel ends with what might be the onset of a heart attack. Moreover, he is arrogant, stubbornly proud and has a vindictive streak. Early in the novel, one of his junior colleagues, Tom Aldous, who has been having an affair with Beard's wife, is killed in a bizarre accident in Beard's home. Beard frames his builder (who has also had an affair with his wife) for Aldous' murder. Towards the end of the novel he encounters the now pathetic figure of the builder, newly released from prison. Ignorant that Beard brought about the perversion of justice that placed him in prison, the builder asks his help in finding employment, but Beard contemptuously refuses him any assistance.

At the *denouement*, these character flaws come together with disastrous results – not only for Beard personally, but also for international efforts to combat climate change. For Beard found an idea among Aldous' papers that he has appropriated and developed into an invention for harnessing solar energy on a massive scale, and as the book draws to a close, a crucial high-profile demonstration of the invention is about to take place in the New Mexico desert. But Aldous' former employer – a research institute directed by Beard, until he was sacked after a high-profile scandal – claims the intellectual property of the invention. Beard's pride and vengefulness lead him to refuse the compromise offer of collaboration and profit sharing, whereupon the institute's lawyer clandestinely hires Beard's former builder to smash the solar array. Beard is left with an unpayable debt for the apparatus and the launch event, criminal charges of fraud and theft, and the prospect of at least five years' legal wrangling over the rights to the invention, when we have already been told that the world cannot afford five years' delay in acting against climate change.

The plot of *Solar* can be read as a parable of how the quite ordinary flaws and failings of human beings and societies, and even perhaps some actors' conscientious performance of their duty according to their lights, can come together with disastrous consequences for global action on climate change. That this state of affairs is not only a fictional scenario is all too evident in the recent history of the international politics of climate change. For example, among the complex of interacting factors that gave rise to the fiasco of the 2009 Copenhagen summit (COP 15), one might identify a 'tragedy of the commons' where the representatives of different nations, rationally pursuing their own peoples' self-interest, brought about a situation that is bad for everyone.[2] To that could be added many people's quite understandable reluctance to face disturbing news, particularly when it calls for uncomfortable or costly action in response, which provided fertile ground for the cynical distortion of evidence discernible in some presentations of the 'Climategate' affair in the run-up to COP 15.[3] In short it is not hard to see how quite everyday human faults and failings and even things done in good faith, in the context of political, social and economic structures that constrain the possibilities for action, can come together with catastrophic results.

If read entirely within a this-worldly horizon, the story of *Solar* – notwithstanding its elements of rich comedy and even farce – is ultimately a tragedy. To the extent that it is a true parable of real-life international failures to address the problem of climate change, despair might seem, in purely secular terms, the most appropriate response. However, if we read these fictional and real-life accounts through a theological lens (admittedly a move hardly likely to commend itself to McEwan) then the picture looks somewhat different. Reading these stories theologically requires us to understand them in terms of *sin*. Paradoxically, this is a *hopeful* thing to do, because to know ourselves as sinners is already to know ourselves reconciled in Christ.

In this chapter I shall attempt such a reading by outlining an account of the Christian doctrines of sin and salvation, and then asking three questions: first, what difference, if any, does it make to this account to read it in the light of climate change? Second, what light is shed on climate change by understanding it in terms of sin? Finally, what can a Christian doctrine of salvation teach us about our response to the crisis of climate change?

Some aspects of the doctrines of sin and salvation[4]

Often, when the language of sin is used in contemporary discourse, it is taken to be a slightly old-fashioned synonym for moral wrongdoing. Sometimes this assumption is made without much thought, but sometimes sin-talk is equated quite deliberately with moral language. For example, Mary Midgley, in her book *Wickedness*, deliberately brackets out any discussion of religious or theological claims, and uses 'sin' simply to mean moral transgression.[5] She does this for understandable reasons, to avoid the danger that a difficult philosophical enquiry into evil will get diverted into a conflict about the (supposed) evils of religion. From a theologian's point of view, however, this move has the unfortunate effect of presupposing what Alistair McFadyen has called 'pragmatic atheism' – that is to say, a state of affairs in which, whether we are believers or not, our belief or unbelief makes no practical difference to the way in which we understand human affairs and act in the world.[6] In opposition to such 'pragmatically atheist' assumptions, McFadyen develops a rich and stimulating reading of the Christian doctrine of sin, as a test-case for the claim that Christian doctrines have real explanatory power in informing an understanding of human affairs and guiding action in response to human problems. He argues (against the assumption made by Midgley and others) that sin must be understood first and foremost as a theological rather than a moral category. So understood, it offers a richer resource for understanding and responding to the 'pathological' in human life than narrowly moral frames of reference.[7]

One move that follows from such a reading is to reverse the conceptual and theological priority of sin and salvation. It might seem that sin is logically prior: first, we have to understand what our problem is, before we can know what God in Christ saves us *from*. But as Karl Barth and others have argued, this gets the order exactly wrong.[8] Barth holds that to pretend to an independent knowledge of our need, prior to learning what God has done in and through Christ to meet that need, is itself an aspect of the sin of pride, in which we set ourselves up as our own 'law-giver and accuser and judge' rather than receiving God's word of judgment and salvation to us.[9] We cannot truly understand our problem independently and (so to say) in advance of God's revelation in Christ: it is *in the light* of God's saving work in the incarnation, life, death and resurrection of Christ that we come to know ourselves as sinners, and discover what that means. This also means – strange as it may seem to anyone accustomed to 'moral' readings of the language of sin – that it is *good* news to learn that we are sinners: to know ourselves as sinners is always already to know that we are the objects of God's reconciling and redeeming love revealed in Christ.

Such an emphasis can be found in the thought of that great Congregationalist theologian of the early twentieth century, P. T. Forsyth, whose constant concern is to re-assert what he calls 'the cruciality of the cross'.[10] If the death of Christ is acknowledged to be at the heart of Christian theology and preaching, it reveals to us that the love of God is *holy* love – to use one of Forsyth's most characteristic phrases. The ordering of the universe is an objective *moral* order, a reflection of God's own holiness. We are confronted by that moral order in our own consciences – in which, says Forsyth, we 'even [find] the voice of God.'[11] The tragedy of our condition is that our sin has breached this moral order, rupturing the relationship between God and humanity, and of ourselves we can do nothing to repair that breach. According to Forsyth, the Cross reveals how serious this is. Forgiveness is not an easy or 'natural' matter, as if God could simply pass over our sin or ignore it: the healing of this broken relationship requires the 'satisfaction' of God's holiness. As Forsyth puts it, forgiveness on this scale 'is natural only to the Supernatural'.[12]

There is much to be learned from Forsyth's rich (though sometimes rather dense) account. His theological insight that the 'cruciality of the cross' discloses the holy love of God and the seriousness of sin is an impressive achievement, particularly against the background of Ritschlian theology in which Forsyth was trained and which he spent his scholarly career critiquing.[13] Moreover, while he echoes Anselm in using the language of 'satisfaction' to speak of the Atonement, he also emphasises in critical response to Anselm that sin and salvation are not a matter of impersonal transactions but of relationships: the breach and restoration of humanity's relationship with the God whose holy love is revealed in the death of Christ.[14] There are aspects of his account, however, that require some critical reappraisal. He aims to develop a theology that is not only 'positive' and 'evangelical', but also 'modern', and one aspect of this programme is (as he puts it) to 'ethicize' the message of the Cross.[15] Thus he speaks of the holiness of God in terms of the *moral* order of the universe, and of sin as a revolt against that moral order. While this is understandable in his own context, a century's hindsight makes it easier to recognise that, in this respect, he laid a false trail for Christian talk of salvation and sin. As McFadyen suggests, an over-'ethicized' account of sin lends itself all too easily to a 'pragmatically atheist' reduction of sin-talk of the kind evident in Midgley's discussion of wickedness, cited earlier.[16]

As McFadyen shows, sin and salvation can be understood in a properly theological way if we recognise that worship is at the heart of the matter. In a sense, *the* crucial issue is whom or what we worship, and how. Sin can be understood most fundamentally as idolatry: the basic refusal to direct our being and energies in joy, faith and worship to the triune God.[17] From this most basic distortion in our relationship with God spring distortions in our relations with our neighbours, ourselves and the creation: '[w]hereas true worship energises the loving dynamics of genuine community, idolatry undermines them (Babel).'[18]

Within this theological frame of reference, more specific ways of understanding sin and salvation can be understood as aspects of idolatry and true worship. For example, Karl Barth's massive presentation of the doctrine of reconciliation weaves together Christology, the 'threefold office' of Christ as Prophet, Priest and King, the Atonement and sin into a rich and complex threefold account.[19] The first aspect concerns 'the humiliation of the Son of God', or his 'journey into the far country', as Barth puts it, echoing the parable of the Prodigal Son (Luke 15. 11–32).[20] Whereas the serpent in Genesis 3 tempted the human beings to grasp at equality with God, the one who 'was in the form of God' refused to do so, 'but emptied himself, taking the form of a slave' (Philippians 2. 6–7). The self-emptying of the Son of God and his willing submission to the humiliation of the Cross disclose that sin is pride: the perverse, deluded and ultimately self-destructive attempt to direct our own lives without reference to God.[21]

The second aspect concerns the exaltation of the Son of Man, 'lifted up' on the Cross and in the Resurrection and Ascension. Jesus Christ is the 'Royal Man'[22]: the true human being, our representative, who fulfils all that humanity is created to be. There is an important connection here with Dietrich Bonhoeffer's core theological concept of 'vicarious representative action' (*Stellvertretung*):

> [Jesus'] entire life, action, and suffering is vicarious representative action. As the one who has become human he indeed stands in the place of all human beings. All that human beings were supposed to live, do and suffer falls on him.[23]

The exaltation of Jesus Christ, the true and representative human, reveals sin as sloth: our *refusal* to become what we were created to be; the disorientation and dissipation of our energies and integrity, which amounts to a rejection of God's 'call to personhood'.[24]

Third, if sin is at root idolatry, the giving of our worship and devotion to that which is not God, then the victory of the divine-human Jesus over sin can be understood as his faithful witness to the truth. Jesus Christ is the Prophet whose truthful witness makes known God's reconciling work, shining as the true light in the darkness and overcoming its opposition.[25] This true and faithful prophetic witness exposes sin as idolatrous falsehood: a fundamental misrepresentation of reality, good and evil, the nature of God and God's relations with humanity.[26]

The magnitude of God's saving work in Christ shows humanity the depth of our need. This is traditionally expressed in Western Christianity in the doctrine of original sin, which is, from a modern perspective, probably the most implausible and offensive-seeming aspect of the Christian doctrine of sin. Some of its apparent implausibility stems from the tension between an evolutionary account of human origins and Christian accounts which trace original sin back to the fall of Adam and Eve; but as I have tried to show elsewhere, the doctrine of original sin does not depend on an historical fall of a first human couple or the transmission of sin through sexual intercourse, and can in fact engage critically and fruitfully with a scientific narrative of human evolution.[27] Much of the offence in talk of original sin, to modern sensibilities, is caused by the inference that we can be guilty of sin that we did not freely choose and from which we are unable to free ourselves. This is, to say the least, counter-intuitive to a modern moral vision deeply influenced by the Kantian slogan that 'Ought implies Can'. Yet as McFadyen and others have argued, the doctrine offers a more complex and genuinely illuminating under-standing, in which sin is a condition that we *both* inherit *and* contribute to. It gives an account of deep distortions of identity, relationships and social structures which transcend individual willing and choosing, yet which *also* incorporate and co-opt them. 'Guilt', in the sense of such a distortion of identity and relationships, becomes a far broader category than the blameworthiness with which it is equated in modern moral frameworks. As McFadyen puts it,

> Guilt as accountability before God ... relates to the call and directionality of the dynamics of God. It means being called to take responsibility in and for our situation in its radical distortion. That is true to the predominant Biblical interest in guilt, not primarily concerned with locating blame, but in calling people to take responsibility for re-energising and re-orienting their situation in relation to God.[28]

The re-orientation of lives and social relationships so fundamentally distorted can only be accomplished by God's grace through the work of the Spirit, catching human beings up into the divine dynamics of love and praise in such a way that their living is energised and transformed.[29]

A further crucial point implicit in what has already been said is spelled out by Forsyth: salvation is not to be understood just in terms of *individual* transformation. Forsyth places a strong emphasis on the solidarity of humanity, so that '[w]e are each one of us saved in the salvation of the [human] race, in a collectivist redemption'.[30] Salvation incorporates us into a new and different kind of human community or *polis*, which we enter by baptism, and whose life is shaped by the Word and the Eucharist (cf. Eph. 2. 11–22). The existence of this 'new humanity' is a sign that the renewal accomplished and promised by God in Christ is not only of individual lives or even personal relationships, but also of political, social and economic structures. The knowledge that salvation is political and structural as well as personal ought to alert us to the structural as well as personal dimensions of sin, such as political, institutional and economic arrangements that constrain individuals' actions and choices, steering them in the direction of evil rather than good.[31] It should make us more attentive to the prophets' denunciations of injustice as well as idolatry – and indeed, to their linkage of the two (e.g. Amos 5. 21–27). However, two caveats must be entered about the category of structural sin. First, it is an indispensable *aspect* of the Christian doctrine of original sin as I have outlined it here – one with obvious importance for a theological analysis of climate change – but, unlike some authors on theology and ecology, I do not regard the concept of structural sin as an *alternative* to original sin.[32] The latter has explanatory power and resources for a theological understanding of our predicament that are not exhausted by talk of structural sin.[33] Secondly, I have observed that the category of structural sin should make us attentive to the linkage between idolatry and injustice, but how are we to know what is meant by 'justice' and 'injustice', or to recognise them when we see them? In Barth's terms, if we were to answer this question by uncritically importing some non-theological account of justice, that would merely replicate our sin of pride by presuming to a knowledge of good and evil independent of humanity's relationship to God.[34] A Eucharistic community, formed by the writings of the Hebrew prophets and by New Testament texts such as the vision of divine generosity set out in the Sermon on the Mount (Matt. 5. 43–48), stories of radical sharing among the first followers of the Way (Acts 4. 32–37), Paul's injunctions about the collection for the impoverished believers in Jerusalem (1 Cor. 11. 17–22) and James' invective against inequalities among the believers (Jas 2. 1–7), ought to have a distinctive vision of justice to bring to bear on problems of climate change.[35]

Salvation and sin in the light of climate change

In the previous section I sketched, partially and selectively, aspects of the Christian doctrines of salvation and sin. What difference (if any) will it make to our understanding of these doctrines if we have the crisis of climate change consciously in our minds as we explore them?

My account of sin, drawing on Forsyth, Barth, McFadyen and others, has represented it as a radical distortion of humanity's relationship with God – in McFadyen's terms, idolatry – that gives rise, in its turn, to distortions of human relationships and social structures. Barth, for example, shows how a basic alienation from God also results in our alienation from one another and ourselves in real and terrible ways.[36] Yet nowhere in his doctrine of sin does he give any extended consideration to our alienation from the non-human creation. The fact that in his ethics of creation he discusses the present 'fallenness' of the non-human cosmos in the light of the future hope promised in Isaiah's vision of the peaceable kingdom (11. 6–9) draws attention to this lacuna in his account of salvation and sin.[37] Not all of his contemporaries and allies ignored this dimension of sin and salvation: Dietrich Bonhoeffer, reading the 'Fall' narrative of Genesis 3 as a sundering of the unity of humanity's created existence, writes of 'the destruction and dividedness of the original relation between humankind and *nature* and the alienation that takes its place'.[38]

The crisis of climate change is the sharpest of reminders that humanity's fate is bound up with that of the whole created earth that we inhabit. As such it can redirect the attention to aspects of salvation and sin in the Scriptures that Christian reflection has too often neglected; it can prompt us to give an account which acknowledges our solidarity with the whole of creation, and remind us of the biblical witness to a divine purpose of transformation and renewal that is not limited to our species: 'See, I am making all things new' (Rev. 21. 5, cf. Isaiah 65. 17–25). Christians whose understanding of God's saving purposes is informed by texts such as Isaiah 11 might reflect that God's promise of peace is extended not only to humans but to all creatures, so that in God's good future, as Barth puts it, 'there will be no more question of the struggle for existence and therefore of slaughter between man and beast'.[39]

In this light, a question arises about the connection between human sin and the brokenness of the whole creation. Life on earth as we know it is inconceivable without the violence, suffering and destruction inherent in the evolutionary 'struggle for existence'. Indeed, evolution raises the problem of natural evil in its sharpest form, because, biologically speaking, it is precisely those violent and destructive processes that *generate* the rich diversity of living beings that Christians celebrate as God's good creatures. Yet a theological vision formed by Isaiah 11 is committed to affirming, with Barth, that the violence of the evolutionary struggle for existence 'does not correspond with the true and original creative will of God, and that it therefore stands under a *caveat*.'[40] While it seems implausible in the extreme that human sin *caused* the pain, waste and destruction inherent in evolutionary processes that were going on for billions of years before humans arrived on the scene, sin can certainly be understood as an *aspect* of the evil threatening God's good creation, evil also reflected in the violence and suffering evident in non-human nature.[41]

Although much of the evil in the natural world cannot be said to have been caused by human sin, some undoubtedly is. Climate change stands as a stark reminder of what Bonhoeffer learns from Genesis 3, that 'the *work* that human beings do on the ground that is cursed comes to express fallen humankind's state of dividedness from nature; that is, work too falls under the curse.'[42] As McFadyen's account of sin might remind us, humanity's state of alienation from the earth is one that we inherit, that is not entirely of our making and is beyond our merely human power to repair, yet we also make our own contribution to this state of alienation by our own willing and choosing. The perversely self-destructive ways in which we continue to use the planet's resources and blight its fruitfulness, even when we are made aware of the damage we are doing, are shaped and constrained by our inherited alienation from the earth; but these same choices and actions also compound and contribute to our alienation from the earth. Yet as Bonhoeffer makes clear, even this story of the curse is not a message of despair but of hope:

> The world is changed and destroyed in that human beings in their dividedness can no longer live with God, with one another, and with nature; yet, in this dividedness between tob and ra, they also cannot live *without God*, without one another, and without nature. They do live in a world that is under a curse. Yet just because it is *God's* curse that oppresses it, the world is not wholly God-forsaken; instead it is a world that even under God's curse is blessed and in its enmity, pain and work is pacified, a world where *life is upheld and preserved.*[43]

Climate change and sin

Alistair McFadyen holds that – contrary to the 'pragmatically atheist' assumptions he criticises – the doctrine of sin has real explanatory power that can help us understand and respond to the pathological in human affairs. If he is right, what might the doctrines of sin and salvation offer our understanding of, and response to, the problem of climate change? In this section I shall indicate some contributions that the doctrine of sin might make to an understanding of the problem, while in the next I shall suggest how a Christian understanding of salvation might guide a response.

As we saw earlier, McFadyen concludes that sin should be understood, at root, as idolatry: a fundamental distortion of our relationship with God.[44] This distortion is the mis-direction of the love, faith and devotion that are properly God's to that which is not God – an ultimately self-destructive move, as Colin Gunton remarks: 'If the created order, or part of it, is treated as god, then it behaves like god for those who so treat it, but for destructive rather than creative ends.'[45]

To diagnose climate change as a symptom of idolatry might seem counter-intuitive to those modern people who are not accustomed to thinking that they worship any god – not to mention those western Christians who are confident that they worship only the God and Father of Jesus Christ. Yet perhaps there is a characteristically modern species of idolatry that consists in the confusion of the ultimate and the penultimate (to borrow more language of Bonhoeffer's)[46]: the conceit that we, as humans, can and must live in the world entirely by our own resources.[47] It is not difficult to discern a connection between the conceit that our ultimate fate is in our hands alone and bounded by the horizon of this world, and other forms of idolatry such as the investment of god-like powers in the global market, which then comes to drive unsustainable patterns of consumption.[48]

Earlier I suggested that the basic distortion of relationship with God named by McFadyen as idolatry can be further specified (following Barth) as pride, sloth and falsehood. Aspects of all three can be discerned both in the human activity in the world that has given rise to climate change and in current responses to the problem. Faced with such an overwhelming threat, three kinds of temptation are obvious. First, it is all too tempting to deny that the problem exists, or that it is a human-caused problem that requires human action in response: a species of *falsehood*. Such falsehood can be egregiously cynical, as for example when the scientific evidence about climate change is distorted by lobby-groups representing powerful commercial interests. However, such distortions also find a receptive audience among ordinary, decent people whose fears and interests strongly motivate them to believe that climate change is not a real problem. Moreover, falsehood can take forms other than outright denial. The philosophically and psychologically curious phenomenon of self-deception is one. Another, closely linked to it, is the 'cognitive evasion' of things that we would rather not know or think about.[49] A third is what Stephen Gardiner calls 'moral corruption': the distortion or subversion of moral discourse by those who are strongly tempted to pass the buck of responding to climate change – which of course means most present inhabitants of the world's wealthy nations. Faced with such temptations we are vulnerable, as Gardiner puts it, to 'corruption that targets our ways of talking and thinking, and so prevents us from even seeing the problem in the right way.'[50] Arguments about what constitutes a just sharing of the burden of responding to climate change, in contexts like COP

15, might well be genuinely difficult to resolve because of the conflicting needs and interests of different populations. But it is also entirely possible that some arguments about fairness are introduced into such negotiations with the conscious or unconscious aim of muddying the waters.[51]

A proper estimate of the value of scientific evidence and knowledge is another important aspect of a theological response to climate change, and a theological analysis of sin as falsehood could support a balanced evaluation. On the one hand, it will be properly appreciative of the notable strengths and achievements of the intellectual and practical project that is modern science, and will be ready to use scientific knowledge and understanding in the service of truthful witness. On the other, it will be properly critical of the cultural, political and economic distortions to which scientific research is by no means immune, and suspicious of responses to climate change which presume that technological fixes alone will solve the problem. To set up the natural sciences as the ultimate arbiter of truthfulness or to invest in them the hope of a this-worldly salvation would be another kind of idolatry.

If, however, the problem is acknowledged rather than denied, two other kinds of temptation could come into play in responses to climate change. One is *pride*, which could take various forms. In Ian McEwan's parable, Michael Beard's intellectual arrogance is one of the factors that comes together with others at the *dénouement* to bring about disaster for him and his invention. But it is possible for pride to manifest itself in a rather different way: the confusion of the ultimate and penultimate to which I have already alluded, which leads us to imagine that our ultimate fate lies in our hands alone, and our actions in this world must bear the burden of our ultimate hopes. In Karl Barth's analysis of sin as pride, the pride that makes us want to be our own helpers has the disastrous effect of turning us away from proper reliance on God, our true helper.[52] In the face of climate change, such misguided self-reliance can easily reinforce the conceit that technical, managerial or political solutions alone will save us from our predicament. It could also manifest itself as a kind of totalitarian activism: faced with such an immense crisis, we must do whatever it takes to combat the danger by any means necessary, and we cannot afford to entertain the luxury of our usual moral scruples about those means.

Perhaps a more likely response when faced with the enormity of the problem, however, is what Gardiner calls 'political inertia', for which he suggests various psychological and other causes.[53] In addition to the explanations he proposes, it seems plausible that a further cause is a kind of paralysing despair: the feeling that whatever we can do will never be enough, so there is no point even trying. The theological analysis offered in this chapter will readily identify such political inertia as a form of *sloth*.

In the first section I drew attention to the social and structural, as well as personal, dimensions of sin. Some authors connect structural sin with the New Testament language of the 'principalities and powers': Lesslie Newbigin, for example, understands this language to refer to 'power and authority which is real, which is embodied in and exercised by individual human beings, but is not identical with them.'[54] He connects this account with Pauline references to the *stoicheia* ('elements') of the universe in Galatians and Colossians: the *stoicheia*, on Newbigin's reading, are to be understood as the physical, social and cultural structures of the world, within which we live our lives. We cannot live without structure, and the *stoicheia* are 'part of God's good ordering of his creation';[55] yet when they are absolutized, they can become tyrannical or demonic, which helps to explain why the New Testament speaks of the death of Christ as the disarming and unmasking of the powers (see Col. 2. 15). In McFadyen's terms, social, political and economic structures might radically constrain individuals' willing and choosing, yet the willing and choosing of those individuals is also incorporated and co-opted by these systems and structures.[56]

The distortions of structural sin can give rise to the tragic and ironic situation that when individuals or groups act conscientiously according to their duty, their conscientious action is co-opted into this distorted dynamic. Descriptions of political processes such as COP 15, by using shorthand language that describes nations or their negotiating teams as personal agents ('The USA argued that X; the African nations protested that Y … '), sometimes mask this reality. No doubt national leaders and representatives are sometimes motivated by self-serving considerations of personal political advantage, but there is no need to doubt that, much of the time, they act in good faith in what they take to be the interests of those it is their duty to represent. Part of the moral tragedy attributable to structures of sin in international relations is that such conscientious performance of duty often results in deadlock, or in some nations' and peoples' interests being systematically marginalized.[57]

Salvation and the human response to climate change

I claimed in the chapter introduction that to understand our human problems theologically as sin is fundamentally good news, because to know ourselves as sinners is always already to know ourselves as the objects of God's saving love in Christ. If that is so, what difference might the good news of God's saving love make to a response to the crisis of climate change? I would suggest that two of the most important things that the Church can offer a world facing climate change are the related gifts of the *practice of repentance* and the *virtue of hope*.

The practice of repentance, in which Christians participate every Sunday when they gather for worship, can be an exercise in a form of honesty only made possible by God's grace. Most of us are only too expert in the kind of self-deception and inward spin-doctoring that makes us the moral heroes of our personal narratives: like the lawyer to whom Jesus told the parable of the Good Samaritan, we want to justify ourselves. The confession of sins in worship is an individual and corporate practice that can strip away such pretence, and it is possible just because the judgement that we are sinners is the shadow of the Gospel of salvation. To know myself a reconciled sinner, the object of God's inexhaustible saving love, can give me the courage to face truths about myself that I could not otherwise bear. Here it is possible to find the courage to look not only the threat of climate change, but also our own complicity in that threat, squarely in the face. The practice of repentance offers resources for truthfulness that can stand against the falsehoods of denial, cognitive evasion, self-deception and moral corruption.[58]

Because the theo-logic of repentance presupposes the saving love of God, this practice is closely associated with God's gift of the theological virtue of hope. God's gracious address to humanity in the Gospel enables us to recognise that our ultimate hope is in God's saving love, and our ultimate destiny is in God's hands, not ours alone. This enables us to place the ultimate and the penultimate in their proper relation. The knowledge that human activity in the world is not to be identified with the ultimate can beckon us away from the idolatrous pride of thinking that we can and must save the world by our own efforts alone. But in unmasking the ultimate pretensions of human activities and abilities, God's last word to us in Christ also confers on those human activities and abilities their proper status and significance as *penultimate*. The knowledge that our actions do not have to bear the overwhelming burden of saving the world makes it possible to resist the inertia born of paralysing despair – in other words, the sloth – that can seem a natural and rational reaction to the enormity of the problem.

To respond in repentant and hopeful ways to the Gospel opens up the possibility of living a truly responsible life in the face of the challenge of climate change. As Bonhoeffer argues, the structure of a responsible human life is defined by '*vicarious representative action* and *accordance with reality* … my *accountability* for my living and acting,[59] and … the *venture* of concrete decision'.[60] This framework offers rich and suggestive potential for mapping the forms that responsible action in the face of climate change could take; I close by sketching a few possibilities, but a full account must await another occasion.

First, understanding responsibility in this way can give a proper perspective to the vocation of climate change activists. The rhetoric of salvation, common in climate activism,[61] perhaps signals a particularly powerful temptation: to attach ultimate importance to the righteous cause, so that '[t]he origin, essence and goal of responsible life is denied … and responsibility has become a self-made, abstract idol.'[62] Against this temptation, to understand climate activism as *Stellvertretung* is to locate its possibility and worth in the vicarious responsibility that Jesus willingly assumed for all humanity. Activism conducted by a few can thus become responsible action taken on behalf of all – not in a way that relieves the others of their responsibility, but in a way which challenges and enables them to become responsible themselves.

Grassroots activism by individual Christians – and even more by local Christian communities – can thus become a form of Christian witness to the hope promised in the Gospel, which is never extinguished by human sin. A church that becomes an 'eco-congregation' will not thereby save the world, but it does witness to God's saving love for the world, express a commitment to live in ways that conform to that love, and invite others to join the enterprise.[63] Furthermore, such grassroots action is often best taken by making common cause with others, and Christian communities which understand their participation as a form of vicarious responsible action might have particular gifts to offer to such alliances by interpreting their activism to themselves and their co-activists.[64] And finally, members of Christian communities have more opportunities than most Westerners to form relationships of solidarity with people and communities in the parts of the world hardest hit by climate change. For example, one congregation in an English city known to the author has formed a link over the past few years with an NGO working with women in part of Mali to mitigate the effects of drought on their communities' agriculture and food security.[65] This example could be replicated countless times in the churches of any Western nation, and its force lies in its very ordinariness: the cumulative potential of all these relationships to erode the barriers that divide rich from poor nations should not be underestimated.

In this chapter, I have tried to show how the Christian doctrines of salvation and sin can radically shift our perspective on what Gardiner calls the ethical tragedy of climate change. In short, if Michael Beard is merely a fatally flawed human being who reflects the moral flaws of us all, then the last word about the 'moral storm' of climate change might indeed be a tragic word. But if he is a sinner who shows us that we are all sinners, then the last word is assuredly one of hope.

Notes

1 Ian McEwan, *Solar* (London: Vintage, 2011).
2 See Stephen M. Gardiner, *A Perfect Moral Storm: The Ethical Tragedy of Climate Change* (Oxford: Oxford University Press, 2011), pp. 24–29 and *passim*.
3 See Celia Deane-Drummond, 'Public Theology as Contested Ground: Arguments for Climate Justice', in Celia Deane-Drummond and Heinrich Bedford-Strohm (eds), *Religion and Ecology in the Public Sphere* (London: T&T Clark, 2011), pp. 189–210. The loaded term 'Climategate' was the nickname widely adopted in the news media for the controversy caused by the leaking of e-mails between climate scientists, which was used by some commentators in an attempt to discredit the scientific evidence presented by the Intergovernmental Panel on Climate Change (IPCC).
4 This section is based in part on an account of salvation and sin developed in Neil Messer, *Selfish Genes and Christian Ethics: Theological and Ethical Reflections on Evolutionary Biology* (London: SCM, 2007), Chapters 7 and 8.
5 Mary Midgley, *Wickedness: A Philosophical Essay* (London: Routledge, 2001 [1984]), pp. 6–7.
6 Alistair McFadyen, *Bound to Sin: Abuse, Holocaust and the Doctrine of Sin* (Cambridge: Cambridge University Press, 2000), pp. 3–13.
7 McFadyen, *Bound to Sin*, pp. 14–42.
8 Karl Barth, *Church Dogmatics*, vol. IV.1, Geoffrey W. Bromiley and Thomas F. Torrance (trans and eds) (Edinburgh: T&T Clark, 1956), pp. 138–42. See also Colin Gunton, *The Actuality of Atonement: A Study of Metaphor, Rationality and the Christian Tradition* (Edinburgh: T&T Clark, 1988), p. 119.
9 Barth, *Church Dogmatics*, vol. IV.1, pp. 388–89.
10 P. T. Forsyth, *The Cruciality of the Cross*, 2nd edn (London: Independent Press, 1948 [1909]).
11 P. T. Forsyth, *Positive Preaching and the Modern Mind* (London: Hodder and Stoughton, 1907), p. 351.
12 Forsyth, *Positive Preaching*, p. 295.
13 See, for example, Trevor A. Hart, 'Morality, Atonement and the Death of Jesus: The Crucial Focus of Forsyth's Theology', in Trevor Hart (ed.), *Justice the True and Only*

Mercy: Essays on the Life and Theology of Peter Taylor Forsyth (Edinburgh: T&T Clark, 1997), pp. 16–36 (17).

14 See further P. T. Forsyth, *The Work of Christ* (London: Hodder and Stoughton, 1910), pp. 156–57, 223, and Hart, 'Morality, Atonement and the Death of Jesus', pp. 32–34.

15 Forsyth, *Positive Preaching*, pp. 293–333.

16 McFadyen, *Bound to Sin*, pp. 40–42. For a fuller discussion of the strengths and pitfalls of Forsyth's programme of 'ethicizing' the Gospel, see Messer, *Selfish Genes*, pp. 166–69.

17 McFadyen, *Bound to Sin*, pp. 200–226.

18 McFadyen, *Bound to Sin*, p. 226.

19 For a summary, see Barth, *Church Dogmatics*, IV.1, pp. 3–154.

20 Barth, *Church Dogmatics*, vol. IV.1, pp. 157–210.

21 Barth, *Church Dogmatics*, vol. IV.1, pp. 413–78.

22 Karl Barth, *Church Dogmatics*, vol. IV.2, Geoffrey W. Bromiley and Thomas F. Torrance (trans and eds) (Edinburgh: T&T Clark, 1958), pp. 154–264.

23 Dietrich Bonhoeffer, *Ethics*, vol. 6 of *Dietrich Bonhoeffer Works*, Ilse Tödt, Eduard Tödt, Ernst Feil and Clifford J. Green (eds), Reinhard Krauss, Charles C. West and Douglas W. Stott (trans) (Minneapolis, MN: Fortress, 2005), pp. 231–32.

24 Barth, *Church Dogmatics*, IV.2, 403–83, cf. Alistair I. McFadyen, *The Call to Personhood: A Christian Theory of the Individual in Social Relationships* (Cambridge: Cambridge University Press, 1990). For a discussion of feminist accounts of sin as sloth (which he differentiates sharply from Barth's), see McFadyen, *Bound to Sin*, pp. 139–54.

25 Karl Barth, *Church Dogmatics*, vol. IV.3, Geoffrey W. Bromiley and Thomas F. Torrance (trans and eds) (Edinburgh: T&T Clark, 1961), §§69.3, 70.1.

26 Barth, *Church Dogmatics*, vol. IV.3.1, pp. 434–61.

27 Messer, *Selfish Genes*, pp. 184–95; see also Richard H. Bell, 'Science and the Bible: Adam and His "Fall" as a Case Study', in Angus Paddison and Neil Messer (eds), *The Bible: Culture, Community and Society* (London: T&T Clark, 2013), pp. 31–46.

28 McFadyen, *Bound to Sin*, p. 245.

29 McFadyen, *Bound to Sin*, pp. 212–16.

30 Forsyth, *The Work of Christ*, p. 114.

31 Pope John Paul II characterised the relationship of personal to structural sin thus: '"structures of sin" … are rooted in personal sin, and thus always linked to the concrete acts of individuals who introduce these structures, consolidate them and make them difficult to remove. And thus they grow stronger, spread, and become the source of other sins, and so influence people's behavior.' *Sollicitudo Rei Socialis*, 36. Available online at www.vatican.va/holy_father/john_paul_ii/encyclicals/documents/hf_jp-ii_enc_30121 987_sollicitudo-rei-socialis_en.html (accessed 22 June 2012).

32 *Contra*, for example, Frederick Simmons, 'Sin and Evil', in Willis Jenkins and Whitney Bauman (eds), *The Berkshire Encyclopedia of Sustainability, vol. 1: The Spirit of Sustainability* (Great Barrington, MA: Berkshire, 2010), pp. 367–68.

33 Cf. McFadyen, *Bound to Sin*, pp. 34–40.

34 Of course, there are many situations where injustice is plain for all to see, but the intractable arguments at COP 15 about what would be fair to the various parties serve to illustrate that, in the context of climate change, securing agreement on what justice requires can be far from straightforward: see Deane-Drummond, 'Public Theology as Contested Ground'. The difficulty of reaching agreement in such situations could be partly because the issues are genuinely complex, though we might also suspect a strong element of what Stephen Gardiner (*A Perfect Moral Storm*, pp. 301–38) calls 'moral corruption': see further below, section entitled 'Salvation and sin in the light of climate change'.

35 For a sketch of this approach to justice in another context, see Neil Messer, 'Healthcare Resource Allocation and the "Recovery of Virtue"', *Studies in Christian Ethics* 18.1 (2005), pp. 89–108.

36 E.g. Barth, *Church Dogmatics*, vol. IV.2, pp. 432–83.

37 Karl Barth, *Church Dogmatics*, vol. III.4, Geoffrey W. Bromiley and Thomas F. Torrance (trans and eds) (Edinburgh: T&T Clark, 1961), pp. 348–56. For a discussion, see Neil Messer, 'Natural Evil after Darwin', in Michael S. Northcott and R. J. Berry (eds), *Theology after Darwin* (Milton Keynes: Paternoster, 2009), pp. 139–54.

38 Dietrich Bonhoeffer, *Creation and Fall*, vol. 3 of *Dietrich Bonhoeffer Works*, Martin Rüter, Ilse Tödt and John W. de Gruchy (eds), Douglas Stephen Bax (trans.) (Minneapolis, MN: Fortress, 2004), pp. 133–34, emphasis original.

39 Barth, *Church Dogmatics*, vol. III.4, p. 353. For further reflection on this theme, see Messer, 'Natural Evil after Darwin', and Neil Messer, 'Humans, Animals, Evolution and Ends', in Celia Deane-Drummond and David Clough (eds), *Creaturely Theology: On God, Humans and Other Animals* (London: SCM, 2009), pp. 211–27.

40 Barth, *Church Dogmatics*, vol. III.4, p. 353; see further Messer, 'Natural Evil after Darwin', and for a critique of my account, Christopher Southgate, 'Re-Reading Genesis, John, and Job: A Christian Response to Darwinism', *Zygon* 46, 2 (2011), pp. 378–84.

41 On the connections between human evolutionary history, sin and salvation, see further Messer, *Selfish Genes*, pp. 133–215.

42 Bonhoeffer, *Creation and Fall*, p. 134, emphasis original.

43 Bonhoeffer, *Creation and Fall*, p. 135, emphasis original.

44 McFadyen, *Bound to Sin*, pp. 200–226.

45 Gunton, *Actuality of Atonement*, p. 72.

46 Bonhoeffer, *Ethics*, pp. 146–70.

47 This is not unrelated to Bonhoeffer's account of the condition of humankind '*sicut deus*': one might say that the serpent in Genesis 3 speaks truly when it promises that the human beings will be 'like god, knowing good and evil' – only the 'god' whom they will be like is a false god, not the true God of the *imago dei* in which they have been created: cf. *Creation and Fall*, pp. 111–14.

48 Cf. Michael S. Northcott, *A Moral Climate: The Ethics of Global Warming* (London: DLT, 2007), pp. 32–39.

49 I owe the point about cognitive evasion to Niels Henrik Gregersen. David Burrell and Stanley Hauerwas, in a classic and disturbing essay on Albert Speer's autobiography, demonstrate the connection between cognitive evasion and self-deception, particularly in relation to a crucial moment described by Speer when he deliberately chose not to ask what was happening at Auschwitz: 'Self-Deception and Autobiography: Theological and Ethical Reflections on Speer's *Inside the Third Reich*', *Journal of Religious Ethics* 2, 1 (1974), pp. 107–8.

50 Gardiner, *A Perfect Moral Storm*, p. 301.

51 Gardiner suggests that in the face of moral corruption, 'practical ethics can help' by promoting critical scrutiny of the arguments, and by '[operating] defensively, to preserve initially sound moral intuitions against unscrupulous or misguided attacks' (*A Perfect Moral Storm*, 357). He may well be right, but of course (as he acknowledges) practical moral reason is itself vulnerable to corruption. A good deal therefore seems to hang on our capacity to recognize 'initially sound moral intuitions', and a theological response to Gardiner's analysis must emphasize our need for the transformation and 'renewing of [our] minds' (Rom. 12. 2) if we are to be capable of resisting moral corruption: see further Bonhoeffer, *Ethics*, pp. 320–26.

52 Barth, *Church Dogmatics*, vol. IV.1, pp. 458–78.

53 Gardiner, *A Perfect Moral Storm*, pp. 191–97.

54 Lesslie Newbigin, *The Gospel in a Pluralist Society* (London: SPCK, 1989), p. 202; see also Gunton, *Actuality*, pp. 53–74, and Walter Wink, *Engaging the Powers: The Language of Power in the New Testament* (Philadelphia, PA: Fortress, 1984), *Unmasking the Powers: The Invisible Forces that Determine Human Existence* (Philadelphia: Fortress, 1986), and *Engaging the Powers: Discernment and Resistance in a World of Domination* (Minneapolis, MN: Fortress, 1992). I am indebted to Victoria Gaile Laidler's *Gaudete Theology* blog for suggesting the connection between structural sin and Newbigin's discussion of the 'principalities and

powers'. Available online at http://gaudetetheology.wordpress.com/2011/11/27/powers-principalities-and-structural-sin/ (accessed 24 February 2013).

55 Newbigin, *Gospel*, p. 208.

56 He explores this particularly in relation to the Holocaust, his concrete 'case study' of corporate sin: McFadyen, *Bound to Sin*, pp. 95–98.

57 Celia Deane-Drummond suggests that to resolve such intractable clashes and imbalances, a shared understanding of the common good is needed: Deane-Drummond, 'Public Theology as Contested Ground'. I agree, though this raises big questions about how such a shared understanding is to be achieved.

58 This is not to suggest, of course, that Christian worship is immune from self-deception, evasion, denial or corruption. Experience suggests quite the reverse, and since Barth calls falsehood 'the specifically Christian form of sin … the form in which sin occurs in the Christian age which begins with the resurrection of Jesus Christ … ' (*Church Dogmatics*, vol. IV.3.1, pp. 434–35), this should not come as any surprise. However, the practice of repentance, together with other central practices of Christian worship, continually puts participants at risk of encountering the gracious judgment of God that confronts our falsehoods with the true witness of Christ. Anyone who wishes to remain secure in their self-deception or denial should avoid going to church, or least choose their church very carefully.

59 In a later formulation this becomes the readiness to take on guilt (*Schuldübernahme*) – one's own or that of others: Bonhoeffer, *Ethics*, p. 288.

60 Bonhoeffer, *Ethics*, p. 257, emphasis original.

61 I owe this observation to Stefan Skrimshire.

62 Bonhoeffer, *Ethics*, p. 259.

63 See the Eco-Congregation portal at www.ecocongregation.org/ (accessed 24 February 2013).

64 One example of such activism in common cause with others is participation in the Transition town movement: see http://ew.ecocongregation.org/node/1096 (accessed 24 February 2013). For an example of its theological interpretation, see Timothy J. Gorringe, 'On Building an Ark: The Global Emergency and the Limits of Moral Exhortation', *Studies in Christian Ethics* 24, 1 (2011), pp. 23–33.

65 See www.jolibatrust.org.uk/index.html (accessed 25 February 2013).

Bibliography

Barth, Karl. *Church Dogmatics*, 13 vols. Geoffrey W. Bromiley and Thomas F. Torrance (trans and eds) (Edinburgh: T&T Clark, 1956–1975).

Bell, Richard H. 'Science and the Bible: Adam and His "Fall" as a Case Study', in Angus Paddison and Neil Messer (eds), *The Bible: Culture, Community and Society* (London: T&T Clark, 2013), pp. 31–46.

Bonhoeffer, Dietrich. *Creation and Fall*, vol. 3 of *Dietrich Bonhoeffer Works*, Martin Rüter, Ilse Tödt and John W. de Gruchy (eds), Douglas Stephen Bax (trans.) (Minneapolis, MN: Fortress, 2004).

——*Ethics*, vol. 6 of *Dietrich Bonhoeffer Works*, Ilse Tödt, Eduard Tödt, Ernst Feil and Clifford J. Green (eds), Reinhard Krauss, Charles C. West and Douglas W. Stott (trans) (Minneapolis, MN: Fortress, 2005).

Burrell, David, and Stanley Hauerwas. 'Self-Deception and Autobiography: Theological and Ethical Reflections on Speer's *Inside the Third Reich*', *Journal of Religious Ethics* 2.1 (1974), 99–117.

Deane-Drummond, Celia. 'Public Theology as Contested Ground: Arguments for Climate Justice', in Celia Deane-Drummond and Heinrich Bedford-Strohm (eds), *Religion and Ecology in the Public Sphere* (London: T&T Clark, 2011), pp. 189–210.

Eco-Congregation portal. Available online at www.ecocongregation.org/ (accessed 24 February 2013).

Forsyth, Peter Taylor. *Positive Preaching and the Modern Mind* (London: Hodder and Stoughton, 1907).

——*The Work of Christ* (London: Hodder and Stoughton, 1910).

——*The Cruciality of the Cross*, 2nd edn (London: Independent Press, 1948).

Gardiner, Stephen M. *A Perfect Moral Storm: The Ethical Tragedy of Climate Change* (Oxford: Oxford University Press, 2011).

Gorringe, Timothy J. 'On Building an Ark: The Global Emergency and the Limits of Moral Exhortation', *Studies in Christian Ethics* 24, 1 (2011): 23–33.

Gunton, Colin. *The Actuality of Atonement: A Study of Metaphor, Rationality and the Christian Tradition* (Edinburgh: T&T Clark, 1988).

Hart, Trevor A. 'Morality, Atonement and the Death of Jesus: The Crucial Focus of Forsyth's Theology', in Trevor Hart (ed.), *Justice the True and Only Mercy: Essays on the Life and Theology of Peter Taylor Forsyth* (Edinburgh: T&T Clark, 1997), pp. 16–36.

John Paul II. *Sollicitudo Rei Socialis*, available online at www.vatican.va/holy_father/john_paul_ii/encyclicals/documents/hf_jp-ii_enc_30121987_sollicitudo-rei-socialis_en.html (accessed 22 June 2012).

Joliba Trust website. Available online at www.jolibatrust.org.uk/index.html (accessed 25 February 2013).

Laidler, Victoria Gaile. *Gaudete Theology*, available online at http://gaudetetheology.word-press.com/2011/11/27/powers-principalities-and-structural-sin/ (accessed 24 February 2013).

McEwan, Ian. *Solar* (London: Vintage, 2011).

McFadyen, Alistair. *The Call to Personhood: A Christian Theory of the Individual in Social Relationships* (Cambridge: Cambridge University Press, 1990).

——*Bound to Sin: Abuse, Holocaust and the Doctrine of Sin* (Cambridge: Cambridge University Press, 2000).

Messer, Neil. 'Healthcare Resource Allocation and the "Recovery of Virtue"', *Studies in Christian Ethics* 18, 1 (2005): 89–108.

——*Selfish Genes and Christian Ethics: Theological and Ethical Reflections on Evolutionary Biology.* (London: SCM, 2007).

——'Humans, Animals, Evolution and Ends', in Celia Deane-Drummond and David Clough (eds), *Creaturely Theology: On God, Humans and Other Animals* (London: SCM, 2009), pp. 211–27.

——'Natural Evil after Darwin', in *Theology after Darwin*, Michael S. Northcott and R. J. Berry (eds) (Milton Keynes: Paternoster, 2009), pp. 139–54.

Midgley, Mary. *Wickedness: A Philosophical Essay* (London: Routledge, 2001).

Newbigin, Lesslie. *The Gospel in a Pluralist Society* (London: SPCK, 1989).

Northcott, Michael S. *A Moral Climate: The Ethics of Global Warming* (London: DLT, 2007).

Simmons, Frederick. 'Sin and Evil', in Willis Jenkins and Whitney Bauman (eds), *The Berkshire Encyclopedia of Sustainability, vol. 1: The Spirit of Sustainability* (Great Barrington, MA: Berkshire, 2010), pp. 367–68.

Southgate, Christopher. 'Re-Reading Genesis, John, and Job: A Christian Response to Darwinism', *Zygon* 46, 2 (2011): 370–95.

Wink, Walter. *Engaging the Powers: The Language of Power in the New Testament* (Philadelphia, PA: Fortress, 1984).

——*Unmasking the Powers: The Invisible Forces that Determine Human Existence* (Philadelphia: Fortress, 1986).

——*Engaging the Powers: Discernment and Resistance in a World of Domination* (Minneapolis, MN: Fortress, 1992).

9

THE CHURCH[1]

Tamara Grdzelidze

One of the ways to take an action with regard to climate change is through an ecclesiological prism. Taking into account the complexity of the life of the church today, *ekklesia* – a community of like-minded believers sharing faith in the incarnate Son of God who suffered the sacrificial death on the cross out of love for human kind and for all God's creation and was resurrected – leads to the assumption that the division (*diaresis*) among Christians on climate change reflects the division among human beings. In fact, all churches show signs of 'impoverished ecclesiologies', with some of the basic principles of the church having been forgotten or distorted. The complexity of the contemporary ecclesiologies refers to the role of the church in society as well as to the understanding of its foundations: what is the communion, *koinonia*, that the church promotes? This chapter takes it for granted that the purpose of the church in this world is salvation, and so the question it will pose is: what does climate change mean in the life of the church? Or, in other words, how can Christians understand climate change theologically and where can they look for a solution?

1.

This chapter aims to recover the biblical-liturgical tradition of the church, according to which it was founded by Christ himself for the salvation of the created order following the broken covenant between God and human beings. Through the sacrificial death on the cross of the incarnate Son of God, primordial unity between God and the divine creation became, again, a reality in the bosom of the church. Today, however, the reality of the biblical-liturgical tradition has become more allegorical than symbolical[2]: the real part of a liturgical symbol has diminished considerably and the liturgical or sacramental aspect of the church does not always correspond to its true nature but rather turns into allegory or ritual. The 'back and forth movement' between the church and the world is getting weaker, if not already lost. A good illustration of this loss of reality in church symbolism would be, for example, the interdependence of the spiritual and the material in the liturgical life of the church. It is in the liturgy that the blessing/sanctification of matter takes place. From this ecclesiological perspective, the goodness of the matter is not called into question.[3] Material products such as wine, wheat/bread, water, oil, wood and fruits are blessed in the church and some of these products are given back to God during the church service. That is what the prayer of the Anaphora (the offertory prayers for the gifts) says about the offered bread and wine – 'Thine own, of thine own, we offer unto thee, on behalf of all and for all'[4] – but these words extend to other material goods as well. However, the real part of the sanctification symbolism has been largely lost today because, in most cases, especially in urban areas, the offered products used in the liturgical celebration (if we have in mind the offered wheat or bread and wine) are not the product of the church community. The blessing of the waters performed at the feast of the Epiphany or the blessing of the crops and fruits at the Feast of the Transfiguration are restricted to local communities so that their universal dimensions – to bless the crops of the world, to sanctify the waters of the earth – have lost their links with wider reality. An important dimension of the connection between reality and the sanctification of matter in the liturgical year is its cyclical character, which coincides with the natural cycle.

The question to pose in this context is: will it make a difference in the age of climate change to recapture the depth of the biblical–liturgical understanding of the church? Will it reconnect with the holistic approach of the tradition, according to which the divine creation does not imply the dominion of human being over other creatures but promotes loving care for the other?

A chapter on ecclesiology in a time of climate change has the potential to turn into a catechesis. If Christians have forgotten, neglected or 're-branded' the essence of what the Christian faith and the Christian life are about, then Systematic Theology must concern itself with the re-discovery of the language to express the truth and its relevance to the present times. This new language cannot avoid having catechetical elements. Unfolding anew the faith by accentuating the need for repentance, or re-interpreting the mediating role of the church in the world, carries a specific task in a time of climate change, where there are visible signs of the physical collapse of the environment. In this context, it seems the time is right to explore the role of the church in Christian life. This exploration will lead towards an exhortation, teaching and spiritual guidance in order to apply theology to the reality; in this particular case, theology attempts to engage with life which is threatened by destruction.

Does the mystical vision of the last days in Revelation (Rev. 11. 18) resonate with the on-going reality of present days – 'rewarding your servants, the prophets and saints and all who fear your name, both small and great, and for destroying those who destroy the earth'? The biblical verse does not speak of vengeance on the part of the creator for disobeying his will; it rather says that the time has come for destroying those who destroy the earth, without saying who will do so. The implication is that it is human beings who act destructively against the earth, and so against themselves.

This chapter starts by retrieving the understanding of the church in the biblical-liturgical tradition. It is interesting to see what the tradition of the church offers when seeing the church as the mediator in the divine economy of salvation, as it has been planned by God for human beings and the rest of the divine creation.

2.

The early church affirmed the biblical vision, according to which the Fall and its consequences caused the disorder of the creation.[5]

In her work about Creation, Margaret Barker argues that human failure in keeping the covenant safe brought about the destruction of the earth and thus it has become a spiritual problem,[6] and that the covenant renewed in the New Testament was fundamentally the creation covenant.[7] Breaking the covenant, then, amounts to making one's own reality by transgressing the limits; setting up one's own conditions differently to those intended by God in the covenant.

The covenant between God and humans is of a particular design. When bestowing the freedom of choice on human beings, God does it within his own plan of salvation. The sun, moon and stars keep to their paths and the sea stays within its bounds – all obeying the decrees of the Creator, says I Clement.[8]

There is a clear vision which keeps things together in the divine economy: the vision extending from the specific rules to the overarching reflection. The rules to be followed by human beings are: moderation and self-discipline, caring for others and for all of God's creation, and bringing justice and peace into life. The overarching reflection of the divine economy concerns the salvation of all of God's creation.

> The bonds of creation cannot be renegotiated, and so some manmade systems – moral, political, economic – will have to change, since the bonds of creation are breaking. The seven sins – pride, envy, gluttony, lust, anger, greed and sloth – have now been rebranded and become socially acceptable. ... sin has been redefined.[9]

What can the church do in this situation, if the environmental crisis is a spiritual crisis? Churches would gain from becoming more politically engaged – or, as it will be argued later, churches must reveal their true political nature – in order to bring the message about the close link between the broken covenant and failing spirituality, and its connectedness with political choices and actions, to their respective societies. Spirituality and politics have been inseparable in the church, but this link – open or hidden, formal or unofficial – has been unpacked in different ways in different contexts, depending on whether Christians are in a majority or a minority.[10]

At the end of the day, one wonders what theology is about if it is not concerned with what is happening to the world we live in, to the world of God's creation. The church is described as the mediator for the salvation of all of God's creation through the human response to the sacrificial love and care of the Son of God, and it has to unfold this message in everyday life, bringing the Body of Christ into the world in a more vivid and meaningful way.

Can a theory remain valid if it is not put into practice? Can Christians remain faithful to Christ if the message of his incarnation and redemptive death is not related to life? However difficult it may seem, the church – *ekklesia* – must set an example by following its foundational principles, set an example by striving for the salvation of God's creation.

The church, because of its theandric origin and salvific purpose, has many implications in the world. The church has been glorified for its destiny and the church has been condemned for being blind to the ongoing reality. In the church what is physically seen and scientifically proven is complemented by the unseen reality and by the human spiritual experience (of both of these realities).

'Behold I make all things new … ' (Rev. 21. 5) – this is *the* universal truth, which in the church becomes a particular moment of a history.

3.

There exists in the church today a theological discourse which describes human beings damaging the natural world as 'sin against nature'.[11] Climate change is the result of the sin that has been manifested in degraded spirituality, the breaking of the covenant; in economic injustice towards one's neighbour – the other – and the rest of the creation;[12] and in the tendency to rule over the other and over the rest of the creation.[13]

On the other hand, this 're-discovery' of profound spiritual themes is about the renewal of Christian ethical vows in the light of the sacrificial death and bodily resurrection of the Son of God. The greed, the excess in consumption and the everlasting desire for possessions destroy these vows that were originally embedded in the belief that grace supersedes nature and faith fulfils reason.

Against the background of the biblical–liturgical tradition of life in the church, human beings realise their own errors, such as going beyond the limits of the permissible in exploiting natural resources. The roots of the sustainability problem are largely political. Excessive consumption and greed at the individual level in different societies have been widely supported by the respective political systems. Greed cannot be seen as a problem of individuals without strongly connecting it to the societies that promote it, based on political direction of those societies.[14]

As Konrad Raiser has shown, the churches were having ecumenical discussions about issues of wealth as early as the 1920s. There were various attempts 'to restate the essential principles of the Christian tradition and apply them to the con-temporary situation,'[15] through the AGAPE-Process[16] of the World Council of Churches and study documents such as *Christian Faith and the World Economy Today*

(1992). Addressing issues of the essential goodness of the created order, the free-dom of each human being, the covenant in Christ between humanity and God and caring for the poor[17] – all derived from biblical tradition – the study document could be used by the churches as a guide for ethical judgement:

> When we assume that human needs are virtually limitless, the scarcity increases (especially non-economic good), regardless of the level of human prosperity. Many seem to have lost the perception of enough. ... Just as humanity has more or less developed a sense of a required minimum of consumption to ensure a decent life, so we should be considering where maximum limits may lie, and how those might be implemented, before excess leads to ruin.[18]

A later ecumenical document – *Lead Us Not into Temptation* (2001) – speaks more openly about ecological responsibility in the light of Christian economic life. Such an emphasis on the human dependency on creation is largely, Raiser says,

> a result of the first United Nations conference on Environment and Devel-opment in Stockholm in 1972 and the publication of the Club of Rome's report on the Limits to Growth that same year. This shift is reflected in ecumenical discussion in the growing concern for sustainability of the use of resources.[19]

As in many other cases, the results of these useful discussions do not seem to have been received by the churches and so they have not stepped into dialogue with the governments and big corporations that oppose sanctions on the use of natural resources.

The contemporary lifestyle often encourages the so-called 'fortress mentality' which is contrary to the vision of a church rooted in the biblical and liturgical tradition. The church often expresses, in different ways, the communion of the living and the departed; it trusts in the ontological communion of saints, those distinguished witnesses of faith. This human interconnectedness speaks of the loving care that exists between all creatures and that spreads over the rest of crea-tion. The human focus on oneself is the foundation of the crisis of the created order. Acknowledgement of the witnesses of faith – expressed by means of the liturgical commemoration of saints or by reading out their life-stories – grants to their lives a paradigmatic character.[20] Christian social life, witnessed to by the communion of saints, is fundamentally opposed to the so-called 'fortress men-talities' which is the tendency not only among nations but also among churches. Individuals, or corporations, or states with an impoverished spiritual life have less concern, or no concern at all, for anything else but their own interests and are deprived of the sacred communality that the church envisages for all in the divine order.

4.

The communal life of the church links the body of Christ with the world – the whole of God's creation – and also assists in its transformation.

The fundamental question asked by evangelical theologian Simon Chan is whether the church as the body of Christ is a metaphor or something more than that. Struggling with the question of whether the church can 'regain its position as a community whose way of life has a decisive bearing on individual Christians', the answer is sought in unfolding a theological understanding of the church coupled with a strong liturgical practice.[21] To be a Christian is to be incorporated into the church by baptism and nourished with the spiritual food of the body and blood of Christ in the Eucharist.[22] Ecclesial communion is first and foremost a eucharistic communion, and the prevailing foci of the church life are *koinonia* and *agape*.[23] The world must derive its *raison d'être* from the church, by dying to itself and being reborn into the polity of the church.[24]

Rediscovering the potential of the church as polity requires engagement with spiritual themes which are part of systematic theological reflection on the Church. In doing so, it is reasonable to start with an ancient understanding of the church, set in the framework of the biblical-liturgical vision.

A well-known Byzantine theologian of the seventh century in his treatise on the church – tentatively called Mystagogia – sees the church as an image of God and the world, of human being and the sensible world. Maximus the Confessor follows many of his predecessors in viewing the sacramental life of the church as a means of divine adoption: the imminence of the eschatological formula 'already, but not yet' occurs at the eucharistic celebration. In a broader ecclesial framework, the human image–likeness distinction sets forth the motion towards the salvation of the divine creation: rendering the image unto likeness imitates the loving care of the Son of God for all of God's creation. The interest today in this rather ancient understanding of the church lies in its intention to keep all beings and their relations together: material and spiritual, noetic and sensible, cyclic time and linear history, the present moment and eternity. Only through this sense of the wholeness of all the created beings with the uncreated principles (i.e. angels, archangels etc.) may human beings see their life as indissoluble from the rest of the creation and of the divine economy. The sacramental life of the church witnesses to life (and, indeed, to the creation) being not only bound to the material, physical, rational aspects of the divine order but being equally bound to the invisible divine principles.[25]

> Participation in the energies of the Holy Spirit – always within a Trinitarian framework – signifies that these liturgical celebrations form, in this particular phase in the history of the church the Paraclete, a fully organic part of the whole ecclesial body of Christ and, therefore of the whole created reality.[26]

The strong sacramental implications of this understanding of the Church indicate a special role for the Holy Spirit in salvation history together with the sacrificial death (and resurrection) of the incarnate Word of God and the will of God the Father. Unless the destiny of the divine creation is seen as interwoven with the destiny of the redeemed human image, the purpose of the Church with regard to the created order is inexplicable.

> ... God becomes a human being, in order to save lost humanity. Through Himself He has, in accordance with nature, united the fragments of the universal nature of the all, manifesting the universal logoi that have come forth for the particulars, by which the union of the divided naturally comes about, and thus He fulfils the great purpose of God the Father, 'to recapitulate everything both in heaven and earth in Himself' (Eph. 1. 10), 'in whom everything has been created' (Col. 1. 16).[27]

Since the church bears the imprint and image of God, Maximus says, it reflects God as the image reflects the archetype.

> For numerous and of almost infinite number are the men, women, and children who are distinct from one another and vastly different by birth and appearance, by nationality and language, by customs and age, by opinions and skills, by manners and habits, by pursuits and studies, and still again by reputation, fortune, characteristics, and connections: All are born into the Church and through it are reborn and recreated in the Spirit ... to be and to appear as one body formed of different members is really worthy of Christ himself. ... As the center of straight lines that radiate from him, he does not allow by his unique, simple, and single cause and power that the principles of beings become disjoined at the periphery but rather he circumscribes their extension in a circle and brings back to himself the distinctive elements of beings which he himself brought into existence. The purpose of this is so that the creations and products of the one God be in no way strangers and enemies to one another by having no reason or center for which they might show each other any friendly or peaceful sentiment or identity.[28]

The church exists for the sake of the creatures of God, not being strangers to one another nor enemies, through their unity in Christ. By keeping created and uncreated together, the church focuses on their relations. The church is endowed with immense significance as the place where the faithful become united with God and with one another in the eucharistic celebration; the church itself is also the unity without confusion, the kind of unity that is not distorted by the diversity of its constituent parts.

5.

The church is the worldly embodiment of the eschaton of creation, as revealed in the New Testament account of the Christ events. Its cyclical vision of time, together with linear history and well reflected in the liturgical year, co-exists with the expectation of the final consummation. Maximus, and the tradition he belongs to, comprehends eschatological imminence through the sacramental life of the church.

The church, due to its divine-human – or theandric – nature, is embedded in the fleshly appearance and bodily resurrection of Christ and witnesses to the break-through of the Kingdom that has already taken place in the Incarnation and has been actualised with Christ's redemptive death and resurrection. The church embraces past, present and future in a unity that is fundamental to Christian eschatology. The complex interpenetration of different times generally causes uncertainty about the time of the realisation of the divine promise – the church resolves this uncertainty, however, in the eucharistic rite. In the liturgical celebra-tion, one reaches the height of earthly transformation, but full realisation will take place only with the consummation of the cosmos. The liturgical rite reinforces the presence of the Kingdom in the church, though its full realization is still to come. This eschatological imminence involves the anthropological theme of the trans-formation of human being, known in the tradition to which Maximus belongs as divinisation or deification – theosis.

Deification is not a destruction of human nature – in union with the Trinity a person transforms, changes. This dialectic, like certain other patterns of dialectic in the early church, is based on the dialectic implied in the Incarnation: a change, without changing essence. A similar structural framework marks deification: human being becomes god, without destroying human nature.

6.

The Bible encourages human beings towards holiness: 'You shall be holy, for I the Lord your God am holy' (Lev. 19. 2). Or, again, 'Be perfect, therefore, as your heavenly father is perfect' (Matt. 5. 48). Human beings are destined to seek holiness and perfection. But the question is, how can one seek holiness? In Matthew 6, Jesus tells his followers that life is not restricted to food or other material goods – 'Strive first for the kingdom of God and his righteousness, and all these things will be given to you as well.' (Matt. 6. 33)

The potential for perfection distinguishes human beings from the rest of creation and relates him/her distinctively to the creator (in contrast to other beings). All the fathers of the church in the East and in the West agree that there is a primordial correspondence between the human being and the divine being because of the *Imago Dei* but there have been various opinions as to where and how this image is located. The image is seen in a particular quality of the human soul, in the ability to know God, in mind or intellect (*nous*),[29] in reason (*logos*), in freedom.[30] Some of the fathers said that not only the soul but also the body shares in the character of the image.[31] Freedom is

> formal image, the necessary condition for the attainment of perfect assimila-tion to God. Because created in the image of God, a human being is to be

seen as a personal being, a person who is not to be controlled by nature (i.e. human nature) but who can himself control nature (i.e. human nature) in assimilating it to its divine Archetype.[32]

The uniting capacity of *Imago Dei* has its historical roots. As John Zizioulas has commented:

> Logos or rationality had a particular meaning at that time, and it had mainly to do with the capacity of the human being to collect what is diversified and even fragmented in this world and make a beautiful and harmonious world (cosmos) out of that. Rationality was not, as it came to be understood later, simply a capacity to reason with one's mind. Instead, as the ancient Greeks thought of logos, it is man's capacity to achieve the unity of the world and to make a cosmos out of it. Human being has the capacity to unite the world.[33]

The church, on the other hand, has been founded (not founded *just once,* as until its consummation it is a continuing process) with a view to being a medium for bringing human beings and the created world to the archetype.[34] (In this context, a human being, because of its distinguished role, is also responsible for the rest of the creation.) The original unity intended for the divine creation is re-established in the body of Christ that is the church, by the synergy of the grace of God and the human freedom to acquire the divine likeness.

The image–likeness distinction – the verse from Genesis which became foundational for the Christian anthropology: 'Then God said: "Let us make humankind in our image, according to our likeness"' (1:26) – prepares the ground for speaking about the church as the image of God and its relation to the material world and sensible beings. The image–likeness distinction indicates the transformative potential of the church. The transformation from image to likeness also extends to society, and political and economic systems. This is what the church should be striving for: a transformation according to the principles lying at the heart of the image–archetype and image–likeness distinction.

Since the church contains continuity but also reflects constant renewal, its fundamentals need to be revisited in order to give a proper meaning to the renewal of both humanity and creation in the light of the scientific revelations of a coming crisis for creation and the human condition from climate change. But where and how does the church speak?

7.

'Wherever the relevance of speech is at stake, matters become political by definition, for speech is what makes man a political being.'[35] The 'language' of the church should convey a particular message of unity and loving care for the other which extends to the rest of God's creation. The church, for the sake of being the church, brings into one prism multiple aspects and dimensions of the Creation and its language must be adapted to this multiplicity of expression.

To come to grips with the teaching of the church and its incompatibility with politics in today's world, it is timely to refer to the issue of how the church can maintain its political nature following the final institutionalization of secular nation-states in our age, as the world has gradually come to witness 'a loveless power and an impotent love.'[36] Here I invite three conversation partners from Roman Catholic, Anglican and Orthodox traditions.

As William Cavanaugh points out, political theologies of the twentieth century – among which should also be counted the churches in solidarity against environmental injustice – emerged in response to the tendency to interiorize the Gospel, removing the church from the public sphere and placing it into the private sphere.[37] The message that Jesus came not to destroy the law but to fulfil it has been neglected. Cavanaugh, however, very much in accordance with Oliver O'Donovan, sees another approach to the dominant separation of the church and politics in the twentieth century by retrieving the political nature of the church itself. Although it is very difficult to argue against the prevailing views regarding the spiritualization and interioriziation of the church in the modern nation-state, the answer is sought in examining the politics in core Christian theological themes and by a return to the Augustinian conviction that politics is truly politics when mapped into salvation history.[38]

To pursue the political nature of the church in our age is a big ecclesiological challenge; however, there are strong claims that theology is about politics and that the church plays a central role in the transformation of the social order.[39] In this context, O'Donovan repositions politics within salvation history by recovering the eschatology – with a strong emphasis on 'already' – missing from most of the contemporary political theologies.[40] The church is not a mystery cult but it reaches into all aspects of life by offering a new way of reconciled life in the world. By offering a new way of life, the church teaches that the kingdom of God is in this world although it is not of the world (John 18. 36). The church has a fundamental role in the salvation of the world because of its political nature. The church – the already inaugurated Kingdom – is not compatible with its marginalized image in nation-states today. 'Without seeking to rule, the church has more to contribute precisely because it is the bearer of God's politics, and because it is catholic, trans-national, transcending the parochial borders of the nation-state.'[41] This dialectic should be kept in mind: the church does not have ready answers to all problems in the world; the church, however, constantly reminds us of Christ's salvific death on the cross and thus urges us to live and act in accordance with it. 'The church's job is to try to discern in each concrete circumstances how best to embody the politics of the cross in suffering.'[42]

'Political is mystical', says Aristotle Papanikolaou in his recently released book.[43] Papanikolaou works with two principles of political theology: on the one hand, there are churches which survived communist regimes and which found it difficult to deal with political theology whilst they were stuck between the ideas of the

Byzantine symphonia and the unacceptable modernity; on the other hand, some eastern and western theologians believe (for different reasons) that liberal democracy is incompatible with Christian ecclesiological ideals. The strength of his approach lies in starting from the core orthodox principle – divinisation. If the human being is created for union with God, the Christian principle of love of the other becomes foundational for political theology, insofar as politics 'can be construed as an engagement with the neighbor/stranger.'[44]

The destiny of all creation to participate in the divine life, 'to actualize God's presence as the body of Christ in the material', is grounded in the logic of divine–human communion.[45] Thus what was assigned to the private sphere is shown to have public ramifications, the mystical is the political. The very mission of the church is to eucharistize the material creation.[46]

The view on eucharistization of the world, however, comes into conflict with the pluralism, multi-religious and multi-confessional reality of today's life. Resolving this conflict of the eucharistization of all of God's creation through Christian worship and life with democratic pluralism is the most urgent ecclesiological agenda for Christian churches, regardless of their traditional or (quasi) non-traditional roots. This is clearly articulated by Papanaikolaou in the chapter on Eucharist or Democracy. There are greater possibilities of reaching a less compromised solution to reconciling democracy and Christian ecclesiology than one may assume from the first glance. The religious voice can participate in public discussion without coming into conflict with freedom, equality or other democratic principles; however, the debate goes around the question of 'how religion can be a part of public life'.[47] In fact, Papanikolaou argues, liberal democracy offers ample possibilities for the Christian church to be a genuine voice among other voices, possibilities that become evident from the church's nature as an eschatological community.[48] On the other hand, the church, while recognizing its limits, may become active in bringing diverse voices into the search for the common good. Accepting the diversity of liberal democracy must be voluntarily accepted by the church – an eschatological community. 'Christians can only think politics within the horizon of the eschatological, though potentially immanent, goal of divine-human communion.'[49] Papanikolou offers a timely solution to the question of 'curing' a gap between the eschatological vision and existing ecclesial structures: the former should unceasingly feed the latter,[50] the material world should be transformed by the divine.[51] Although, the theandric nature of the church comes into conflict with the atheistic voice of liberal democracy, the principles of liberal democracy do not come into conflict with the theandric nature of the church.

The church is continuously on a mission to speak the truth, to bring the Kingdom to the earth and to eucharistize all God's creation, but in order to define what it means in reality – in other words, how to realize it – one needs to become a *zoon hermeneutikon*. Without interpreting and re-interpreting one's everyday life within one's local and global communities, without constantly posing questions in relation to one's local and global communities, it is impossible for Christians to relate to the existing pluralism. There are fewer visible and formal signs of Christian presence in the modern world than in the pre-modern world. The Christian presence is actualized through the Christian life itself. So, the modern Christian, who has been living the faith throughout the modern age, has become *zoon hermeneutikon*, habitually addressing the modern pluralistic world from Christian convictions which, on their part, demand the eucharistization of all of God's creation. And the crucial question here is – how to manage this? Another interesting question in this context will be whether it can be argued that a notion of Christian denomination does not diminish the significance of eucharistization. Can the church, as an eschatological community, contain within itself the potential for overcoming the diminution of the eucharistization by some other factors?

And what is wrong if this is an ideal level of discourse on the church? There should be an inexhaustible source of nourishment: the eschatological vision and ethical principles which help the church to be itself and guide Christians to fulfil their lives in Christ. Truly, the church is *the vision* of an ideal society.[52]

> We must begin to understand God's revelation in history as the apocalyptic reality fulfilling itself, that reality which leads to the end of history; and this is something more than a simple cataloguing of events according to their pragmatic significance. A further dimension needs to be in view – a living sense of the incompleteness of history (history as 'prehistory'), which still leaves room for 'utopia', for what is not yet but is to come, for the ideal, for hope. Christianity, in its idea of the Kingdom of God, possesses just such a comprehensive and inexhaustible ideal, including in itself all good human goals and achievements. But it also still has its promise, signified in the symbolic language of the Apocalypse as the inauguration of the thousand-year reign of Christ on earth (Rev. 20). This symbol, which is the guiding star of history, was for a long time locked in by a one-sided interpretation, so that the rejection without remainder of this dominant interpretation was immediately reckoned as heresy. But this ultimate manifestation of the Kingdom of God on earth, symbolically rendered in this way, cannot remain a purely passively understood prophecy (worthy of ideological rejection on account of this passivity): it must become an active utopian ideal, a hope.[53]

In my view, eucharistic ecclesiology unfolds the inherently political nature of the church – to speak the truth and to strive for the common good until the end comes.

Two features define the church as political in its manifold dimensions: it speaks in order to be heard; and it speaks the truth and strives for the common good for the sake of all of God's creation.

Post-scriptum

The recent international meetings on climate change – Copenhagen (2011) and Rio+20 (2012) – were considered 'a failure' and 'almost a failure' respectively. The world is blind when it comes to changing one's pattern of life. The points of concentration, especially for those who are powerful politically and materially, remain materialistic and the alternative human approaches have become fragmented. Christians are in an unfavourable position as they 'know' but are not able to endorse their conviction in a more effective way. This is especially pitiful in the light of the understanding of the church described above: the church teaches the loving care for one's neighbour and for the rest of the creation, and it makes the people of God members of the Body of Christ. This reality has to draw on more creative approaches than frustration and nihilism. Christians believe that the world is to be made anew and the church – *ekklesia* – has to play a major role in this new creation. And again, the purpose of the church with regard to the created order is fulfilled only if the destiny of the divine creation is interwoven with the destiny of the redeemed human image.

Notes

1 Note on terminology: divine order is the same as the created order; sometimes also referred to as the whole of the created order.
2 The meaning of the Greek word *sumballo* is to bring or throw two realities together. In fact, both parts of a symbol are grounded in their respective realities.
3 See Peter Scott, 'Thinking Like an Animal: Theological Materialism for a Changing Climate', *Studies in Christian Ethics* 24 (1) (2011): 50–66.
4 'We can easily make the mistake of thinking that materiality is itself the problem; but the whole structure of Greek patristic and medieval Christian thinking should recall to us the conviction of the sacredness of matter which stands at the heart of classical Christian doctrine,' writes Rowan Williams in his review – 'Such a thing: An invigorating journey on the frontier between science and religion' – of Conor Cunningham's *Darwin's Pious Idea: Why the ultra-Darwinists and Creationists both get it wrong* (*The Times Literary Supplement*, April 22, 2011, No. 5638, 8).
5 Lars Thunberg, *Microcosm and Mediator, The Theological Anthropology of Maximus the Confessor*, 2nd edn, Foreword by A. M. Allchin (Chicago: Open Court, 1995), p.136.
6 Margaret Barker, *Creation, A Biblical Vision for the Environment*, Foreword by His All Holiness Ecumenical Patriarch Bartholomew, (London: T&T Clark, 2010), p. 2. Barker names human choices that make lifestyles in harmony with the plan of the Creator. The central idea of Barker's book is to trace the roots of the Biblical vision in the Temple theology.
7 Barker, *Creation*, p. 165.
8 I Clement 20; in Barker, *Creation*, p. 96.
9 Barker, *Creation*, p. 140.
10 H. W. Montefiore, *The Question Mark. The End of Homo Sapiens?* (London: Collins, 1969), p. 44.
11 John Zizioulas, 'Towards an Environmental Ethic'. Available online at www.rsesymposia. org/themedia/File/1151678281-Ethic.pdf (accessed September 16, 2013).
12 'You have lived on the earth in luxury and in pleasure; you have fattened your hearts on a day of slaughter. You have condemned and murdered the righteous one, who does not resist you.' James 5. 5–6.
13 Paul teaches us to follow Christ in his self-emptying love: 'Do nothing from selfish ambition or conceit but in humility regard others as better than yourselves. Let each of you look not to your own interests, but to the interests of others.' Philippians 2. 3–4.
14 Here I propose a slight critique of the view that 'the roots of sustainability problems are not political or technological, but principally the inner ethical and spiritual crises, manifested outwardly as human greed.' Lucas Andrianos, 'Structural Greed and Creation: A

Theological Reflection', *The Ecumenical Review* 63.3 (2011): 312. See in the same issue of *The Ecumenical Review* Konrad Raiser's article 'Theological and Ethical Considerations regarding Wealth' supporting the argument in the paper: 'The structural and systemic problem of glaring inequalities nationally and globally has to be addressed first, before individual violations of an accepted rule can be dealt with.' 291.

15 Raiser, 'Theological and Ethical Considerations,' p. 286.

16 AGAPE – Alternative Globalisation Addressing Peoples and Earth.

17 *Christian Faith and the World Economy Today* (Geneva: WCC Publications, 1992), pp. 13–15.

18 *Christian Faith and the World Economy Today*, p. 31.

19 Raiser, 'Theological and Ethical Considerations', 288: 'The ecumenical conference on Science and Technology for a Human Development at Bucharest (1974) called for fixing an upper limit for the use of resources in the developed countries. The Nairobi Assembly of the WCC (1975), in the section on Human Development – the Ambiguities of Power, Technology and Quality of Life found in the assembly's report, addressed the ethical problems in the transition to a sustainable and just society.'

20 However, the faith in the divine powers differs: the Orthodox and Catholics pray to the saints and it implies an ecclesiological difference.

21 Simon Chan, *Liturgical Theology, The Church as Worshipping Community* (Downers Grove, IL: InterVarsity Press, 2006), pp. 166, 21–40. I cannot agree with the approach that sees the church as prior to creation, namely, in the following formulation: 'the church does not exist to fix a broken creation.' 23.

22 Chan, *Liturgical Theology*, p. 24.

23 Chan, *Liturgical Theology*, p. 29. Greek *koinonia* – communion, *agape* – love.

24 Chan, *Liturgical Theology*, p. 26.

25 The teaching on the divine principles – *logoi* – of creatures in Maximus the Confessor manifests the divine order in the created world and its relatedness to the world beyond it. See Torstein Theodor Tollefsen, *The Christocentric Cosmology of St. Maximus the Confessor*, Oxford Early Christian Studies (Oxford: Oxford University Press, 2008). 'The main point in Maximus' concept is the idea that lower reality could neither exist nor be glorified if the cause did not make itself present as that by which this lower reality has a certain mode of being' p. 261.

26 Nikos A. Matsoukas, 'Chemins de la Christologie Orthodoxe', in *L'Eglise, Lieu de la Célébration des Mystères*, Textes réunis par Astériou Argyriou (Paris: Desclée, 2005), 383. See also Nikos Matsoukas, 'The Economy of the Holy Spirit, The Standpoint of Orthodox Theology', *The Ecumenical Review* 41 (1989): 400.

27 Ambigua 41, translation by Andrew Louth, *Maximus the Confessor* (London: Routledge, 1996), p. 159.

28 Maximus the Confessor, *Selected Writings*, George C. Berthold (trans. and notes), The Classics of Western Spirituality (Paulist Press, 1985), p. 187.

29 Clement of Alexandria called mind/*nous* 'the image of the image'. Stromata, 5, 14, quoted in Thunberg, *Microcosm and Mediator*, p. 116.

30 Philo of Alexandria regards the highest part of the soul – *nous* – as the divine image; Evagrius Ponticus sees it in mind (Thunberg, *Microcosm and Mediator*, 116). Maximus the Confessor says that every rational soul is made in the image of God (*Selected Writings*, 130). Or, in another place, he considers freedom as a sign of the divine image (Ambigua 42; PG 91, 1345D).

31 Vladimir Lossky, *The Mystical Theology of the Eastern Church* (Cambridge: James Clark, repr. 1991), pp. 114–18.

32 Lossky, *The Mystical Theology*, pp. 119–20.

33 John Zizioulas, 'Proprietors or Priests of Creation?' Available online at http://www.rse-symposia.org/themedia/File/1151679350-Pergamon.pdf (accessed September 16 2013).

34 Archetype, in this context, means God, according to which human being is created.

35 Hannah Arendt, *The Human Condition*, 2nd edn (Chicago and London: Chicago University Press, 1998), p. 3.

36 Catherine Pickstock, *After Writing, On the Liturgical Consummation of Philosophy* (Oxford: Blackwell Publishers, 1998), p. 157.
37 William T. Cavanaugh, 'The Church,' in *Blackwell Companion to Political Theology*, Wiley-Blackwell Companions to Religion, eds. Peter Scott and William T. Cavanaugh (Oxford: Blackwell Publishers, 2004), pp. 393–406.
38 Cavanaugh, 'The Church,' p. 403.
39 Oliver O'Donovan, *The Desire of the Nations, Rediscovering the Roots of Political Theology* (Cambridge: Cambridge University Press, 1996), p. 199f.
40 Cavanaugh, 'The Church,' p. 403. It must be noted that the recent attempts to come to grips with Orthodoxy and Political Theology address the eschatological dimension of the church in a similar manner. See Pantelis Kalaitzides, *Orthodoxy and Political Theology*, Doxa and Praxis series (Geneva: WCC Publications, 2012)
41 Cavanaugh, 'The Church,' p. 405
42 Cavanaugh, 'The Church,' p. 406.
43 Aristotle Papanikolaou, *The Mystical as Political, Democracy and Non-Radical Orthodoxy* (Notre Dame, IN: University of Notre Dame Press, 2012)
44 Papanikolaou, *The Mystical as Political*, p. 4.
45 Papanikolaou, *The Mystical as Political*, p. 69.
46 Papanikolaou, *The Mystical as Political*, p. 70.
47 Papanikolaou, *The Mystical as Political*, p. 76.
48 Papanikolaou, *The Mystical as Political*, p. 77.
49 Papanikolaou, *The Mystical as Political*, pp. 78–79.
50 Papanikolaou, *The Mystical as Political*, p. 82.
51 Papanikolaou, *The Mystical as Political*, p. 73.
52 Papanikolaou, *The Mystical as Political*, p. 24.
53 Sergii Bulgakov, 'The Soul of Secularism' in *Towards a Russian Political Theology*, Texts edited and introduced by Rowan Williams (Edinburgh: T&T Clark, 1999), p. 257.

Bibliography

Andrianos, Lucas. 'Structural Greed and Creation: A Theological Reflection', *The Ecumenical Review* 63, 3 (2011).
Arendt, Hannah. *The Human Condition*, 2nd edn (Chicago and London: Chicago University Press, 1998).
Barker, Margaret. *Creation, A Biblical Vision for the Environment*, Foreword by His All Holiness Ecumenical Patriarch Bartholomew (London: T&T Clark, 2010).
Bulgakov, Sergii. 'The Soul of Secularism' in Rowan Williams (ed.), *Towards a Russian Political Theology* (Edinburgh: T&T Clark, 1999).
Cavanaugh, William T. 'The Church', in Peter Scott and William T. Cavanaugh (eds), *Blackwell Companion to Political Theology*, Wiley-Blackwell Companions to Religion (Oxford: Blackwell Publishers, 2004), pp. 393–406.
Chan, Simon. *Liturgical Theology, The Church as Worshipping Community* (Downers Grove, IL: InterVarsity Press, 2006).
Kalaitzides, Pantelis. *Orthodoxy and Political Theology*, Doxa and Praxis series (Geneva: WCC Publications, 2012).
Lossky, Vladimir. *The Mystical Theology of the Eastern Church* (Cambridge: James Clark, repr. 1991)
Louth, Andrew. *Maximus the Confessor* (London: Routledge, 1996).
Matsoukas, Nikos. 'The Economy of the Holy Spirit, The Standpoint of Orthodox Theology', *The Ecumenical Review* 41, 1989.
Matsoukas, Nikos A. 'Chemins de la Christologie Orthodoxe', in Astériou Argyriou, *L'Eglise, Lieu de la Célébration des Mystères* (Paris: Desclée, 2005).
Maximus the Confessor. *Selected Writings*, George C. Berthold (trans. and notes), The Classics of Western Spirituality (New York: Paulist Press, 1985).

Montefiore, H. W. *The Question Mark. The End of Homo Sapiens?* (London: Collins, 1969).

O'Donovan, Oliver. *The Desire of the Nations, Rediscovering the Roots of Political Theology* (Cambridge: Cambridge University Press, 1996).

Papanikolaou, Aristotle. *The Mystical as Political, Democracy and Non-Radical Orthodoxy* (Notre Dame, IN: University of Notre Dame Press, 2012).

Pickstock, Catherine. *After Writing, On the Liturgical Consummation of Philosophy* (Oxford: Blackwell Publishers, 1998).

Raiser, Konrad. 'Theological and Ethical Considerations regarding Wealth', *The Ecumenical Review* 63.3, 2011.

Scott, Peter. 'Thinking Like an Animal: Theological Materialism for a Changing Climate', *Studies in Christian Ethics* 24 (1), 2011.

Scott, Peter and William T. Cavanaugh (eds). *Blackwell Companion to Political Theology*, Wiley-Blackwell Companions to Religion (Oxford: Blackwell Publishers, 2004).

Thunberg, Lars. *Microcosm and Mediator, The Theological Anthropology of Maximus the Confessor*, 2nd edn, Foreword by A. M. Allchin (Chicago: Open Court, 1995).

Tollefsen, Torstein Theodor. *The Christocentric Cosmology of St. Maximus the Confessor*, Oxford Early Christian Studies (Oxford: Oxford University Press, 2008).

Zizioulas, John. 'Towards an Environmental Ethic'. Available online at www.rsesymposia. org/themedia/File/1151678281-Ethic.pdf

Zizioulas, John. 'Proprietors or Priests of Creation?' Available online at www.rsesymposia. org/themedia/File/1151679350-Pergamon.pdf

10

ESCHATOLOGY

Stefan Skrimshire

All we have to decide is what to do in the time that is given to us.

(Gandalf)

Introduction

Lars von Trier claimed that the inspiration for *Melancholia* (2011) – in which a wedding party is rudely disrupted by news that the earth is about to collide with a rogue planet – came during treatment for depression. Those who have lost all hope, von Trier was told by his therapist, respond more calmly than others in situations of crisis.[1] It isn't hard to see how this revelation pervades the film. The anti-hero is the bride Justine who finds, within a state of profound melancholy, a lucid acceptance of the imminent end of the world. What unfolds is the juxtaposition of this acceptance against the clamour of trivial human desires, plans (including her own wedding) and petty disputes of those who surround her.

Like the character interplay in *Melancholia*, Christian eschatological parables and instructions revolve frequently around the juxtaposition of mundane human concerns alongside the expectation of the eschaton. Eschatology is concerned not only with reasoning about the end, but also the psychological-phenomenological experience and ethical orientation of believers towards it. Which imperatives (or prohibitions) of human action are generated by eschatological pronouncements? What does one *do* when the end is pronounced? It is a familiar literary and cinematic trope (one thinks of Don McKellar's 1998 film *Last Night*), but also well known to the audience of the New Testament. Believers in a newly crucified and resurrected messiah knew exactly what it was to hold anticipation of the messianic age in tension with the sober reality of living in the world in the time that remains.

St. Paul's discourses on the inter-personal and social responsibilities of the interim period thus hold special importance for us: 'the appointed time has grown short; from now on, let even those who have wives be as though they had none ... for the present form of this world is passing away' (1 Corinthians 7. 29–32).

So much for abandoned weddings and encroaching apocalypses. What has this to do with ethical thought in general, and for climate ethics in particular? Eschatology concerns that in which a believer may legitimately place their hope, from purely personal destiny (life after death) to the fate of the cosmos and the 'end of all things'. It is also the doctrine that is most likely to have direct impact upon the direction of political action, generating attitudes that range from resignation and apathy to triumphalism in the face of future crises.[2] A more specific problem facing climate activism is, however, that of radical uncertainty. Not over the reality of anthropogenic global warming, but rather uncertainty with regard to temporal thresholds (those of 'tipping elements', for instance) and their impact upon what is achievable and desirable through activism. If carbon emissions will commit the earth system to irreversible warming, is authoritarian governmental intervention or disruptive (and potentially violent) direct action ethically warranted? What measure of likelihood would be enough to validate such claims? And what sort of actions and behaviours are warranted when we are believed to have passed a critical threshold? Can we know what we ought to do when there is no way of knowing for certain how much time is left to do it? There is a quite broad concern here about the purpose and function of political action. But it invites a further consideration that relates us back to that dilemma facing St. Paul's audience: how much information about future scenarios do we require to make sense of our time on earth, in the 'time that remains'? To what extent does a vision of a different future turn ethical life into a form of mere *waiting* as opposed to that of *transforming* the present?

In the following I attend to these questions of temporal uncertainty, faith and action. I do this first by outlining what I see as the new pressures generated for both ethical and theological thought by anthropogenic global warming, specifically with regard to the meaning of political action given worst case scenarios. Then I look critically at the themes and thinkers in eschatology (with particular attention on Jürgen Moltmann) that have dealt most directly with these pressures: the tension between faith in personal and universal redemption; the tension between an 'incoming' future and that of a transformed present; and, finally, the importance and implications of a discourse of loss and mourning.

Outlining the pressures of a changing climate

Ecotheology, mirroring the evolution of environmental consciousness itself since the 1960s, has been eschatologically framed from the outset. The dedication that Rachel Carson made in *Silent Spring* to the environmentalist and theologian, Albert Schweitzer, is pertinent in this regard. Schweitzer is well known for insisting upon the messianic eschatological expectations of Jesus and his followers. But he also linked this hope with a vision of the liberation of the natural earth from its condition of suffering.[3] Later liberationist perspectives also understood a multitude of ecological woes through the image of the planet that was suffering alongside that of the human being.[4] But the political relevance of eschatology really came to the fore in the light of (and perhaps in reaction to) the first predictive experiments of earth systems analysis, with the report of *Limits to Growth* in 1972. A decade later, process theologian John Cobb asked two fundamental questions of theology: whether, if humanity were to wipe itself out, creation would continue to be good; and how theology must respond to the future prospect of leaving planet earth for another.[5] Since then, Jürgen Moltmann has made clear that theology must respond to the prospect of ecological end times, the 'slow but sure and irreversible catastrophe'.[6]

The emergence of a distinctive discourse about global, *climatic* change, moreover, created two shifts in wider environmental consciousness whose significance for theology should become clear. One is the realisation that humanity has become an agent in the constitution of its own habitat. Talk of entering the Anthropocene era[7] or of humans as geological agents[8] is intended to convey this shift.[9] The second shift might be called the invention of climate as a new subject of ethical concern, in a dual sense. Humans can both cause harm via their interference with the climate, and also be harmed (arguably unjustly) by acts of interference that are not of our doing (carbon emissions from the actions of our ancestors, for instance). Taken together, these shifts portray humanity as both agent of, and constituted by, a system of dynamic change that comes from both within and without. Climatic change is problematic to cultural and theological narratives about the 'trajectory' of the human, therefore, as much as it is to do more straightforwardly with environmental ethics. Mike Hulme's study into the invention of a holistic notion of 'the climate' explains this dilemma. For the cultural, religious and scientific ways in which we have, throughout history, 'load(ed) climate with our ideologies'[10] suggest that we understand climate according to the stories that matter most to us at any given time. And perhaps the most enduring of such ideologies is the story of climate as a carrier of original innocence: 'a repository of what is natural, something that is pure and pristine and (should be) beyond the reach of humans.'[11] It is, for example, a discourse that serves the rhetorical power of Lovelock's arch-metaphor, the self-regulating Gaia, against which human interference threatens to jeopardise the very future of the system.[12]

As a discursive phenomenon, therefore, climate change reflects changes in our social conception of history itself. As Dipesh Chakrabarty argues, the monumental shift in climate consciousness was not triggered by the discovery of global warming by the Swedish scientist Svante Arrhenius in the 1890s, nor the successive scientific advances that followed. Natural history, until relatively recently, was perceived to change so gradually that it could never be conflated with human history and thus human struggle, or liberation.[13] The definitive discovery was a temporal one. The fact that the effects of anthropogenic global warming could be perceived to come soon, and with 'speed and violence',[14] has broken down the conceptual barrier separating recorded human history from the idea of the 'deep history' of the evolution of the earth. Hulme also argues that the shift in social consciousness of climate change was made possible by the key political and scientific developments of the 1980s, which again reflect wider social fears about the future: namely, a cold war predilection for publicising global catastrophes in terms of sudden shocking events; and the rise of a science of earth system modelling, allowing scientists to project and communicate graphically to the public a vision of systemic and planetary catastrophe.[15]

The idea of 'unnatural' change is instructive, therefore, as a category that reveals the cultural embeddedness of eschatological belief. We have an awareness, to adapt St. Paul's terminology, that time can indeed grow (too) short, redefining and putting in question our place in the cosmic narrative. It is, moreover, this category that causes problems in generating any sort of ethical or political consensus. Many science communicators have expressed concern at the public's obsession with defining which threshold or tipping points will dictate that it is 'too late' to curb irreversible climatic change.[16] There may be good scientific reasons to scrutinise such rhetoric. The political ramifications are much simpler: it is hard to secure moral consensus upon what are essentially slippery and subjective scientific thresholds. A report in 2011 from the Tyndall Centre for Climate Change Research typifies this ambiguity when it stated that:

> despite high-level statements to the contrary there is now little to no chance of maintaining the global mean surface temperature at or below 2° C. Moreover the impacts associated with 2° C have been revised upwards sufficiently so that 2° C now more appropriately represents the threshold between 'dangerous' and 'extremely dangerous' climate change.[17]

Updated evidence from the IPCC's Fifth Assessment Report doesn't alter what was originally problematic about this.[18] Passing 'critical' thresholds according to a loosely agreed language about danger, emergency and so on, cannot, on their own, also direct our decisions about what those scenarios mean for ethical and social life. Dangerous for whom? By which standards of living and according to what belief about the human? Here, then, is the first obvious overlap between a study of eschatology and that of humanity (Chapter 7 in this volume). For the fact is that climate change discourse delivers predictions whose orders of magnitude (from the bad to the very, very bad, for instance) matter a great deal to campaigners and policy makers. What idea of humanity could constitute the object of those visions? Survival of *Homo sapiens* at all costs? Not only bare human life, but a just, social life? Combating climate change cannot be about mere survival – a prolongation of humanity's existence by use of life-support technology. It must be about more: about affirmation of better forms of life, of justice in human communities and of mutual respect for both human and non-human life forms. When James Lovelock wrote that, 'before this century is over billions of us will die and the few breeding pairs of people that survive will be in the Arctic where the climate remains tolerable'[19] – despite later recanting the tenor of his rhetoric – he demonstrated the need for a kind of eschatological-anthropology: is such a vision of human being *desirable*? What is it to be human in the anticipation of a catastrophic future? Which attitudes of hope towards the future of creation are adequate to the task of answering this question?

A related challenge thrown up by such predictions is the uncertainty over which physical processes are already committed in the earth system, through climate 'inertia'. An example of this is the suggestion that even in the event of the stabilization of global temperatures following 'aggressive mitigations' scenarios, the sea level rise will continue for hundreds of years.[20] That such a scenario complicates a notion of intergenerational ethics is obvious. Neither has the conceptual challenge evaded theologians. Jürgen Moltmann was aware of the irretrievability of some acts of the 'poisoning' of the earth and biosphere, such that 'we cannot know whether the die has not already been cast and the fate of the human race already sealed.'[21] But Moltmann is right, I think, to venture no further than the suggestion that 'we cannot know'. The problem for the theologian, as Karl Rahner liked to remind us, is not about prediction. It is about clarifying the meaning of hope within states of uncertainty for the planet. The theologian's challenge is no less serious for that. For we might ask, for example, at which point is the preservation, or stewardship, of the natural world beyond repair? At which point would it share no recognisable feature with the creation that God saw was good? It is the father's dilemma in Cormac McCarthy's thought experiment in *The Road*. At which point would we view our world as beyond redemption with regard to the needs and desires of humans to be worth living in, to bring up a child in? Clearly, we are not there yet, but the discourse surrounding projections of irreversibility (or, in other words, the sorts of world we may be committing future generations to through our present actions) should invite a response as much from theology as it does from literature.

The eco-logic of apocalypse

The history of eschatological doctrine describes an attempt to remain faithful to two features of Christian faith. First, that there are grounds for hoping in a future that is given by God. Second, that God's presence in the world makes possible good action – ethics – in the interim period before the end. The dilemma for ethical and social thought is clear. If the Christian hopes that death (whether of an individual, humanity or the planet) does not signal the *ultimate* end, and if the ultimate end or ends of God's salvation is what grounds Christian ethics (there are clear hints of a Kantian influence here), what is it that makes the prolongation of the present world worth fighting for? Is a long future better than a short one?[22] The popular suspicion that Christian eschatological faith answers negatively – generating only ecological pessimism – is not unfounded. But it does rely upon a particular (and false) understanding of apocalyptic and its reception in Christian history. It is an assumption about the violent opposition of human history and natural history which, in the light of my observations about climate change discourse above, theology must resist. Given that much twentieth century theology – Moltmann's in particular – has entailed a revival of apocalyptic eschatology, I will turn now to some of the roots of that thinking in order to clarify its ethical implications.

Eschatological doctrine unavoidably reflects wider social and political contexts. These contexts are typically periods of social, political and ecological crisis – 'storms', as Gerhard Sauter appropriately calls them[23]– in the evolution of doctrine. It is, therefore, easy (and a little simplistic) to relate the 'success' of apocalyptic eschatology to the experiences of social and environmental crisis – indeed, a sense of ecological and social *hopelessness* – in Jewish and Christian cultures. A people whose place and destiny in the world is threatened by Empire – such as was the case for first century followers of Jesus – is, according to such a view, one that will welcome a dramatic narrative of annihilation and restoration of a new order: the 'new heaven and a new earth' revealed in the book of Revelation. It is certainly a view that persists in contemporary attitudes. Evangelical Christianity, in particular, fuelled by dispensationalist, premillennial eschatology, has historically generated deep ecological pessimism. To this is coupled the popular conviction that to attempt to *resist* world destruction is to stand in the way of God's plan.[24] But an emphasis on annihilation ignores a more primary function of Jewish and Christian apocalyptic as the revelation of God's order within the processes of world history. Jewish apocalypses portray a universe in which God is wholly in command, both temporally and spatially.[25] It is a concept that runs deeply with ecological metaphors. Even as early as the writings of the prophet Isaiah, acknowledged by some as the 'first preacher of the eschatological expectation',[26] Jewish thought is littered with allusions to the restoration of order in nature. The exilic notion of the Day of the Lord, for example, was accompanied in prophetic writings by a strong emphasis on God's wrath and victory over the natural order: Mount Zion will rise above all other mountains and order will be established to the natural world. We would have strong grounds for critiquing the image of Nature subdued by God's lordship in this context,[27] but here is not the place to do so. My point is that the apocalyptic roots of Christian eschatology do not provide the foundation for an ecologically and politically pessimistic outlook that many people want to assume. That assumption has depended upon a vision of God's abandonment of the natural order in pursuit of an entirely other one. Christian apocalyptic – particularly the book of Revelation – insinuates with equal force the hope for a redemption of nature and humanity, and a purification of their corrupted elements.[28] Thus we are not *bound* to read into the symbolism of the levelling of the mountains and the disappearance of the sea (for example) an abandonment of the world to its fate. We can read it instead as realignment within God's redemptive future. On this basis, therefore, the task in respect of eschatological doctrine is to clarify which *objects* of hope emerge from the relationship between the destiny of individuals and that of the planet. As the social, scientific and cultural knowledge of the future develops, so must theology interpret and respond to this knowledge.

The objects of hope: between individual and cosmic eschatologies[29]

Lynn White, Jr.'s infamous critique of the desacralisation of nature by Christian culture in 1967 has in fact been a view directed against Christian eschatology since the nineteenth century – first by Nietzsche and then neatly summed up by Feuerbach: 'Nature, the world, has no value, no interest for Christians. The Christian thinks only of himself and the salvation of his soul.'[30] Theologians have also recognised the historic and philosophical roots of such thinking. Wolfhart Pannenberg, for instance, explained the obsession with personal salvation as a failure to understand the whole of theology in terms of eschatological promise.[31] Eschatology in the early church through to medieval scholastic theology was interested almost exclusively with the resurrection of the dead and the life of the soul. Patristic scholars were at pains to demonstrate that God's lordship over creation was already present and did not need the invocation of faith 'to come' to be realized. This was a belief in creation, not in an eschatological future. It was, in other words, an implicit doctrinal defence against Gnosticism.[32] Today the question must resurface in the light of a new challenge to the conception of the 'completeness' of creation: the experience of a damaged earth system. As Pannenberg puts it, what is threatening to Christian orthodoxy is the insinuation that finite matter might have autonomy from the absolute lordship of God: 'If God is truly the creator, why is his will for his creation not always done already?'[33] It is a lament, as much psychological as it is philosophical in origin, and reminiscent of Claire's despair in *Melancholia*: why isn't creation perfect? Where will life persist, if not *here*? Pannenberg's recommendation, in response, is that we acknowledge the authorship of God in all acts of creation and at every stage in the earth's evolution. If we do not, then eschatological promise will always appear in the form of an obsession with heaven and hell. We shall also concede ground to those features of apocalyptic faith (i.e. premillennialism) that await Jesus' return to earth before any commencement of the millennial kingdom (and the restoration of nature, therefore) can be entertained.[34] An individualising millennial trend in the predominantly protestant tradition[35] can be explained in this way as an indifference towards the fate of natural history. What does this bias tell us about humanity's evolving relationship with ecological crisis and climatic change? Moltmann explains, perhaps more forgivingly than Pannenberg, that an eschatology of personal salvation can be the starting point, but not the end point, of articulations of hope:

> Personal hope in the face of one's own death and beyond is certainly the beginning of eschatology. ... But as beginning, it is an integral component of the universal hope for the whole of creation in its present misery. Eternal life is 'the life of the world to come,' as the Nicene Creed says, so it means not just human life but the life of all the living – of 'all flesh' as our Bible puts it.[36]

The connection is implicit in Jewish thought, for instance, in that individual and cosmic eschatologies are not separable in the way that became possible in the western Christian tradition. Indeed, it is significant that Jewish theology came relatively late to a discussion of the destiny of individual souls after death, and that even these discussions need reading in the light of the external political pressures of persecution during the exile.[37] Moltmann also points out that in Orthodox eschatology the unity of the destiny of the natural world, the individual and cosmos, is taken for granted and poses no conflict in offering the salvation of one over the other.[38]

Why is a uniting of individual and cosmic eschatology important in the light of climate ethics? If theology is re-oriented as the promise of God's kingdom in the future throughout the life of creation, then human striving is not distinct from non-human striving, and an escapist eschatology ('bring on the apocalypse') ceases to make sense. Global climatic change reveals fundamental interdependencies of life-systems through the continual loss (and creation, in some cases) of habitats, cultures and species. In popular culture it is tempting to frame climate action in terms of quantified losses and gains on the part of humans engaged in battle against 'the world': the sentiment encapsulated in the tag-line of the Hollywood climate epic *The Day After Tomorrow* as 'save as many [humans, presumably] as you can'. The task of the theologian would appear to be more complicated if, as Rachel Muers has argued in Chapter 6 of this volume, non-human creatures should be considered as participants in the life of God, not reducible to a mere backdrop of human history. Their destinies should very much concern us, and their loss is a genuine catastrophe.

Here, then, is one possible challenge to an eschatological ethics as depoliticizing consolation – as Rowan Williams puts it, the 'safety net that guarantees a happy ending in this world.'[39] In the light of the irreversible effects of global warming, Christian orientation towards the future, whilst insisting on hope, must be at the same time a confrontation with the inevitability of continual loss, and our participation in that loss. Two biblical metaphors lend themselves to this assertion and raise further questions. The first, construed by Pannenberg, is contained in the story of the fall. He compares present attempts to rise above the fate of the world with the attempt of Adam and Eve to be 'like God' in their attempt at denying their finitude:

> the human failure to achieve independence of God has led to an attempt to pursue supposed self-interest not only relative to God but also relative to others and to other creatures. The result is a lack of peace in creation with the consequence that we cannot at once detect the lordship of the creator in it.[40]

The second is St Paul's well-known metaphor of the 'world ... groaning in labour pains' (Romans 8. 22–23) in anticipation of the redemption of the world. A modern political appropriation of this metaphor is well-established in eco-liberationist works.[41] Pannenberg also believes that it cements Christian eschatology to its apocalyptic Jewish heritage:

Jewish expectation linked the hope of the kingdom of God to the idea of an overturning of the natural conditions of human existence itself. Nothing less than a new heaven and a new earth (Rev. 21. 1; cf 20. 11 and Isa. 65. 17) is demanded.[42]

Some recent interpretations of the infamous 'groaning' metaphor, in fact, tend away from a linear apocalyptic view in a way that I think is more attentive to our present context. Paul operates within the concept of messianic time: a time of overlap between the present and the age to come. As Brendan Byrne has argued, Paul achieves this by recapitulating a creation theme from Genesis in which creation is bound up in (and suffers *from*) the fate of human beings. Creation is 'subject to futility' following the sin of Adam.[43] But there is an implicit demand for justice in the present, here. Non-human nature did not ask for this state of corruption but was 'compelled to be the innocent victim'[44] in playing out the story of sin. Byrne thus reads creation's 'groans' as eschatologically attuned, as participating in the hope that humanity and creation can be restored in harmony. Discord between human action and non-human flourishing on this view is to be resisted and overcome. And this refusal of a dichotomy between the eschatological destinies of the individual and the world, humanity and nature, are important responses to climate change. Such a view avoids, for example, the image of a fallen humanity pitted against a ticking clock (with its attendant warring metaphors: the 'fight against climate change') for the salvation of a pristine, innocent nature. Such could be interpreted once again in Lovelock's Gaia, for instance, whose latest incarnation saw her turn from nurturing mother to vengeful goddess.[45] As dystopian 'climate thrillers' such as *The Happening* and *The Day the Earth Stood Still* suggest, hopelessness about the prospects of human survival can flip easily into desires for its speedy annihilation. Eschatology, insofar as it creates a dichotomy between personal and cosmic hopes, may also be implicated in this tendency.

New heaven, new earth?

In Moltmann's well-known framing of eschatology, the idea of *adventus* – hope in an incoming, completely new reality – is contrasted with that of *futurans* – hope predicated upon expectations gleaned from the past. But if eschatology is future-oriented in this radical, apocalyptic sense, what significance could be placed on the *loss* of the natural habitat and humanity's struggle alongside this loss? To repeat my claim in the introduction, eschatology must be able to articulate not only what may be endured before the eschaton, but what motivation there is to act in the light of it. Moltmann's claim is that he *can* explain such a motivation, principally through an eschatological Christology. The Resurrection event operates not only within human history but also natural history. Easter symbolizes and enacts the promise that *all* nature will be reconciled, 'which opens up the horizon of expectation in which the nature wounded by human violence can be healed through a human history of peace.'[46] In other words, Christian hope for creation is not meant to be passive. It does not simply await the apocalyptic levelling and annihilation of creation as we know it now, in anticipation of a new heaven and a new earth. Nor does it await the myth of a return to Eden. A cosmic Christology suggests, instead, that faith in the resurrection of creation both promises a radically new thing in the future – a utopian rebirth of creation – as well as motivating and sustaining an ethics of ecological action in the present.

But our concern has been to sustain a theology that justifies action in the present at the same time as acknowledging mortality and loss. What is lost, what is preserved, in the promise of this ecological form of transfiguration in the cosmic Christ? Ernst Conradie has something like this concern in mind when he draws attention to the centrality of transience and perishing at the personal, global and cosmic levels of creation.[47] Drawing on process theology, he answers this by speaking of God's 'cosmic memory' in which either (or both) individual lives of creatures or the whole history of natural process is 'inscribed' eternally in the mind of God, so that 'nothing that is past can pass away ... This inscription will be completed when the history of the cosmos finally comes to an end (*finis*).'[48] However, this presents a dilemma with regard to the threat of irreparable loss encountered in climatic 'points of no return'. Inasmuch as human life is bound to cycles of physical decay, eschatological hope cannot be a search for immortality. Conradie argues that with the idea of material inscription both redemption and justice for the earth are possible, since

> every moment in the earth's journey is not only of ecological but also of eternal significance. That is why it remains imperative to care for the earth and all its creatures and to prevent any tragic accidents on this journey.[49]

But the challenge of anthropogenic change is precisely the possibility that death *is* brought about prematurely, and against God's will. There is no reckoning, in Conradie, with the sense that we are witnessing the escalating and unfolding of a tragic and avoidable global accident, nor how such a realisation provides for an imperative to resist its progress. I concur with Deane-Drummond's worry that an eschatology of inscription is too forgiving, therefore, providing unlimited forgiveness of the (ecological) sins of the present, and thereby denying motivation for action against injustice.[50] If all is preserved in the mind of God, what do we mourn in its passing from present existence, or what do we resist in the passing of species and cultures from our natural history?

The challenge of making sense of an eschatological ethics is, it would seem, particularly acute in the context of climate change. The Christian claims that despair is always sin: no amount of damage to the climate is cause to give up hope. On the other hand, she must resist the interpretation of hope as the expectation of a reconciliation or return to Eden. This reflects a wider cultural dilemma: one frequently finds either extreme forms of earthly disengagement (hope for personal salvation), or else the fantasy that life must continue, of necessity, in some form or another, into infinity. The lament of Justine's sister Claire, in *Melancholia*, demanding desperately that there must be life, or the hope of life, elsewhere, that this cannot be 'the end', is a very present anxiety. And yet the desire for infinity in the sense of 'continuing indefinitely into the future' is a danger that Karl Barth rejected as the deceptive belief in 'infinite-finiteness'. For what this really conjures is the maintenance of perpetual control over one's environment without the threat of mortal annihilation. And it is, according to Rosemary Radford Ruether and other eco-feminists, very much a man's vision. Ruether suspects eschatological language to be an implicitly macho attempt to 'survive' through eternity.[51] The typical alternative – to emphasise life's cycles of death and rebirth against a desire for personal immortality – brings with it its own problems, however, particularly with concern for a changing climate. For Moltmann's (and Conradie's) criticism of Ruether's position is that it assumes a morally neutral, 'pantheist appreciation of the cycles of matter and energy'.[52] This leaves no room for a critique of the current suffering of the earth and its need for future redemption. Furthermore, a narrative of cosmic, cyclical balance provides no obvious grounds for critiquing specific injustices implicit to global warming. There is, to repeat, something about global warming that demands that we account for the premature disappearance of certain habitats and civilisations over others, for example, or the inability of certain cultures to protect themselves against resource depletion: this is the problem of climate justice.

There is, nevertheless, something of Ruether's suspicions about the machist orientations of apocalyptic eschatology that I think are worth holding on to. They are related also to Kathryn Tanner's suggestion that eschatological thinking may have been 'overly temporalized' in twentieth century theology to the detriment of its spatial elements. Just as Christopher Rowland has argued that Jewish apocalyptic is as much concerned with the spatial as with the eschatological, so for Christian thought. For eschatology can be read as an alternative vision of the demands of the present world rather than a vision directed by the vision and hope of its future, cosmic restoration. Tanner insists that such a perspective presents no case for political apathy. On the contrary, 'complacency is ruled out not by a transcendent future but by a transcendent present – by the present life in God as the source of goods that the world one lives in fails to match';[53] and again,

> even if one knows that all one's achievements will come to nothing with the world's end, one is obligated to act, simply because this is the only way of living that makes sense in the light of one's life in God.[54]

Can the core of Christian theology make sense without *any* reference to hope in a future and its apocalyptic heritage? This seems dubious, tending towards an overly 'realised' eschatology, and denying Christianity the full and materialist power of its message of hope in the world *to come*.[55] Indeed, it was precisely the kind of Barthian (and Tillichian) eternalizing of the present 'now' that Moltmann was concerned to overcome in order to remain true to the political and millenarian future – 'the life of the world to come' – at the heart of Christian doctrine.[56]

Timothy Gorringe is right (in Chapter 2 of this volume),[57] in any case, to allay Tanner's fears: the intention behind a theology of hope is not to console present generations through the promise of a happy ending. On the contrary, the message is to act in *spite* of the likelihood of failure. Moltmann (particularly in his latest works on theologies of catastrophe)[58] thus makes it just as clear as Tanner does that he wishes to deter eschatologies of triumphalism in the face of suffering. I wish to emphasise, nevertheless, that eschatology needs to work harder than this if it is to disassociate itself from the lure of a millennialist apocalyptic vision that anticipates an incoming paradise as a cosmic relief from the struggles of the present. In secular terms, that fear is already present in what some have called the 'consolations of extinction'.[59] Faced with the almost certain failure to halt runaway global warming, cultural attention shifts to that of a wider, macro cosmic (far-future) vision. The question is not so much whether such a vision can coexist alongside political commitment, but what *sort* of commitment it allows. Moltmann cites Luther's pithy (and now hackneyed) expression of planting an apple tree even were the world to end tomorrow.[60] It is an expression that fails to capture what is ethically distinctive about the pressure of a changing climate. One, in other words, that magnifies social injustices, and condemns the majority of the world to premature annihilation. Of course, one must say yes to life in the face of certain (irreversible) death. But one must equally find grounds to refuse the conditions, scale and process by which death is being dealt. Theology, too, must provide grounds to 'rage against the dying of the light', to risk another pithy expression (this time from Dylan Thomas).[61] For this one needs to retain a sense of apocalyptic that is radically and materially critical of the present age. Tanner's view of Eternity as participation in the true life of God creates its own wider problems to a coherent systematic scheme, for which we have not the space here to discuss.[62] But her attempt to unchain an obligation to take action from the (already uncertain) assurances of some future victory have important resonances with the ethical challenges I have tried to outline. It also gives eschatology a route away from clinging to hope in life at all costs. Christianity, as Pannenberg reminds us, positioned itself guardedly against the Platonic philosophy of the immortality of the soul, by re-emphasising the ultimate condition of finitude and death that is an irreducible human condition. Death still has some finality for the human individual, and it is our task to extend this emphasis to the crisis of climate change. The death of biodiversity, the passing of points of no return, the irreversible alteration of the earth's capacity for sustaining human communities – these are scenarios whose finality theology must not dilute, as many Christian millennialists do, via anticipation of a 'new heaven and a new earth'. The world is not eternal: this belief is fundamental to orthodox Christian thought. But if theology is to articulate this in a way that is meaningful to the activist, it may need to be through the lamenting – and resisting – of future *failures* within the time allotted to us, not the utopian, consoling vision of some future one.

Conclusion

Inasmuch as it is capable of generating different attitudes towards political action, I have argued, eschatological belief is clearly implicated in the way we talk about and respond to climate change. Amongst the theological arguments I have found most relevant, the Christian desire to reflect its Jewish apocalyptic roots looms large. Is this desirable, given the obsession with predictions and fatalism to which such a tradition is susceptible? Thus put, the problem echoes in some ways the philosophical debate about the messianic character of contemporary politics.[63] Thus Slavoj Žižek's obsession with the apocalypticism of Jesus and St. Paul. For both, according to Žižek, apocalyptic and messianic faith was accompanied with a prohibition against predicting the future with any numerical precision (the censure against 'false prophets'). There is, further, a lesson in this for our own response to climate crisis. Living in 'apocalyptic time' means admitting that the climate crisis is already a reality. But at the same time it means resisting the urge to predict and calculate precisely when any ultimate end-point will occur, and thus any basis to give up struggling against injustice.[64] Or again, in the terms of Giorgio Agamben's study of St. Paul, to live in the Messianic age is not simply to 'wait around' for the second coming, but to affirm a 'form of life' that lives the reality of the *parousia* already, in new political formations.[65]

Can our (ethical) commitment to the present be founded not by a sense of waiting for the end to come, but by a vision of future justice that inspires the refusal of the conditions of the present? Can we draw inspiration to act, 'irrespective of the likelihood of success or failure'?[66] The question is a pressing one. For who could judge today whether or not, and on what grounds, human attempts at combatting global warming are going to be successful, when there is so much uncertainty already around the impact of our actions and inactions upon the earth system? The Fifth Assessment Report of the IPCC has suggested already that exceeding the critical global threshold of 2 degrees Celsius before the end of the century may be unavoidable. An eschatology that denies despair in the face of such epic failures, and encourages action in the face of the death that such failures will bring, may be an extremely welcome one in the light of such a report.

Notes

1 Per Juul Carlsen, Danish Film Institute, 'The Only Redeeming Factor is the World Ending', available online at www.dfi.dk/Service/English/News-and-publications/FILM-Magazine/Artikler-fra-tidsskriftet-FILM/72/The-Only-Redeeming-Factor-is-the-World-Ending.aspx (accessed 3 May 2012).
2 Kathryn Tanner, 'Eschatology and Ethics' in Meilaender, G. and Werpehowski, W. (eds), *The Oxford Handbook of Theological Ethics* (Oxford: Oxford University Press, 2005), p. 41.
3 Ara Barsam and Andrew Linzey, 'Albert Schweitzer, 1875–1965' in Joy Palmer, David Cooper and Blaze Corcoran (eds), *Fifty Key Thinkers on the Environment* (London: Routledge, 2001), p. 172.
4 Leonardo Boff, *Cry of the Earth, Cry of the Poor* (New York: Orbis, 1997).
5 John. B. Cobb, Jr. *Process Theology as Political Theology* (Manchester: Manchester University Press, 1982), p. 123.
6 Jürgen Moltmann, *The Coming of God: Christian Eschatology* (Minneapolis: Fortress Press, 1996), p. 208. Moltmann did also mention global climatic changes by way of stressing the universally integrated nature of the crisis, its causes and effects.

7 J. K. Gibson-Graham and Gerda Roelvink, 'An Economic Ethics for the Anthropocene' in Noel Castree *et al.* (eds), *The Point is to Change it: Geographies of Hope and Survival in an Age of Crisis* (London: Wiley-Blackwell, 2010).

8 Dipesh Chakrabarty, 'The Climate of History: Four Theses', *Critical Inquiry* 35 (2009): 204.

9 I take Peter Scott's hesitancy in accepting Chakrabarty's claim that humanity thus becomes a 'force of nature' as a not particularly useful turn of phrase. However, my concern here is – in agreement with Chakrabarty – to highlight the new ethical demands that humanity places upon itself by its own awareness that its present actions might shape the integrity of ecological systems in the future (and certainly of biodiversity) perhaps *irreversibly*.

10 Mike Hulme, *Why We Disagree About Climate Change: Understanding Controversy, Inaction and Opportunity* (Cambridge: Cambridge University Press, 2009), p. 26.

11 Hulme, *Why We Disagree*, p. 25.

12 Hulme, *Why We Disagree*, p. 27.

13 Chakrabarty, 'The Climate of History', p. 204.

14 Fred Pierce, *With Speed and Violence: Why Scientists Fear Tipping Points in Climate Change* (London: Beacon Press, 2009).

15 Hulme, *Why We Disagree*, p. 67.

16 Solomon, S. *et al.* 'Irreversible Climate Change due to Carbon Emissions', *Proceedings of the National Academy of Sciences (PNAS)* vol. 106, no. 6 (2009).

17 Kevin Andersen and Alice Bows 'Beyond "dangerous climate change": scenarios for a new world', *Philosophical Transactions of the Royal Society A: Mathematical, Physical and Engineering Sciences*, 369 (2011), pp. 20–44. For an analysis of the 'deep uncertainty in climate scenarios prediction', see also Milind Kandlikar, James Risbey and Suraje Dessai, 'Representing and communicating deep uncertainty in climate-change assessments', *C. R. Geoscience* 337 (2005): 443–55.

18 For a discussion of the uses of this term in science and policy documents, see Suraje Dessai *et al.* 'Defining and Experiencing Dangerous Climate Change', *Tyndall Centre for Climate Change Research* Working Paper 28. Available online at www.tyndall.ac.uk/sites/default/files/wp28.pdf (accessed 23 January 2013).

19 James Lovelock, 'The Earth is about to catch a morbid fever that may last as long as 100,000 years', *The Independent*, 16 January 2006. Available online at www.independent.co.uk/voices/commentators/james-lovelock-the-earth-is-about-to-catch-a-morbid-fever-that-may-last-as-long-as-100000-years-523161.html (accessed 30 September 2013).

20 Gerald A. Meehl *et al.* 'Relative outcomes of climate change mitigation related to global temperature versus sea-level rise', *Nature Climate Change* Vol. 2, No.8 (2012), 576–80.

21 Moltmann, *The Coming of God*, p. 209.

22 This question is also addressed by Peter Scott, 'Are We There Yet? Reaching the End of the Line – a Postnatural Enquiry', in Stefan Skrimshire (ed), *Future Ethics: Climate Change and Apocalyptic Imagination* (London: Continuum, 2010), pp. 260–79

23 Gerhard Sauter, *What Dare We Hope? Reconsidering Eschatology* (Harrisburg: Trinity Press International, 1999), p. 25. Typically these include the perceived failures of Enlightenment optimism; the experience of two world wars on twentieth century German systematic theology; and the influence of revolutionary politics on historical theologies of the postwar era.

24 Harry O. Maier, 'Green Millennialism: American Evangelicals, Environmentalism and the Book of Revelation' in David G. Horrell *et al.* (eds), *Ecological Hermeneutics: Biblical, Historical and Theological Perspectives* (London: T&T Clark, 2010), p. 253.

25 John J. Collins, *The Apocalyptic Imagination: An Introduction to the Jewish Matrix of Christianity* (New York: Crossroad, 1984).

26 Vriezen, quoted in Hans Schwarz, *Eschatology* (Cambridge: Eerdmans, 2000), p. 45.

27 Michael Northcott, for instance, insists that the Christian belief in the life, death and resurrection of Jesus Christ is a fundamental break from the tradition of understanding God's intervention in world history via a model of mastery and domination. See Michael

Northcott, *A Moral Climate: The Ethics of Global Warming* (London: Darton, Longman and Todd, 2000).

28 I am indebted to Celia Deane-Drummond's analysis here, in Celia Deane-Drummond, *Eco-Theology* (London: Darton, Longman and Todd, 2008), p. 167.

29 I am using a distinction similar to that of Hans Schwarz for whom 'individual eschatology (concerns) … the destiny of the individual after death' whereas 'cosmic eschatology … includes the destiny of this earth or of the whole cosmos' (Schwarz, *Eschatology*, 26).

30 Quoted in Douglas J. Moo, 'Nature in the New Creation: New Testament Eschatology and the Environment', *Journal of the Evangelical Theological Society* 49 (2006): 449.

31 Christiaan Mostert, *God and the Future: Wolfhart Pannenberg's Eschatological Doctrine of God* (London: T&T Clark, 2002), p. 3.

32 Wolfhart Pannenberg, *Systematic Theology Vol. 3* (Edinburgh: T&T Clark, 1998), p. 528.

33 Pannenberg, *Systematic Theology*, p. 580.

34 Premillennialism – the belief that the millennial period of grace is yet to come, and can occur only after Jesus' return to earth – often coincides with a particular form of social and ecological pessimism with regard to progressive political movements and a remoralising of puritan societies.

35 It is also far from just a protestant phenomenon, of course. Figures such as Joseph Ratzinger and Ladislaus Boros loom large in twentieth century versions of personalized eschatology. See William J. La Due, *The Trinity Guide to Eschatology* (London: Continuum, 2004).

36 Moltmann, *The Coming of God*, p. 131.

37 La Due, *The Trinity Guide*, p. 1.

38 Moltmann, 'Cosmos and Theosis', p. 258.

39 Rowan Williams, 'Renewing the Face of the Earth: Human Responsibility and the Environment', *Ebor Lecture*, Wednesday 25th March, 2009. Available online at http://rowanwilliams.archbishopofcanterbury.org/articles.php/816/renewing-the-face-of-the-earth-human-responsibility-and-the-environment (accessed 1 October 2013).

40 Pannenberg, *Systematic Theology*, p. 580.

41 Boff, *Cry of the Earth*.

42 Pannenberg, *Systematic Theology*, p. 584.

43 Brendan Byrne, 'An Ecological Reading of Rom 8. 19–22' in David G. Horrel *et al.* (eds), *Ecological Hermeneutics*, p. 89.

44 Byrne, 'An Ecological Reading', p. 89.

45 James Lovelock, *The Revenge of Gaia* (London: Penguin, 2007).

46 Moltmann, *The Way of Jesus Christ*, p. 256.

47 Ernst Conradie, 'Resurrection, Finitude and Ecology', in Ted Peters, Robert John Russell and Michael Welker (eds), *Resurrection: Theological and Scientific Assessments* (Grand Rapids: W.B. Eerdmans, 2002), p. 282.

48 Conradie, 'Resurrection, Finitude and Ecology', 292. See also Deane-Drummond, *Eco-Theology*, 174 for a summary and critical assessment of Conradie's position.

49 Conradie, 'Resurrection, Finitude and Ecology', p. 293.

50 Deane-Drummond, *Eco-Theology*, p. 175.

51 Grace Jantzen makes essentially the same point in noticing the emergence in the first centuries BCE, alongside the invention of Christian martyrdom, of the seemingly opposite practice of overcoming (or 'reconfiguring') death through the Neoplatonic ascetic practices of 'reaching' eternity. Grace Jantzen, *Foundations of Violence* (London: Routledge, 2004).

52 Conradie, 'Resurrection, Finitude and Ecology', p. 278.

53 Tanner, 'Eschatology and Ethics', 52. See also Kathryn Tanner, 'Eschatology Without a Future?' in John Polkinghorne and Michael Welker (eds), *The End of the World and the Ends of God: Science and Theology on Eschatology* (Harrisburg: Trinity Press International, 2000), pp. 222–37.

54 Tanner, 'Eschatology and Ethics', p. 54.

55 For a critical description of the three distinct approaches of Moltmann, Pannenberg and Tanner, see Timothy Harvie, *Jürgen Moltmann's Ethics of Hope: Eschatological Possibilities for Moral Action* (London: Ashgate, 2009).
56 Miroslav Volf, 'After Moltmann: Reflections on the Future of Eschatology', in Richard Bauckham (ed.), *God Will Be All in All: The Eschatology of Jürgen Moltmann* (Edinburgh, T&T Clark, 1999), p. 234.
57 Gorringe, 'The Trinity', this volume page 28.
58 See in particular Moltmann, *In the End*.
59 Christopher Cokinos, 'The Consolations of Extinction', *Orion* (May/June 2007). Available online at www.orionmagazine.org/index.php/articles/article/268/ (accessed 1 October 2013).
60 Moltmann, *The Coming of God*, p. 235.
61 Thomas, D. *Dylan Thomas Selected Poems, 1934–1952*, revised edition (New York: New Directions Publishing, 2003), p. 122.
62 But see Stephen Barton, 'New Testament Eschatology and the Ecological Crisis in Theological and Ecclesial Perspective' in Cheryl Hunt *et al. Ecological Hermeneutics*, pp. 266–82.
63 See, for example, Arthur Bradley and Paul Fletcher (eds), *The Politics to Come: Power, Modernity and the Messianic* (London: Continuum, 2011).
64 Slavoj Žižek, and Boris Gunjevic, *God in Pain: Inversions of Apocalypse* (London: Verso, 2012), p. 71.
65 Giorgio Agamben, *The Time That Remains*, Patricia Dailey (trans.) (Stanford: Stanford University Press, 2000).
66 Tanner, 'Eschatology and Ethics', p. 46.

Bibliography

Agamben, Giorgio. *The Time That Remains*, Patricia Dailey (trans.) (Stanford: Stanford University Press, 2000).
Andersen, Kevin and Alice Bows. 'Beyond "dangerous climate change": scenarios for a new world', *Philosophical Transactions of the Royal Society A: Mathematical, Physical and Engineering Sciences*, 369 (2011), pp. 20–44.
Barsam, Ara and Andrew Linzey. 'Albert Schweitzer, 1875–1965', in Joy Palmer, David Cooper and Blaze Corcoran (eds), *Fifty Key Thinkers on the Environment* (London: Routledge, 2001).
Barton, Stephen. 'New Testament Eschatology and the Ecological Crisis in Theological and Ecclesial Perspective', in David G. Horrell, Cheryl Hunt, Christopher Southgate and Francesca Stavrakopoulou (eds), *Ecological Hermeneutics: Biblical, Historical and Theological Perspectives* (London: T&T Clark, 2010), pp. 266–82.
Boff, Leonardo. *Cry of the Earth, Cry of the Poor* (New York: Orbis, 1997).
Bradley, Arthur and Paul Fletcher (eds). *The Politics to Come: Power, Modernity and the Messianic* (London: Continuum, 2011).
Byrne, Brendan. 'An Ecological Reading of Rom 8. 19–22', in David G. Horrell, Cherryl Hunt, Christopher Southgate and Francesca Stavrakopoulou (eds), *Ecological Hermeneutics: Biblical, Historical and Theological Perspectives* (London: T&T Clark, 2010).
Callicott, J. Baird. 'The Temporal and Spatial Scales of Global Climate Change and the Limits of Individualistic and Rationalistic Ethics', *Royal Institute of Philosophy Supplement* 69 (October 2011) (Cambridge: CUP): 101–16.
Carlsen, Per Juul. Danish Film Institute. 'The Only Redeeming Factor is the World Ending', available online at www.dfi.dk/Service/English/News-and-publications/FILM-Magazine/Artikler-fra-tidsskriftet-FILM/72/The-Only-Redeeming-Factor-is-the-World-Ending.aspx (accessed 3 May 2012).
Chakrabarty, Dipesh. 'The Climate of History: Four Theses', *Critical Inquiry* 35 (2009): 197–222,

Cobb, John. B. *Process Theology as Political Theology* (Manchester: Manchester University Press, 1982).

Cokinos, Christopher. 'The Consolations of Extinction', *Orion* (May/June 2007). Available online at www.orionmagazine.org/index.php/articles/article/268/ (accessed 1 October 2013).

Collins, Adela Yarbro. *Crisis and Catharsis: Power of Apocalypse* (London: Westminster/John Knox Press, 2002).

Collins, John J. *The Apocalyptic Imagination: An Introduction to the Jewish Matrix of Christianity* (New York: Crossroad, 1984).

Conradie, Ernst. 'Resurrection, Finitude and Ecology', in Ted Peters, Robert John Russell and Michael Welker (eds), *Resurrection: Theological and Scientific Assessments* (Grand Rapids: W. B. Eerdmans, 2002).

Deane-Drummond, Celia. *Eco-Theology* (London: Darton, Longman and Todd, 2008).

Dessai, Suraje, W. Neil Adger, Mike Hulme, Jonathan Koehler, John Turnpenny and Rachel Warren. 'Defining and Experiencing Dangerous Climate Change', *Tyndall Centre for Climate Change Research Working Paper 28*. Available online at www.tyndall.ac.uk/sites/default/files/wp28.pdf (accessed 23 January 2013).

Gibson-Graham, J.K. and Gerda Roelvink. 'An Economic Ethics for the Anthropocene', in Noel Castree, Paul A. Chatterton, Nik Heynen, Wendy Larner and Melissa W. Wright (eds), *The Point is to Change it: Geographies of Hope and Survival in an Age of Crisis* (London: Wiley-Blackwell, 2010).

Harvie, Timothy. *Jürgen Moltmann's Ethics of Hope: Eschatological Possibilities for Moral Action* (London: Ashgate, 2009).

Horrell, David G., Cherryl Hunt, Christopher Southgate and Francesca Stavrakopoulou (eds). *Ecological Hermeneutics: Biblical, Historical and Theological Perspectives* (London: T&T Clark, 2010).

Hulme, Mike. *Why We Disagree About Climate Change: Understanding Controversy, Inaction and Opportunity* (Cambridge: Cambridge University Press, 2009).

Jantzen, G. *Foundations of Violence* (London: Routledge, 2004).

Kandlikar, M., James Risbey and Suraje Dessai. 'Representing and communicating deep uncertainty in climate-change assessments', *C. R. Geoscience* 337 (2005): 443–55.

La Due, William J. *The Trinity Guide to Eschatology* (London: Continuum, 2004).

Lovelock, James. *The Revenge of Gaia* (London: Penguin, 2007).

——'The Earth is about to catch a morbid fever that may last as long as 100,000 years'. *The Independent*, 16 January 2006. Available online at www.independent.co.uk/voices/commentators/james-lovelock-the-earth-is-about-to-catch-a-morbid-fever-that-may-last-as-long-as-100000-years-523161.html (accessed 30 September 2013).

Maier, Harry O. 'Green Millennialism: American Evangelicals, Environmentalism and the Book of Revelation', in David G. Horrell, Cherryl Hunt, Christopher Southgate and Francesca Stavrakopoulou (eds), *Ecological Hermeneutics: Biblical, Historical and Theological Perspectives* (London: T&T Clark, 2010), pp. 253.

Meehl, Gerald A., Aixue Hu, Claudia Tebaldi, Julie M. Arblaster, Warren M. Washington, Haiyan Teng, Benjamin M. Sanderson, Toby Ault, Warren G. Strand and James B. White III. 'Relative outcomes of climate change mitigation related to global temperature versus sea-level rise', *Nature Climate Change* 2, 8 (2012): 576–80.

Moltmann, Jürgen. *The Way of Jesus Christ* (London: SCM Press, 1990).

——*The Coming of God: Christian Eschatology* (Minneapolis: Fortress Press, 1996).

——'Cosmos and Theosis: Eschatological Perspectives on the Future of the Universe', in George F. R. Ellis (ed.), *The Far Future Universe* (London: Templeton Foundation Press, 2002).

——*In the End – the Beginning: the Life of Hope* (London: SCM Press, 2004).

Moo, Douglas J. 'Nature in the New Creation: New Testament Eschatology and the Environment', *Journal of the Evangelical Theological Society* 49 (2006): 449–88.

Mostert, Christiaan. *God and the Future: Wolfhart Pannenberg's Eschatological Doctrine of God* (London: T&T Clark, 2002).

Northcott, Michael. *A Moral Climate: The Ethics of Global Warming* (London: Darton, Longman and Todd, 2000).

Pannenberg, Wolfhart. *Systematic Theology Vol. 3* (Edinburgh: T&T Clark, 1998).

Pierce, Fred. *With Speed and Violence: Why Scientists Fear Tipping Points in Climate Change* (London: Beacon Press, 2009).

Sauter, Gerhard. *What Dare We Hope? Reconsidering Eschatology* (Harrisburg: Trinity Press International, 1999).

Schwarz, Hans. *Eschatology* (Cambridge: Eerdmans, 2000).

Scott, Peter. 'Are We There Yet? Reaching the End of the Line – a Postnatural Enquiry', in Stefan Skrimshire (ed). *Future Ethics: Climate Change and Apocalyptic Imagination* (London: Continuum, 2010), pp. 260–79.

Solomon, Susan, Gian-Kasper Plattner, Reto Knutti and Pierre Friedlingstein. 'Irreversible Climate Change due to Carbon Emissions', *Proceedings of the National Academy of Sciences (PNAS)* 106, 6 (2009): 1704–9.

Tanner, Kathryn. 'Eschatology Without a Future?' in John Polkinghorne and Michael Welker (eds) *The End of the World and the Ends of God: Science and Theology on Eschatology* (Harrisburg: Trinity Press International, 2000), pp. 222–37.

——'Eschatology and Ethics', in Gilbert Meilaender, and William Werpehowski (eds), *The Oxford Handbook of Theological Ethics* (Oxford: Oxford University Press, 2005).

Volf, Miroslav. 'After Moltmann: Reflections on the Future of Eschatology', in Richard Bauckham (ed.), *God Will Be All in All: The Eschatology of Jürgen Moltmann* (Edinburgh: T&T Clark, 1999).

Williams, Rowan. 'Renewing the Face of the Earth: Human Responsibility and the Environment', *Ebor Lecture*, Wednesday 25th March, 2009. Available online at http://rowan williams.archbishopofcanterbury.org/articles.php/816/renewing-the-face-of-the-earth-hu man-responsibility-and-the-environment (accessed 1 October, 2013).

Žižek, Slavoj and Boris Gunjevic. *God in Pain: Inversions of Apocalypse* (London: Verso, 2012).

INDEX